THE ARCHITECTURE OF LEISURE

HOUSES OF THE HAMPTONS
1880–1930

THE ARCHITECTURE OF LEISURE

HOUSES OF THE HAMPTONS

1880–1930

GARY LAWRANCE AND ANNE SURCHIN

FOREWORD BY JAQUELIN T. ROBERTSON

ACANTHUS PRESS
NEW YORK : 2007

ACANTHUS PRESS, LLC
54 WEST 21ST STREET
NEW YORK, NEW YORK 10010
WWW.ACANTHUSPRESS.COM
212-414-0108

Library of Congress Cataloging-in-Publication Data

Lawrance, Gary.
  Houses of the Hamptons, 1880-1930 / Gary Lawrance and Anne Surchin.
    p. cm. — (The architecture of leisure)
  Includes bibliographical references and index.
  ISBN-13: 978-0-926494-44-2 (alk. paper)
  ISBN-10: 0-926494-44-9 (alk. paper)
  1. Architecture, Domestic—New York (State)—Hamptons. 2.
Architecture—New York (State)—Hamptons—19th century. 3.
Architecture—New York (State)—Hamptons—20th century. I. Surchin, Anne.
II. Title.

  NA7235.N72H356 2007
  728'.37097472109034--dc22
                                        2006037934

FRONTISPIECE: SCULPTURE OF APHRODITE AT PORT OF MISSING MEN

PRINTED IN CHINA

THE ARCHITECTURE OF LEISURE

AFTER U.S. CITIES EXPANDED in the 19th century, Americans sought respite from the stress of urban life by renewing their bond to the landscapes they saw as enduring symbols of American greatness. From the icy waters of Maine's Northeast Harbor to the gentler shores of Palm Beach, from Bailey's Beach in Newport to the faux-rustic camps of the Adirondacks, the creators of America's great fortunes communed, played, and cut deals. They hired the future fathers of American architecture to build French châteaux, Scottish castles, old-money cottages, and Venetian villas. Mile-long driveways, private docks for ocean-cruising yachts, horse paddocks, acres of greenhouses, private bowling alleys, and movie rooms were essential amenities in this gilded world where time spent at the club and sit-down dinners for 50 lakeside were the natural counterparts to lunch at the city club and evenings on Fifth Avenue.

Recognizing that the story of American residential architecture is not complete without the history of American resort architecture, Acanthus Press has issued "The Architecture of Leisure" series to complement the Acanthus Urban and Suburban Domestic Architecture series.

CONTENTS

~

FOREWORD

❧

LONG ISLAND'S East End, settled 366 years ago, remains today one of our country's most compelling, evolving settings, in which the past and the present, the natural and the built world, the rustic and the chic have become inextricably intertwined. Once a region of old, unpretentious farming and fishing villages with small wooden houses and open fields, the Hamptons today are an internationally known resort—another overdeveloped, over-promoted hot spot of our wealthy, celebrity-driven culture.

There are interesting histories to be written about how the region's gradual transformation from colonial to modern times is clearly revealed in its architecture. One of these is *Houses of the Hamptons, 1880–1930*, by Gary Lawrance and Anne Surchin, the most recent in a noteworthy series on traditional American architects and architecture published by Acanthus Press.

What I find particularly appealing is that this architectural history of houses is presented in terms of those who commissioned and lived in them, as well as those who later bought, preserved, or changed them. The houses are not treated as architectural objects but as extensions of people's lives and ambitions.

How did social change and the changing meanings of society, style, and precedent reorganize the domestic program and change the way we live today? What about "old" and "new" money in terms of the increased size of things during this 50-year period? Are there new uses? Yes, indeed, there were new sorts of rooms for different kinds of entertaining; more formal layouts; extensive new servants' quarters; more prominent and substantial materials, such as stone, brick, and stucco (as upgrades over wood); grander landscaping; and more complex detailing. Simply put, the design of East End "summer cottages" and formal estates was (and still is) clearly about the changing needs, tastes, priorities, and pretensions of rich clients and changing economics. It is also about architects' roles in having to serve and educate their clients and simultaneously find ways to "strut their own stuff." The design of houses, after all, not only launched the careers of many architects but also provided them later with a good bit of high-end residential work in which they were free to experiment with a great variety of architectural issues. Most particularly, it allowed them to develop a reusable language of details about how new and old things go together. Houses are in fact ideal "idea labs," in which new knowledge is created that changes the way we think about a design both for our houses and our lives. And in this regard we are again reminded that—to paraphrase Churchill—we shape our buildings and they, in turn, shape us, something understood equally well by Andrea Palladio, Thomas Jefferson, Stanford White, John Russell Pope, and Frank Gehry, as well as by many of the architects in Houses of the Hamptons. Houses, more than any other building type, most clearly reveal what we think about the past, the future, and ourselves.

But what makes the East End such a telling and successful place to live in and write about is that in addition to its location, climate, and light, the plan and structure of its villages set out a clear, communal order of things in which houses are at the center, along with a variety of public and commercial buildings, infrastructure, and open spaces. If one passes through Southampton, Water Mill, Bridgehampton, East Hampton, and Amagansett on the way to the end at Montauk, the area covered in Lawrance and Surchin's history, one is struck by the repetition of these generic place-making elements—town greens, ponds, burial grounds, windmills, monuments, flagpoles, houses, churches, schools, shops, newspaper offices, libraries, banks, theaters, restaurants, and fences, all fronting tree-lined main streets. Although each of these villages differs from the others, they are also the same, all recognizable branches of the same "idea tree." They offer a variety of choices within a cultural consensus about what's important. In the past, these villages were separated by agricultural lands—a necessary balance between town and country that has sadly been lost today. Nonetheless, this historic recipe of communal life, which contains both small cottages and large estates, each influencing the other, remains one of the East End's architectural achievements, a continuing challenge to some of the best architects of their day and ours—both modernist and traditional.

Lawrance and Surchin, in an exemplary introduction about origins, show how the growth of an architecture of leisure is understood only in the context of the area's history. While other high-end places such as Palm Beach started as resorts, the Hamptons were working villages that became valued summer resorts only at the end of the 19th century, 240 years after their founding. This means that the more humble, smaller-scaled architecture of the past has continued to inform and help constrain evolving upmarket tastes. And for this reason, the Hamptons still retain an appealing historic working-place authenticity missing in pure resorts.

It is worth commenting further on how the factors of location and history—geography, economic patterns, the influx of new people and professions—affected building practices. The first of these shaping factors is

the presence of the Gulf Stream, which moderates the weather, producing relatively mild winters, short springs, and endlessly long summers and autumns, all characterized by an extraordinary golden painterly light caused by water vapor in the air. And, of course, hurricanes result, as well, changing shorelines and disciplining where and how one builds.

A second shaping factor is the nature of the land, which is at the southern edge of a glacial moraine and allows huge beech trees and superb flower gardens to thrive close to the ocean; farther inland, one finds scruffy pine barrens, so that two quite different ecosystems exist side by side.

Thirdly, there are several distinct and quite different shorelines: the Atlantic beaches, running from West Hampton to Montauk; the bays between the North Fork and South Fork, which were once rich in shellfish; and Long Island Sound, which is shared with New England and has shaped its history, outlooks, politics, and economics since its founding.

Still another factor affecting the Hamptons' development is the absence of real money until the emergence of the "whaling oil business" that made Sag Harbor the country's third great whaling port and gave it high-style buildings and exotic furnishings before there were any summer resorts. Sag Harbor was a real mixed-use working village based on an international enterprise in which great sailing ships were at center stage.

In addition, artists played an important role in discovering and promoting the area's natural beauty, helping persuade their richer friends and clients to come to what was indeed an unspoiled rural Arcadia well into the 20th century. Although "society" had begun to come on their own in larger numbers after the railroad was built in 1872, and Southampton became their first mecca, it was the artists from 1818 through the 1940s and 1950s who increasingly gave the region its special aura and imagery. One thinks of Chase, Mount, Gifford, Homer, Whiteredge, Moran, Hassam, Twachtman, Pollock, de Kooning.

So what about the histories of the houses, some 32 of them? Are they as stimulating as the lively introduction? Yes. Each house is presented in terms of its date, location, client, architect, builder, style, materials, layout, and massing. To this the authors add the spice of local gossip, current prejudices, and changing social mores, all of which make each chapter more entertaining and culturally instructive. When presented together, you know just what it was like making your mark in the Hamptons during this critical period of its transformation.

Because I live in East Hampton, I turned first to Pudding Hill, a new architectural take on an old historic property at a prominent corner—across the street from Thomas Moran's new Studio Cottage, in itself a pacesetter. Not only was Everett Herrick, the new owner, the founder and first president of the Maidstone Club, but he had the money and the gumption to tear down the old Osborn House and somewhat level the famous hill on which it stood overlooking Town Pond and Gardiner's Windmill. The Gardiners were local aristocrats, having been given a crown grant at Gardiners Island, and the Osborns were one of the oldest founding families. Needless to say, neither the act of tearing down nor the new architecture was well received. Yet Pudding Hill, the first Shingle style summer house built in East Hampton, remains today one of the best examples of how the existing regional small-scale architecture was both radically amended and included in what became a distinctive new way of building, a seemingly timeless style that is continually being revisited and altered even today.

I then went to Villa Maria in Watermill, which this volume's authors call properly "a tale of two houses and multiple owners." This curiosity is located on a spectacular bay front and is the biggest thing you see as you drive eastward from Southampton. Since almost everyone who has passed by this site has wondered about what it is and why it is there, you have to thank the authors for telling you exactly what happened. And at this point you realize what really good hands you're in, that this is both good history and good fun. I could go on and on, with Stanford White's brilliant and still studied Montauk Association Houses (known as the Seven Sisters); the Art Village; William Merritt Chase's homestead, The Orchard, The Port of Missing Men, et cetera, but it's much better for you to start reading this remarkably sophisticated book, which is equally interesting to laymen and professionals. It's a great read.

All of us who live in the East End now and have come to appreciate its architectural DNA—its iconic villages, buildings, beaches, trees; and its still beautiful (but diminishing) open vistas and fields—owe Gary Lawrance and Anne Surchin, as well as Acanthus Press, a big thanks. They have given us a superb chapter in the family history of "our place."

—Jaquelin T. Robertson

ACKNOWLEDGMENTS

THE RESEARCH for this book would not have been possible without the aid of numerous individuals: staff members of many libraries, historical societies, and museums; families past and present associated with these houses, as well as friends and colleagues who shared archival materials, knowledge, and insight on our subject matter. We are indebted to the following for their help.

For their assistance in researching historical information and aiding us in the procurement of archival materials, we wish to thank the Amagansett Free Library; Susan Smyth at the John Jermain Library in Sag Harbor; Sherry Birk at the American Architectural Foundation; Anne LoMonte and Joseph Scarpulla at the Long Island Chapter of the American Institute of Architects; Janet Parks and Julie Tozer at the Avery Architectural & Fine Arts Library at Columbia University; the Bird Library at Syracuse University; John Eilertsen, executive director of the Bridgehampton Historical Society; Brooklyn Historical Society; Brooklyn Public Library; Frick Art Reference Library; Frederick Law Olmsted National Historic Site; Hampton Bays Library; Julie Green at the Hampton Library in Bridgehampton; Alix Reiskind, visual resources librarian at Harvard University; Historic American Buildings Survey at the National Parks Service; Debi Murray at the Historical Society of Palm Beach County; the Library of Congress; the Long Island Studies Institute at Hofstra University; Arlene Travis at Mansions & Millionaires at Greenvale; Robin Strong at the Montauk Library; Melanie Bower at the Museum of the City of New York; Harrison Hunt, senior curator of history, Nassau County Department of Parks, Recreation and Museums; National Register of Historic Places at the National Parks Service; New York Historical Society; New York Institute of Technology Architecture library; New York Public Library; James Warren at the New York State Office of Parks, Recreation and Historic Preservation; Nichols House Museum; Trudy Kramer; Alicia Longwell and Jacqueline Pizza at the Parrish Art Museum; Patchogue-Medford Library; Philadelphia Horticultural Society; Paul Miller at the Preservation Society of Newport County; Quogue Library; Riverhead Free Library; Rogers Memorial Library in Southampton; Sag Harbor Historical Society; Sister Honora Nolty at the Sienna Spirituality Center; Shelter Island Public Library; Joyce Connolly at the Smithsonian Institution, Archives of American Gardens; Charla Bolton and Robert MacKay at the Society for the Preservation of Long Island Antiquities; Geoffrey K. Fleming at the Southold Historical Society; Sandy Costa, Jon Foster, and Christopher M. Talbot at the Southampton Village Building Department; Southampton College Library; David Goddard and Tom Edmonds at the Southampton Historical Museum; Southampton Town Historian Henry Moeller; University Library at the State University at Stony Brook; David Kerkhoff at the Suffolk County Historical Society; Sharon A. Pullen, C.A. County Clerk Archivist for Suffolk County;

William Whitaker, Collections Manager at the Architectural Archives, University of Pennsylvania; Marlene Haresign and Joan Wilson at the Water Mill Museum; Westhampton Free Library; Heather Clewell and Maggie Lidz at the Winterthur Museum Library and Archives.

For her help and invaluable assistance throughout the project we give special thanks to archivist and research librarian Nancy Hadley at the American Institute of Architects Library, Washington, D.C. We are also grateful to Marci Vail and Steve Boerner, who shepherded us through East Hampton Library's extraordinary Long Island Collection. And to Richard Barons, who first at the Southampton Historical Museum and then at the East Hampton Historical Society shared his wealth of knowledge and helped obtain access to rare photos and archival materials, we offer heartfelt thanks.

The authors would also like to thank our many colleagues—architects, authors, photographers, artists, designers, realtors—who provided observations, documentation, access, and introductions to properties for us: Steven Amiaga, Arlene Ball, Peter Bertrand, Maria and Renato Cerini, Peter Cook, Mary Cummings, Zita Davisson, Mark Fasanella, Francis Fleetwood, Sherrill Foster, Jeff Gibbons, Timothy Greer, Mac Griswold, Albert Hadley, Robert Hefner, Michael Kathrens, Roger Lovett, Robert Lenahan, James and Susan Merrell, Frank Newbold, Victoria Budd Opperman, Pamela Holmes Pospisil, John Rainey, Marco Ricca, Ann Sandford, William A. Sclight, Betty Sherrill, Raymond Spinzia, Richard Stott, Anne Swint, Andre T. Tchelistcheff, Robert Verbanac, Samuel G. White, and Walter Wilcoxen.

Special thanks to Doran Mullen and Steven Stolman for their continuous enthusiasm and help.

We wish to thank the many former and current homeowners and occupants, and homeowners' descendents, for their reminiscences and cooperation and for graciously welcoming us into their homes:

Roberta Gosman (Montauk Association); Alan Cordingly, Elford King, Therese Bernbach (Rosemary Lodge); Monica and Walter Noel Jr. (The Dolphins); Beth DeWoody, William Steube, Alexandra Lotsch (Art Village); Jim and Ann Harmon (William Merritt Chase Homestead); Anne Eisenhower Flottl (Claverack); Schuyler Campbell, Suzette de Marigny Smith (The Orchard); William G. McKnight III (Wooldon Manor); Judith and Irving Shafran (Onadune); Lynn Krominga and Amnon Shiboleths (Meadowcroft); Cecile Havemeyer (Villa Mille Fiori); Judith Makrianes, Dianne Wallace, and Lowell Schulman (Coxwould); Lorna Livingston, Brad Shaheen, Michael Shaheen, Donald Burns, Greg Connors (Old Trees); Diane and Charles Holmes (Ballyshear); Dr. Richard and Mirra Brockman (Woodhouse Playhouse); Catherine Sickles (Bayberry Land); Ruth Lord (Chestertown House); Countess von Salm-Hoogstraeten (Port of Missing Men); Maria and Bruce Bockmann (Four Fountains); Julia Carter (Ocean Castle); and Gail and Harry Theodoracopulos (The Shallows).

For their assistance in procuring research materials: Andrew Cuneen, Claude Gagna, and Susan Bradfield. Richard Marchand shared his expertise in graphic presentation and produced new plans from existing ones as well as reconstructing others. In addition, he shared generously from his archives, as did Orin Finkle, Joseph Tyree, and Eric Woodward.

To James Bleecker and Jeff Heatley for their new photography and for capturing the spirit of these wonderful houses.

And to Jane Rinden, Priscilla Dunhill, Annie Jaroszewicz, and Dianne Rennard for reading numerous chapters and providing their suggestions and criticisms, which in turn buoyed our enthusiasm.

We also want to thank Ellen Loos for her technical assistance and generous support in the creation of this book.

For their assistance in providing information and resources we express our gratitude to Judy Bliss, Richard

Casabianca, Aaron Daniels, Roz Edleman, Pandora and Yves Hentic, Valerie M. Jones, Barbara Lord, William M. Manger Jr., Lucy Puig Neis, John W. Rae Jr., Pamela Walker, Patricia Weiss, and Solveig Williams. To others who helped but whose names don't appear here through omission or lack of space, many thanks.

At Acanthus Press we offer our appreciation to Bill Morrison for his critical edits, Angela Buckley for her copyediting, Peter Archer for managing this project and pulling it all together at the end, and, of course, Barry Cenower, our publisher, whose vision for this volume was a guiding light.

INTRODUCTION

THE HAMPTONS began as a group of Puritan villages along Long Island's South Shore. Because of the area's dense woods, moors, rolling grass-covered hills, and topsoil-rich land, the Hamptons developed initially as a farming community. By the end of the 19th century, it became a quiet resort community that by the 1920s had evolved into an elegant, glamorous, renowned community—the American Riviera.

The eastern end of Long Island is geographically split into two land masses, known as the North and South Forks, by a series of interlocking bays. Fifty miles long, 12 miles at its widest point, and 80 miles east of New York City, the Hamptons occupies the South Fork of eastern Long Island. Situated west of Montauk Point and east of Westhampton Beach between the Atlantic Ocean on the south and Great and Little Peconic Bays, Gardiner's Bay, and Block Island Sound on the north, the area encompasses the townships of East Hampton and Southampton. These in turn contain the four Hamptons: the villages of Westhampton Beach, East Hampton, Bridgehampton, and Southampton. The latter is the historical resort epicenter of the Hamptons, which in its day regarded everyplace else as a suburb. As well, the Hamptons includes numerous hamlets and villages.

THE EARLY SETTLERS

Southampton was founded in 1640 by colonists from Lynn, Massachusetts, with land acquired from England's Charles I. They arrived by boat at Conscience Point and encountered a landscape of fields, bays, marsh, moors, beach, ocean, and forest. The first settlers, helped by the Shinnecock Indians, an Algonquin tribe whose ancestors had inhabited the area for thousands of years developed an agrarian and fishing community. By the 19th century, Southampton Township grew to include the incorporated villages of North Haven, Quogue, Sag Harbor, Westhampton Beach, and other communities. With the exception of Sag Harbor, in the late 1700s a port of trade larger than New York's and in the mid-1800s a booming and cosmopolitan whaling port, Southampton remained a sleepy backwater until the 1872 expansion of the Long Island Railroad line.

East Hampton, considered one of Southampton's many "suburbs," followed a similar developmental trajectory. In 1648, East Hampton's Puritan settlers purchased 31,000 acres from the colonial governors of both Massachusetts and Connecticut who had previously purchased it from the Montauk Indians. Some of these early residents came from Maidstone in Kent, England, and called their new home Maidstone, as well. For its first eight years it functioned as an independent "plantation" and, in 1662, became known as East Hampton. Two years later it joined the province of New York as part of what would become New York State. Farming, cattle-raising, fishing, and whaling comprised the basis of the settlers' early economy.

Before becoming a vacation resort, East Hampton's allure had been spread by writers such as Walt Whitman in his 1849 exposition on the "wonders and beauties" of

"The Dunes," residence of Dr. Theodore Gaillard Thomas, social founder of the Southampton Summer Colony

Montauk in "Letters from a Travelling Bachelor." As well, William Cullen Bryant's *Picturesque America* of 1872–74 stated that "perhaps no town in America retains so nearly the primitive habits, tastes and ideas of our forefathers as East Hampton."

The case of Watermill was typical of the many villages that sprang up in the area. It was founded by English colonists, who created the town by dividing their land according to how much was invested by each individual. Lots were sold to "outsiders," but the title to the common grounds belonged to the original investors, respectfully known as "proprietors." Farms and cattle pastures were established along with a water mill (a common sight in the Hamptons) used for the grinding of grain and corn.

When the Long Island Railroad came to the area in 1872, visitors built summer houses along Mill Creek,

Mill Pond, and Mecox Bay, originally a whaling community. Some even helped preserve relics of an earlier time, such as Howell's Mill. Water Mill's Hayground Mill, featured in the 1916 motion picture *Hulda of Holland* with Mary Pickford, operated until 1919.

A RESORT IS BORN

Until the 1870s, when the first summer houses began to appear in the village, local residents in the towns of the Hamptons opened their homes and farms to boarders during the warmest months. Some residents either expanded their houses to accommodate paying boarders or converted them to inns; small hotels also appeared.

Boarders often came from great distances and stayed

Main Street, Southampton

for a substantial amount of time. When a two-hour train trip from New York gave Southampton's first vacationers easy access to the village, the town began to prosper. In the early 1870s, Leon Depeyre de Bost, a New York dry goods merchant, bought a South Main Street house to use as a summer cottage. Prominent New York physician Theodore Gaillard Thomas, at the invitation of de Bost, his patient, visited Southampton and became enamored of the village and, according to *The New York Times*, "the purity of the air, the dry and healthy soil, and the perennial breezes which blew continually, and no matter which quarter they came, brought coolness and health with them." Shortly after his visit, Dr. Thomas built The Dunes, sited on the ocean at the foot of Lake Agawam, a quarter-mile wide by one mile-long sheet of fresh water stretching from the base of the village to the ocean

beach. Dr. Thomas' house was also known as The Birdhouse for its many wraparound porches. He communicated his love for Southampton and its health benefits to his wealthy friends and patrician patients, and they followed his lead. This infusion of visitors known as "Yorkers, rusticators or cottagers" by the locals, built cottages along the dunes, Lake Agawam, and at the beginning edge of what is today considered the estate section, forming the "summer colony."

Owing to the proximity of the town to New York and the ability for men to work in the city while their families stayed by the ocean, Southampton became a "social annex" to New York. In 1890, the Brooklyn Eagle reported that from 1877 to 1890, Southampton Village's combined summer and winter population of 1,400 had doubled in the summer alone. The article's author

Goodhue Livingston with Mrs. Oren Root

"Mocomanto," Betts residence on Lake Agawam, Southampton

Yacht at anchor, North Haven

writes, "the summer residences are nearly all large and expensively furnished. They stand amid level lawns that are kept as closely cropped as a small boy's cranium. . . . It is quiet – so quiet and peaceful that one's brain ceases to worry and one wonders what use there is of anything more elaborate in the world than Southampton and Southampton life."

During America's Gilded Age (1870–1930), the comings, goings, and extravagant doings of Newport, Rhode Island's rich were the talk of the society columns. Later resorts were considered mere alternatives to Newport, so that the Berkshires were called "the Inland Newport," and the Hamptons earned the nickname "the Island Newport" or "Little Newport." Even locally, the Hamptons' charms were appraised relative to Newport's: "As a summer resort for New Yorkers," noted *The Southampton Press*, "Southampton is not far behind Newport. The elegance of its equipages, luxury in its

cottages and display at its entertainments compare favorably with the older city." Or, as Southamptonite Mrs. Albert Jaeckel, said, "Southampton is a little backwater of God."

In fact, other vacation communities, including Bar Harbor in Maine and the Adirondacks in upstate New York, sometimes had more to offer than Newport. These locales offered true relaxation, whereas Newport was renowned for its social pressures and glittering formality.

Long Island sea air was considered a cure-all, and the perceived health benefits contributed to the development of the Hamptons as a popular resort. Mrs. Goodhue Livingston, one of Southampton's grandes dames, or "Dreadnaughts," a group of ladies reigning as mistresses of the social seas said, "Southampton has the strongest air in the world. . . . It's the suction, you know. You feel it the minute you leave Westhampton."

"Ready for the hunt," Bridgehampton

Despite beautiful surroundings and the serene environment that so contributed to mental and physical well being, *The Southampton Press*, in 1899, reported some visitors desiring more. "It is said that three or four of the newcomers to Southampton have openly announced that they will die if something is not forthcoming in the way of excitement. They have sent for all of their gayest friends, but when their friends arrive they soon fall into the quiet easygoing life that is supposed to be peculiar to this section of the country. As one woman says, " 'It's all very well to talk about air. There doesn't seem to be anything down here but air and heaven knows we have enough of that to get heartily sick of it'."

The Hamptons not only served as a social center, but captivated thinkers and artists. The famed "painter's" light from the reflection of the sun on the Atlantic Ocean and landscape that surrounded the early towns inspired painters such as Thomas Moran and Winslow Homer, whose work captured a romantic vision of pastoral America. Plein-air art colonies in East Hampton, which journalists called "the American Barbizon," and in Southampton, home to William Merritt Chase's Shinnecock Summer School of Art, attracted well-known artists and students who helped popularize Long Island's East End.

In 1877, *Scribner's* magazine brought attention to East Hampton when it hired writers and artists, many belonging to the Tile Club, to give accounts of Long Island villages. Artists such as Childe Hassam and Albert and Adele Herter became permanent residents of the summer colony in East Hampton. In 1884, artist Moran, with his wife Mary Nimmo, designed their Queen Anne–Shingle style house/studio on Main Street.

Ladies at the Shinnecock Hills Golf Club

By the mid-1880s, the first summer residences outside East Hampton Village in Montauk were erected. Development proceeded slowly in East Hampton, as builders still had to cart materials from the end of the rail line in Bridgehampton, six miles to the west. With the extension of Long Island Railroad's train line to East Hampton in 1895, a real estate boom came to the area, similar to Southampton's 20 years earlier. Nonetheless, East Hampton's fashionable and innovative houses, by remaining at a more modest scale compared to those of the metropolis further west, echoed Charles de Kay's 1898 New York Times essay, reflecting the commonly held hope that "no large hotels and no very costly country places will ever be built there. . . ."

Among the earliest summer residents were old socially prominent families who helped popularize Long Island's East End communities. From the remains of the colonial aristocracy came the Van Rensellaers, the Livingstons, James Breese, and the family of Ellery James. Bankers and brokers such as Alfred Hoyt and Charles Sabin as well as S. Fisher Johnson and C.B. MacDonald followed, as did heirs to the prominent du Pont, Herter, Mellon, and Rogers families.

THE HAMPTON LIFE

The elite of America's architectural profession built in the Hamptons. McKim, Mead & White, John Russell Pope, F. Burrall Hoffman, Harrie T. Lindeberg, and Cross & Cross were some of the most prominent names. They built alongside self-taught practitioners such as Edward Purcell Mellon, Isaac H. Green Jr., and John Custis Lawrence. Highly credentialed but little-known architects such as Edward Delano Lindsey—who was only the fourth

Playing golf at the James Parrish house, Shinnecock Hills

American to train at the Ecole des Beaux-Arts—also made important contributions. Lindsey created Maycroft, one of his few residential commissions. Some architects dealt in the popular styles of the era, whereas others— often those who lived in the area—related their commissions to the regional design idioms. Many were independently wealthy and could choose their clients and projects. In an era without building or zoning regulations, these architects had a freer hand to express their own artistic ambitions, as well as their clients.

A look at the early vernacular buildings in the area offers clues for the solutions that would later evolve and define the unique qualities of its architecture. The early builders of the leisure community used the vernacular forms of the earliest houses. These forms were characterized by the use of indigenous materials and built by local tradesmen with techniques that addressed the local climate, traditions, and economy. Such building forms initially had everything to do with survival and nothing to do with style.

For example, the shingled lean-to house, known today as the saltbox, was an iconic New England form created to retain warmth and preserve dryness. The saltbox's long north roof with its severe pitch combating the prevailing winter winds, allowed just enough height for a door under the eave. The low-pitched south roof provided two stories and adequate fenestration for light and air. According to architect Jaquelin Robertson, "the shingle was the best raincoat ever invented" and the best material available for the harsh seacoast environment.

Interior of the Parrish Art Museum, Southampton

Gambrel houses, also common in 17th-century America, were shaped to shed snow from their two-tiered roof system.

Gradually, the early forms became stylistic instead of purely functional. They constituted what would become the rural regional architectural style. Later resort architects incorporated the lean-to and the gambrel roof, and borrowed freely from the earlier venacular idiom forms to design crisply detailed summer cottages with porches for solar screening, light, and cross ventilation. Shingles with patterned courses and articulated trim still served to prevent water penetration, but their applications became decorative. Architects R. H. Robertson, Grosvenor Atterbury, and John Russell Pope, among others, seized on the distinctive aspects of the regional architecture and its historical embellishments, incorporating those elements into their designs to associate their new houses with the culture and spirit of the place. Architects were able to tie their buildings into the landscape through their relationship to the regional idiom. One of the aspects that made many Hamptons' houses architecturally unique was this identification by architects with local vernacular and rural regional forms.

The resort architecture that appeared in the Hamptons during the Gilded Age was somewhat atypical for its time. There were no marble palaces; even the sumptuous Villa Mille Fiori could boast only marble-dusted halls. Houses were impressive but not overly ornate, reflecting a desire for simplicity and a lack of pretension.

The mythology of place also played a part in the creation of a contingent of houses related to a romanticized view of the area's English heritage. Such estates as Wooldon Manor, Woodhouse Playhouse, and Onadune used distinctively English details such as thatched roofs, and half timbering. Meadowcroft and Bayberry Land were inspired by the English Arts and Crafts movement. And no Gilded Age resort would be complete without the more conventional styles of the era such as Mediterranean Revival and Beaux Arts.

Often, the varied demands and tastes of wealthy clients determined the architecture and landscape design of Hampton houses. Bayberry Land was created for events, for public people leading very public lives, whereas Coxwould was a getaway that offered respite while still providing the amenities required in a substantial country house.

The unique gardens that complemented the architecture of the houses are widely known for their luxuriant abundance. The Hamptons' flat, sunny landscape and cool ocean breezes offered superb opportunities to dedicated gardeners. Anna Gilman Hill, in her book *Forty Years of Gardening*, wrote, "Gardening in Suffolk County spoils you for gardening in North America."

Most of the Hamptons' houses, built for guests and grand entertainments, had large staffs and ran like first-class hotels where every need was met. The guest rooms, sometimes self-contained suites, came with phones and numbers to dial for the maid, refreshments, or a car; writing desks stocked with postcards depicting the house; and stationery emblazoned with the cottage's name. Also not unlike great hotels, the houses were run by powerful managers, usually the wives of equally powerful men.

These grandes dames, from whom an invitation for lunch, dinner, or a dance was not to be turned down, presided over the Hamptons' summer colony. Mrs. Goodhue Livingston of Old Trees, considered Southampton's first lady—or dictator, as some thought— had the final say on social acceptability. In his column

called the "Social Set," Barclay Beekman wrote of her: "Unlike most first ladies, Mrs. Livingston isn't a joiner. She doesn't even belong to the Colony Club, New York's most exclusive organization for women. Being a Livingston, she believes her name is glory enough."

In a large house, leisure was a complicated affair, and a typical day could involve myriad activities. In the Hamptons, the morning often began with toe dipping in the sea at a beach club like the Southampton Bathing Corporation. This exercise concluded by 1:00 p.m., because afterward the beach belonged to nannies and children. Afternoons started with lunch, followed by golf, tennis, croquet, cards, or backgammon at the area's numerous clubs. The Meadow, Maidstone or Shinnecock Golf Club, the National Golf Links, Westhampton Country, and Southampton Clubs were bastions of leisure. Coaching, horseback riding, and fox hunting at Shinnecock Hills; sailing at the Devon Yacht Club; and motoring, bicycling, and walking were also popular activities.

For the civic-minded, there was volunteer work for Garden Society functions and tours for the Garden Club of Southampton, and teas, event-planning committees, charity work, and meetings for East Hampton's Ladies Village Improvement Society and other organizations. Art aficionados took drawing or painting lessons; looked in on classes at the Art Village, located just to the west of Southampton; served on committees at Southampton's Parrish Art Museum or East Hampton's Guild Hall, or just looked at paintings. If this was not enough, there were always reading groups, lectures on how to simplify life, or the ultimate leisure activity, having one's portrait painted. After spending a day engaged in these pursuits, a little rest was required to prepare for an evening of dinners, clambakes, dances, and debutante balls held at the clubs or in private homes.

All of this leisure activity was carefully orchestrated by the ladies of the Colony and their social secretaries. Some of the many details to be concerned about were invitations and social correspondence, planning dinners,

Viewing tennis at the Meadow Club, Southampton

dances, parties and their respective menus, linens, place settings, flowers and seating arrangements, along with coordinating staff. The staff often consisted of butlers, footmen, maids, cooks, nannies, groomsmen, stable boys, gardeners, groundskeepers, night watchman, coachmen/chauffeur, etc. Often, when an unusually big party was to be given, attractive members of the male gardening staff at the du Pont's Chestertown House, for example, would double as extra footmen. On footmen and entertaining, Mrs. Livingston was quoted by Cleveland Amory in *The Last Resorts* as saying:

In comparing Southampton to Newport, Mrs. Livingston has this to say about Miss Julia Berwind using gold service, 'I don't even bring my real silver she says, 'I just use plate.' In the same way Mrs. Livingston is indignant that the two resorts should be lumped together merely because Mrs. Henry F. du Pont and a few other grandes dames still have, in the manner of Newport, footmen. 'Southampton has footmen,' she says, 'but we've never had footmen in knee britches.'

Joining clubs and organizations and attending social functions was the norm for the Hamptons social set, who were seen at the same gatherings and in the same write-ups in all the social columns of New York and national papers. In society, one's associations with other people were always lifelong. This longevity at times posed problems for hostesses, who were obliged, for example, to plan seating arrangements so as not to place a guest near an ex-spouse or lover. Summer sojourns from the Hamptons often included visits to Long Island's North Shore for events such as the Duke of Windsor's polo match in Old

"The Meadow Club," Southampton

Westbury. Newport, only a short yacht trip away from the Hamptons, was always good for a dinner or a ball.

Balls, festivals, and debutante parties in the Hamptons were just as popular as in any of the other resorts, and those events may have been more creative, thanks to the many artists in the area. At Ballyshear in 1928, Mrs. Charles E. Van Vleck Jr., the famous society portrait painter and heiress to the Palmolive Company fortune, gave a ball for 200 guests to celebrate her 10th wedding anniversary. Everyone attended wearing the fashions of 1918. According to a *New York Times* account on August 4, 1928:

> The west terrace of Ballyshear had been transformed into a Parisian night club of 1918. Strings of colored lights along the trees outlined

the curving driveway from the road to the house. A blue 'moon' shone on a fountain in the center of the formal garden on the south side, and picked out each flower and shrub caught by its rays. Ornamental pomegranate trees and hydrangeas decorated the terrace, which was lighted with floor lights and with lanterns swinging from clusters of bamboo poles. Dancing contests and games popular in the Paris nightclubs were interspersed with numbers by entertainers. An orchestra played throughout the French gala night.

Despite the 1929 stock market crash and the beginning of the Great Depression, social life did not come to an abrupt end in the Hamptons. In July 1931 at the Devon Yacht Club, Mr. and Mrs. A. Wallace

Chauncey gave a dinner dance for 200, called the Poverty Ball, at which the guests arrived in costumes depicting hard times. In Southampton, the George Warrington Curtis family, in August 1932, held a barn dance at their estate to benefit the Southampton unemployment fund. The grounds and a barn on their property were fitted out with buggies, carriages, hay stacks, and pumpkins. The guests came properly attired in rustic or "hayseed" costumes.

A Changing World

The era of splendor by the sea in the Hamptons did not end suddenly. The decline of the great resorts began with the adoption of personal income tax in 1913, and World War I saw the disintegration of the formal lifestyle. The Roaring Twenties brought in a world that was fast, shiny, and new became the vogue. The stock market crash and the Great Depression forced even the wealthiest to scale back. But the final blow to the Hamptons came with the 1938 hurricane, which reduced to rubble many of the oceanfront houses of America's elite. Although a sigificant number of the houses that withstood the damage were rebuilt, War World II soon occupied the thoughts of the summer colony's young socialites and staff, who signed up to serve in the armed forces. In 1941, Mrs. Livingston, whose life spanned the rise and demise of the Hamptons' golden era, let all her footmen go, and after the war, her butler told her that the life she had known on the East End was over.

To escape taxes and the high costs of staffing, maintaining, heating, and cooling houses built solely for summer use, owners subdivided their large properties, leaving the main residences on small acreage or demolishing them. The age of elegance had been replaced by the era of mass production, the values of craft with machine-age efficiency, the quietude of the natural landscape diminished by the forces of greed and development. But despite all the changes, the heritage of the Hamptons has endured as the remaining houses from America's Riviera of the Gilded Age, with few exceptions, are being restored and preserved for enjoyment by a new generation, not only telling the story of the past but also that of the future.

The Southampton Bathing Association, circa 19th century

MONTAUK ASSOCIATION

c. 1882–84

Residences of Dr. Cornelius Agnew, William Loring Andrews, Arthur Benson,
Henry and Robert de Forest, Alfred Hoyt, Alexander E. Orr,
and Henry Sanger

The Seven Sisters

Benson house

IN 1879, Arthur Benson, the millionaire developer of Bensonhurst, Brooklyn, bought most of Montauk from the East Hampton Town Trustees for $151,000. Two years later, Benson and his wealthy friends and business associates established the Montauk Association to create a select summer hunting and fishing retreat on the Atlantic bluff just east of Ditch Plain. The Montauk Association members included renowned ophthalmologist Dr. Cornelius Agnew, one of the founders of the Manhattan and Brooklyn Eye and Ear Hospitals; businessman Henry Sanger; banker Alfred Hoyt; attorneys Robert and Henry de Forest; merchant and financier Alexander E. Orr; and author William Loring Andrews, a trustee of the Metropolitan Museum of Art and founding member of the Grolier Club.

The Association hired landscape architect Frederick Law Olmsted. His 1881 site plan for the 100-acre enclave reveals the optimal placement of houses atop knolls at the highest point along the rolling landscape, to take advantage of the ocean views and the prevailing southwest breezes needed for summer cooling. The staggered arrangement of houses provided each with spacious surroundings and expansive views. The residences were interconnected via a sequence of dirt paths

Benson and Sanger houses

that meandered through the natural terrain and allowed the moorland marshes and native vegetation to remain untouched. Olmsted's intention at Montauk was to minimize transgressions into the natural landscape, a scheme clearly influenced by the design of his earlier masterpiece, New York's Central Park.

The young architectural firm of McKim, Mead & White was commissioned to design the houses, to be built on a ridge north of De Forest Road between 1882 and 1884. Seven houses, a centrally located clubhouse (destroyed by a fire in 1933), a laundry, and a large stable formed the original complex. Known locally as "the seven sisters," the Montauk Association houses represent significant early examples of the Shingle

style, which McKim, Mead & White had a hand in popularizing. Not only do the houses show an understanding of the Colonial idiom in their use of shingled and clapboard walls and gabled roofs, they also reveal a distilled relationship to their historic vernacular precursors in Montauk: First House, Second House, and Third House.

Each of the firm's plans for the original seven houses was unique, but the structures are unified as a grouping through the use of scale, massing, form, materials, and finishes. Ranging between 4,000 and 7,000 square feet, the houses are stylistically they are transitional, incorporating Queen Anne design elements within the Shingle style. Their exterior cladding consists of

Agnew house

painted or unpainted clapboard on the first floors, and cedar shingles from the second floor up into the gables. The first-floor cladding acts as a plinth, a detail commonly seen in Queen Anne-style houses. The articulation of the shingle coursing, bumping out slightly between floors, serves to denote the change in floor levels. The shingles come in an assortment of patterns and shapes, with specialty cuts such as diamonds and fish scales appearing in the upper gables. Sloping, wide gabled roofs, with cross gables and dormers placed as accents, extend over gracious porches. Features such as a cupola, turrets, and eyebrow windows, which appear almost haphazardly in the overall mass, add to the informality of the composition.

Simple painted casings surround the windows and doors. Railings with square balusters sit between plain porch posts, deliberately placed to establish a harmonious rhythm for each facade. Spindles, produced on a lathe, were used to create open screens that framed exterior views. The porches themselves have a gravity-defying quality, as so much roof structure is supported on so little. Chimneys appear to anchor the buildings to the earth. The rambling nature of the exteriors, the tautly stretched shingles, and the contrast of solid and void in the positive-negative projection of balconies and porches are hallmarks of the Shingle style.

The interior plans of the Montauk houses fall into two basic groups. The first features a living hall adjacent

Hoyt house

to the major public spaces. In each of these interiors, the living hall encompasses a sitting alcove and stairwell with a decorative window on its landing, thereby becoming a volumetrically interesting space, reminiscent of some of H. H. Richardson's residential work and seen locally as well in Frederick Stickney's design for Rosemary Lodge in Water Mill.

The second plan theme features a center hall in the colonial tradition, with stairs set off to one side. Interior spaces are free-flowing and open, in part owing to the use of wood-spindled screens, rather than walls, to separate rooms. Finishes include beadboard wainscoting on walls and ceilings, wood paneling and planking, and

turned spindles on the stairwells.

In comparison to McKim, Mead & White projects done in the same time frame, such as the Newport Casino (1879-81), the Cyrus McCormick house (1880-81), and the Isaac Bell House (1882-83), the Montauk houses seem like experimental concept models for the larger commissions that lay ahead. Designed with restrained exuberance and excruciating attention to detail, they achieved a fresh, simple solution. None of these houses stands out in particular, yet each, perched in the face of the sea, offers a poetic and romantic glimpse of its neighbor. More than 120 years after their construction, they retain their access to a landscape of

Clubhouse

moorland and vistas, as well as their harmonious relationships to one another.

In 1976, the Montauk Association houses were
included on the National Register of Historic Places.
The complex is particularly important, not only for
Olmsted's precedent-setting vision for land use and
McKim, Mead & White's early work in the Shingle
style, but also for its documentation of a unique era in
the history of the resort economy of East Hampton. The
Montauk Association was one of the area's first enclaves
devoted to the architecture of leisure. It represents the
evolution from the boardinghouse era to one in which
vacationists lived in their own homes.

In 1997, a fire destroyed the Orr residence, named
Tick Hall after the insect that populates the region.
Owned by television personality Dick Cavett and his
wife, actress Carrie Nye, the house was painstakingly
reconstructed, from documentary materials and artifacts,
to be historically accurate. In 2004, East Hampton Town
designated the Montauk Association Historic District,
including Tick Hall, with the purpose of maintaining the
integrity of the original houses and their setting. The
preservation goals and guidelines, which offer protec-
tion, were developed to ensure the compound's
well-being for the long term.

ROSEMARY LODGE

1884

~

Residence of Reverend Henry Turbell Rose and Mary Cromwell Rose

East elevation, present-day view

Southwest elevation, present-day view

A HOUSE that has stature without size, breadth without length, detail without ornament, and charm and sophistication without contrivance is a very rare thing. Even more remarkable is the fact that the personal iconography of the owners is literally embedded in the walls. As such, Rosemary Lodge may be the quintessential East End summer cottage.

With the building of Rosemary Lodge in 1884, the Reverend Henry Turbell Rose began an odyssey that combined personal history with design and craftsmanship. Over a 37-year period, Rose took a simple Shingle- style cottage in Water Mill and transformed it into a creation all his own, infused with charm, wit, and warmth.

In 1883, Rose approached his uncle Henry for permission to "build a little house" on a piece of his family's Water Mill farmland. Glancing across Montauk Highway, his uncle replied, "You may have half an acre over there; but it must not be where it will shut off my view of the ocean." The following spring, Reverend Rose paid his uncle $50 for the property and commissioned architect Frederick W. Stickney of Lowell, Massachusetts, to design a summer cottage for $25. Stickney opened his Lowell office in 1883, the same year Rose moved there to serve as minister of the John Street Congregational Church.

Stickney completed the plans for the shell of the cottage in two weeks. Rose balked at the high bids submitted by local builders, so he decided to contract the job himself, purchasing his own materials and overseeing the hired carpenters and a mason. In August 1884, a mere month after it began, construction of

Living hall and stair, present-day view

Rosemary Lodge was completed. Reverend Rose named the house for his wife Mary Rose, who died shortly thereafter in 1886.

On both its exterior and interior, Rosemary Lodge's design elements are cohesive and thematically consistent. The exterior possesses all the character traits inherent in the Shingle style: facades layered with projecting volumes in the form of dormer windows, porch roofs, and eaves; an oriel bay cantilevered and supported on brackets; and an asymmetrical massing, all contained within the larger silhouette. Erosions into this silhouette—for example, in the form of sheltered space under the porch roof—contribute to the play of solid and void so typical of the style.

Except for the south and east first floor facades, which are covered in painted beveled siding, the walls are clad in cedar shingles. The main pedimented gables face east and west, whereas the shingled roof pitches steeply from

Stair landing detail, present-day view

the ridge north and south. Above the banding in the gables, the shingles curve outward to cast a shadow line on the wall below, which looks like a cantilevered projection yet is actually in the same plane. For all the complexity of the exterior, the basic plan of Rosemary Lodge is rectangular.

As a child, Henry Rose watched and probably assisted with his father's numerous woodworking projects. For Rosemary Lodge, he designed and built paneling, cabinetry, settees, doors, mantels, washstands, and more than 50 pieces of furniture and built-ins that appeared in every room in the house. He crafted these

Oak Room, present-day view

details for one room at a time, with each room containing a different species of wood. Predicting that "the cottage will never be finished in my lifetime," every winter for 27 years the reverend labored on the interior details of the house in his Lowell attic workshop. His work reflected both knowledge of the Aesthetic movement and familiarity with the Craftsman style. He hand carved more than 75 inscriptions for the wood paneling and furniture, shipping them to Water Mill to be

installed by local carpenters before the start of each summer season.

The layout of the interior rooms on all floors is strangely episodic. Each room leads directly to the next, through either a passageway or opening. The rambling sequence of rooms creates the illusion of an expansive dwelling. The central living hall, which also serves as the house entry, is paneled in ash. Its one-story south end opens on the north to a two-story volume with an L-

Dining room detail, present-day view

shaped staircase leading to a mezzanine and, several steps farther up, the second-floor bedrooms. Tooled balusters and newels topped with urnlike finials anchor the staircase to the base landing.

A sizable fireplace, decorated with green ceramic tiles above the surround, is the dominant element in the living hall. Centered below a balcony supported by curving wood brackets, this fireplace is flanked by inset paneling containing numerous hidden cupboards. The woodwork contains carved floral motifs, ships, butterflies, the family cat Sarah, birds, and inscriptions, such as Shakespeare's "Hold fast all I give thee," which is found in the desk cupboard.

Adjacent to the living hall through a lowered doorway is the Oak Room, an octagonal sitting room with a coffered ceiling. The wainscoting contains carved mottoes from Shakespeare's *As You Like It*, including "He may play the fool nowhere but in his own house." Above a corner fireplace surrounded by greenish-pink Roman tiles, a cornice, supported on narrow turned columns, bears the inscription "Old wood to burn, Old Books to read, Old Friends to love."

A low opening on the west side of the Oak Room leads to the dining room, originally the kitchen. For Henry Rose's second wife, Grace, this small and intimate Arts and Crafts style room, conceived to resemble the inside of a ship's cabin, was the favorite. Lockers under the ceiling with leaded-glass doors ring the room to form a dropped soffit. On the south wall, stained-glass windows, incorporating the initials *R* and *L* for Rosemary Lodge, came from the J. & R. Lamb Studios of New York City. The afternoon sun filters through them, filling the room with a warm glow. Cherry paneling adorning the walls and ceiling contains mottoes in German, such as one that translates to, "It's very nice to think/the world is full of meat and drink." Six dining chairs (1900) surrounding

a round cherry table, are also carved with inscriptions about food and drink, from poets , Stevenson, Khayyám, Shakespeare, Kipling, and Tennyson. The original corner fireplace was resurfaced in 1896 with blue tiles from Traitel Brothers of New York City.

To the north of the dining room is the 1895 sycamore-paneled kitchen wing, adjacent to the back stair hall that reached the second-floor bedrooms. The White Room belonged to Rose's only child, Helen, and the Green Room served as master bedroom for Reverend Rose and his wife. Added in 1909, the attic bedrooms feature Arts and Crafts built-ins in the form of window seats, a drop-down desk, bookshelves, cubby holes, drawers, plate rails, and brackets, all integrated into the odd nooks and crannies created by the rooflines. Every conceivable space was put to good use.

The history of the house remains as intact as the house itself. From 1883 through 1919, the year of his

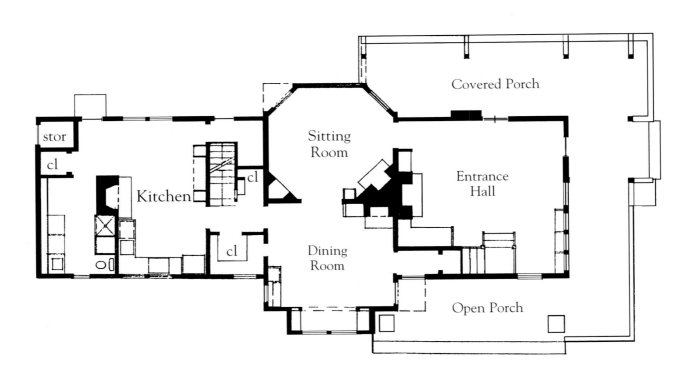

First floor plan

death, Rose maintained a handwritten, leather-bound journal titled *The Story of Rosemary Lodge*. It documents the house's building, decorating, renovations, expenses, and additions, and it contains newspaper articles, photographs of house and family, a log of boarders and guests, and records of the yearly pilgrimage from Lowell to Water Mill.

During his summers in Water Mill, Reverend Rose was active in the community and frequently gave sermons at the church in Bridgehampton. His journal entries chronicle summer picnics, a day trip by horse and buggy to Montauk's Camp Wikoff to hear President William McKinley speak, and commentary on the Boer War and World War I, experiences and concerns that reflect involvement in issues far beyond the scope of day-to-day matters. The mundane details of home ownership were also duly noted with such comments as "Senile [the lawn caretaker] mowed the lawn today."

The journal is the story of family life set against the backdrop of the major events that shaped the times in which the Roses lived. As a depiction of the summer colony and life among the cottagers, it is a remarkable testament to the history of the era.

In 1968, architects R. A. Cordingly and E. A. King bought Rosemary Lodge. In 1985 they moved the building four-tenths of a mile south of noisy Montauk Highway to the west side of Rose Hill Road. The house was rotated 180 degrees on its new site and placed on a new foundation. The architects extended the porch roof beyond the supporting posts, upgraded the mechanical systems, and added a porch, a dormer, and a shed on the north end of the house. Modern casement windows were installed in the dining room, and a glassed-in enclosure was added at the main entry. These changes, performed respectfully, allowed the house to evolve for current needs yet retain its character. It was recently sold to

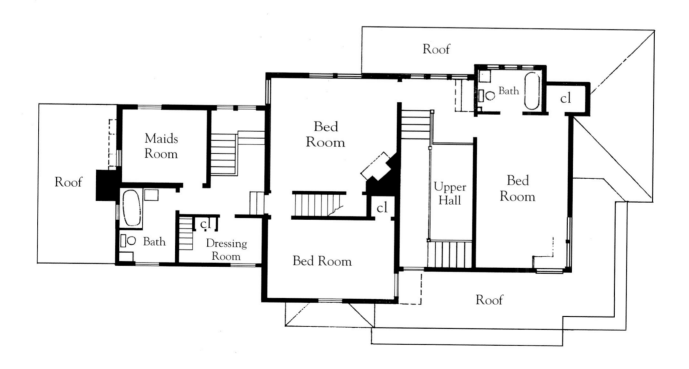

Second floor plan

White bedroom, present-day view

Therese Bernbach, who grew up in a similarly detailed house belonging to a lumber merchant in the Park Slope section of Brooklyn.

Rosemary Lodge was placed on both the State and National Registers of Historic Places in 1999 and cited for "the exceptional integrity of the original interior and exterior design and the degree to which they have been preserved," making it "a museum quality example of Shingle Style architecture and the Queen Anne and Craftsman interior design aesthetic."

The architect Grosvenor Atterbury once wrote about the very important fourth dimension in architecture as "not so very much a matter of seeing as of feeling." He goes on to say that "the quality of beauty and charm—what we are so apt to think of as a footnote to the architecture—which is oftentimes due to the owner as much as to the designer—appears in the final analysis to be the only real, vital, immortal part of the whole business." Rosemary Lodge embodies this notion of a unity between beauty and personal fulfillment.

THE DOLPHINS

1885

*Residence of James Hampden Robb and
Cornelia Van Rensselaer Thayer Robb*

Lake Agawam elevation, present-day view

Front elevation, present-day view

THE DOLPHINS, one of few remaining authentic houses by the architectural firm of McKim, Mead & White, was built in 1885 for the James Hampden Robb family on the west shore of Lake Agawam. It was among the earliest summer cottages in Southampton and helped inspire the trend toward sprawling seaside villas, rambling Shingle-style houses, and 50-room cottages of every conceivable style.

James Hampden Robb (1846–1911), the son of a New Orleans banker, was born in Philadelphia and educated in Europe; at the military school at Ossining, New York; and at Harvard University. In 1868 he married Cornelia Van Rensselaer Thayer, and the couple had three children, Nathaniel, Cornelia, and Louisa who later married architect Goodhue Livingston and lived at Old Trees, the estate he designed next to The Dolphins.

A banker and cotton merchant, James Robb also led a distinguished career in public service. He was elected to the New York State Assembly in 1882 and the state senate in 1884. He participated at the 1888 Democratic

Stair hall, present-day view

National Convention, where he submitted Grover Cleveland's name in nomination for president. Robb was offered the position of assistant secretary of state in the Cleveland administration, but he declined, preferring to devote himself to preserving the scenic resources of New York State. In 1888 he was appointed parks commissioner of the City of New York by Mayor Abraham Hewitt, and he subsequently received praise for his vigilance and effectiveness in keeping the parks of New York intact.

The Dolphins possesses a kind of deliberate informality, exemplified by an exceedingly wide veranda of tall posts and low railings that surround the house on three sides. The house's many doors, generous thresholds, and tall windows open to commodious interiors cooled by summer breezes off Lake Agawam. These portals create such a welcoming air that the visitor can easily ramble without feeling the least bit compelled to use the signature McKim, Mead & White Dutch door in front as the point of entry, particularly because it sits

Library, present-day view

intentionally off-axis with the walkway that leads to the house.

The house is oriented parallel to the lake and overlooks a lawn leading down to the water with the ocean in the distance. The rectilinear structure wears its gabled roof like a hat, adorned with major cross gables and dotted with small dormers. Only the rounded wall of windows in the master bedroom on the southeast corner breaks with the square geometry of the rest of the building. McKim uses this Baroque trick to pull the viewer's eye toward the panoramic water view. The exterior details clearly employ the architectural vocabulary of McKim, Mead & White's early Shingle-style work. The chimney on the east facade pierces through the cross gable, as well as the main roof below, to anchor the house in the landscape. As with the Montauk Association

Dining room, present-day view

houses (1882–84), the first-floor wall cladding forms a plinth of painted cedar bevel siding, and a stringcourse replaces window head casings and wraps around the entire building to establish the differentiation between floor levels, particularly at the gable ends.

The interior of the house is somewhat more formal in its configuration. The living room, which faces Lake Agawam, is centered between the dining room to the North and the library to the South. All three rooms, connected to each other through framed openings with pairs of pocket doors, have fireplaces and raised paneling above the mantels, characteristic of the McKim, Mead & White design repertoire. Entry to these rooms is through the tall living hall, whose ceiling height is diminished by wainscoted panels that terminate at the tops of the windows. Its ceiling is a combination of beams and purlins set against beadboard infill. A dramatic stair features substantial newel posts separated by closely spaced turned balusters and is illuminated by windows, below and above the porch roof, that shed light on both the landing and the second-floor hall. The woodwork, all painted crisp white, most likely had a natural finish originally. The second floor houses the major bedrooms, almost all with water views, and the third story consists of former staff quarters that serve as overflow bedrooms for relatives.

After her parents died, Louisa Livingston inherited The Dolphins, which remained in the family until the 1950s. Since then it has changed hands several times,

receiving upgraded bathrooms in 1985 along with other infrastructure improvements. In 2005, new owners Walter and Monica Noel hired architect Tim Greer to extensively renovate the building. Remedial work involved the removal of modern skylights in the veranda roof and replacement of fish-scale with wave-pattern shingles in the gables. These changes dovetail nicely with the first-floor addition of a small turreted breakfast room, very much in keeping with the spirit of the Shingle style. Having been returned to its former splendor, with added comforts for contemporary living, The Dolphins remains a reassuring presence on the serene shores of Lake Agawam.

Porch overlooking Lake Agawam, present-day view

MAYCROFT

1886

~

Residence of James Herman Aldrich and Mary Edson Aldrich

Entrance elevation

Top: Approach elevation; bottom: rear elevation

Maycroft from the water

MAYCROFT, the country residence of James Herman and Mary Edson Aldrich, exemplifies the late-19th-century East End waterfront estate. When James Aldrich visited an old friend in Sag Harbor in the 1870s, he became enamored of the once bustling whaling port, which was beginning its transformation into a thriving resort community renowned for the quietude of its bays and coves and its pristine, natural landscape all surrounding a village whose quaint character was reminiscent of small, New England seaside towns.

In 1882, the Aldriches purchased a 43.5-acre property and hired the well-known, innovative commercial architect Edward Delano Lindsey of New York. The house he designed for the Aldrich family in 1886 is a phantasmagoric melding of the Shingle and Queen Anne styles. Originally sited in the center of the property at the highest point, the two-and-a-half-story house is surrounded by thick woods and rolling lawns. Conceived to be seen from the water, the house also took full advantage of the panoramic views of lower Sag Harbor Cove. Its name, Maycroft, combines Mrs. Aldrich's name, Mary (aka May), with croft, a Middle English word meaning "field" or "very small farm."

Clearly, the approach to the estate was planned to heighten a sense of anticipation. The driveway winds through a wooded area, past a towering copper beech tree and an open lawn, and it originally formed a circle at the porte-cochere and front door. It continued through the building between the main block and kitchen wing before terminating at the carriage house a few hundred

Top: Tennis court with pavilion; bottom: porch looking towards pavilion

yards away. A separate service road from the carriage house also connected to the street, and an esplanade of catalpa trees linked the house to the tennis pavilion.

Broad, sweeping lines, reflective of the Shingle style, are expressed in the original skin of slate shingles stretched tautly over small hipped dormers that pierce through the larger roof. Massive red brick chimneys, projecting bays, gables, hipped roofs, and porches—both screened and open—form an asymmetrical and eclectic composition. The most prominent element on the west facade is a two-story semicircular tower with a conical skirted roof. Four small triangular windows punctuate the tower's spire in a staccato-like gesture, filling its attic with light. On the east front, a smaller yet taller tower pierces the main roof. The main entrance to the house consists of a pair of French doors beside a colored-glass lantern by Shelter Island's nationally renowned marine mosaic artist Walter Cole Brigham.

The interior of Maycroft—original wood finishes, hardware, light fixtures, and mantels—remained relatively unchanged for more than 125 years. In the main stairwell, a large ogival stained-glass window, commissioned in 1911 from Brigham, featured a reproduction of the facade of a somewhat drab 1650 house from Chester, England. The window is made mostly of amber and green glass, with slithers of opaque pearl delineating the window mullions of the Chester house, and the Aldrich family motto, "Providence Is Mine Inheritance," is inscribed across its face

French doors adjacent to the stairwell lead to the dining room, sitting room, and drawing room. With fenestration on three sides, the drawing room overlooked

Carriage house

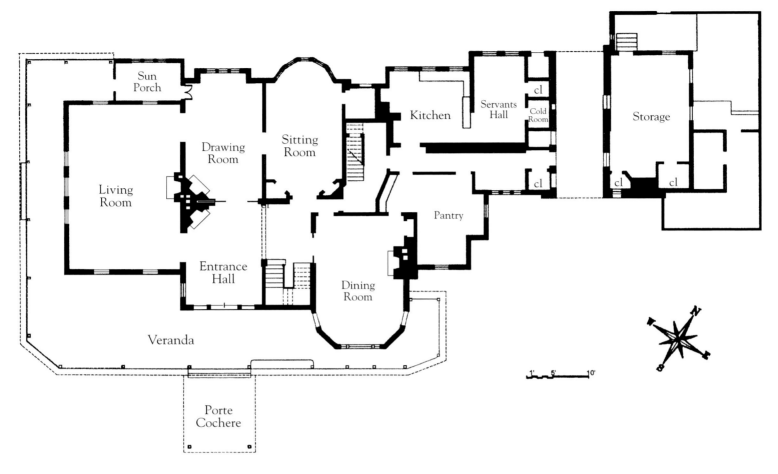

First floor plan

the cove and was remarkably light and airy despite being surrounded by a wraparound porch. The service wing contained the original kitchen, along with ancillary storage rooms and a back stair to the servants' quarters above. The second floor housed large bedrooms, with the master bedroom occupying the tower.

Son of New York dry goods magnate Herman Aldrich, James Herman Aldrich was a merchant prince; his wife, the former Mary Gertrude Edson, was descended from a long line of Long Island sea captains. The Aldriches resided on Central Park South during the winter and were deeply committed to charities, causes, and organizations affiliated with the Episcopal Church, including the building of the Cathedral of St. John the Divine.

The couple were intensely involved in all aspects of community life and contributed money, time, and initiative to many Sag Harbor projects, regularly opening their property for tennis, social, and yachting events associated with the Volunteer Boat Club. Sailing enthusiasts, they also sponsored races in the sharpie class for the Maycroft Cup.

James Aldrich died in 1917. Following the death of Mary Aldrich in 1924, Maycroft was given to the Episcopal Diocese of Long Island. Run by the Girls' Friendly Society and known as the Maycroft Holiday House, the property served for many years as a summer camp and as a retreat for businesswomen. In 1952 the Episcopal Diocese turned the property over to an order

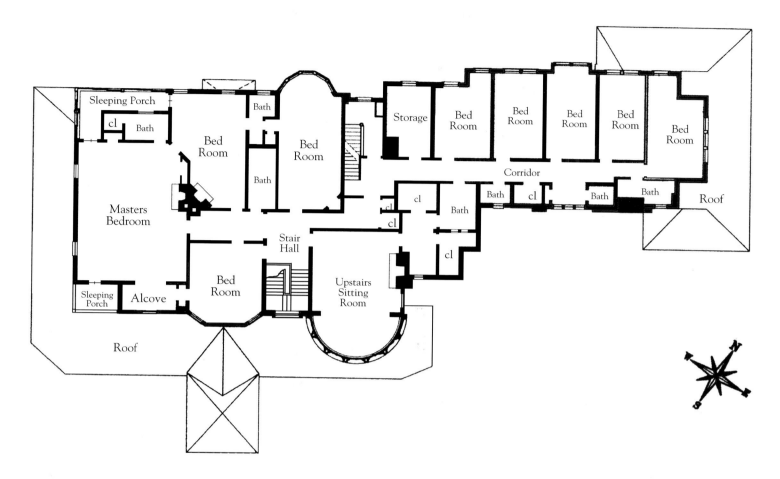

Second floor plan

of nuns, the teachers of the Children of God, who ran the Tuller School there until recent years. Very much neglected since the days of the Aldrich family and despite odd alterations done in the 1890s, Maycroft has remained relatively intact precisely because so little money was put into the structure. Now on the National Register of Historic Places, in 2004 the property was sold for $25 million, and after extensive renovations by architect James Merrell, which included moving the house closer to the water's edge and rotating it on a new foundation to regain views unblocked by foliage, a reinvigorated Maycroft will be used as a vacation retreat by its new owners.

PUDDING HILL

1887

∽

Residence of Dr. Everett and Harriet Ford Herrick

Front elevation

Sketch of Terry residence

HIGHLY VISIBLE on the corner of Woods Lane and Ocean Avenue, the first Shingle-style summer house built in East Hampton was that of Dr. Everett Herrick and his wife, Harriet. An 1854 graduate of Jefferson Medical College, Everett Herrick (1830-1914) began practicing medicine in New York in 1859. A member of the New York County and New York State medical societies, and of the American Medical Association, he also served as a president and trustee of the New York Academy of Medicine. Everett Herrick first came to East Hampton as a vacationist in 1878, and his wife, the former Harriet Ford, arrived in 1875. The couple married in 1880 and purchased the property known as Pudding Hill seven years later.

The decrepit 17th-century Thomas Osborn house on the site, reputed to be haunted, was the stuff of legend, immortalized by a rousing incident that occurred during the Revolutionary War. The bicentennial plaque on Woods Lane reveals how Pudding Hill was named: "At Sag Harbor the British soldiers were given loaves of bread. In East Hampton, they met with a different reception at another patriot's home. At the old Osborn house

the good dame of the home was making a suet pudding, which the soldiers tried to seize, but she seized the boiling pot and threw it blazing hot down the hill."

In 1887 the Herricks razed the old Osborn house and somewhat leveled the famous hill on which it stood overlooking Town Pond and Gardiner's Windmill. The couple commissioned architect Isaac Henry Green Jr. of Sayville, Long Island, to design a house similar to one he had created in his hometown 40 miles to the west for William Terry; that house had appeared in the April 1887 issue of Architecture and Building, a publication analogous in its day to *Architectural Digest*. The groundbreaking occurred in the fall of 1887, and the new house was virtually identical to the Sayville house, except its plan had been reversed.

Pudding Hill's plan is characteristic of the Shingle style. Its living hall features an oak-paneled stairwell with tall windows at its landing leading to the second-floor bedrooms. Multiple porches are set against the facades, room widths run the depth of the house, and a kitchen wing, only one room wide, is placed perpendicular to the house's long mass. Asymmetry rules the

Entrance hall, present-day view

exterior facades. On the east end, a gambrel roof containing an eyelid window with bulging hood is positioned as a cross gable against the main mass of the roof. A bell-topped turret flanks the opposite end of the wall, and a shed roof, later changed in a 1909 addition by Green, appeared as a lean-to on the south end. Diamond window panes in some windows, 15-over-15 panes in others, some with transoms of 24 panes all sitting under built-up drip-caps, force the eye to dart about in cinematic fashion to grasp subtle changes in scale.

Many of the prominent features, such as the side lean-to, allude to colonial elements found in East Hampton's surviving 17th- and 18th-century vernacular dwellings. Green designed several other houses in the village, but the influence of this particular house, with its oddball charm, can be seen throughout the environs.

Everett Herrick was the driving force behind the founding of East Hampton's Maidstone Club in 1891. As a trustee and the club's first president, he presided over its affairs until his death in 1914 at the age of 84. A revered figure in the community, he was also perhaps somewhat eccentric. At the Maidstone Club, he insisted that a bucket of water and oats be left for the tennis players, not to be partaken of until 10 minutes after the completion of play, it being considered dangerous to imbibe anything cold after being "heated." Most members considered Herrick's concoction an abomination.

An aficionado of ocean bathing and a stickler concerning issues of modesty, the good doctor would not hesitate to ask members to leave the beach if inappropriately attired. One Maidstone Club member reminisced, "The beach and its life loomed large in the world. Dr. and Mrs. Herrick were the Maharajah and Maharanee of

Book hall, present-day view

the place. At the bathing hour none dared enter the ocean until Dr. Herrick, in long flannel 'bathing dress' with all the dignity of a High Priest officiating at a rite in honor of Neptune, would advance like a pontiff, immerse his huge wooden thermometer in the surf, and holding it aloft, announce the temperature to the breathless assemblage." The strapping six-foot-three-inch Herrick also barred dogs from the Maidstone grounds, except for his own wheezing pug, Belle. He never went anywhere without the little dog sauntering alongside him. Impromptu notices, created by the Maidstone's younger set, noted the inequity: "NO DOGS ALLOWED IN THE CLUB—Except Belle."

A childless couple, the Herricks left Pudding Hill to Harriet's brother, James Ford, who rarely used it, and the house was passed on to various cousins over the years. In 1999, current owners gave both the interior and exterior a traditional makeover. Today, Pudding Hill remains a pristine presence at the gateway to what many have called "America's most beautiful village."

VILLA MARIA

1887–1919

Residences of Josiah Lombard and Marshall Ayres &
Edward Phinley Morse and Ada Martha Gravel Morse

Front elevation, original Lombard–Ayers residence

Front elevation, 1919 alteration, present-day view

VILLA MARIA, on Montauk Highway in Water Mill, is a tale of two houses and multiple owners. Situated at a bend in the road overlooking Mecox Bay, the highly visible 14.6-acre estate serves as a landmark and point of interest for people passing through the Hamptons, particularly all those drivers crawling along the road at 5 miles per hour during the summer season.

The first version of Villa Maria was built for merchant industrialists Josiah Lombard and Marshall Ayres, owners of both the Seaboard Lumber and Tidewater Oil corporations. Lombard and Ayres initially purchased

eight acres at the intersection of Halsey Lane and Mecox Bay and later added 1.8 acres containing the Corwith Windmill and more waterfront property. In 1887 they erected a sprawling Queen Anne–Shingle-style house known as Red Gables, for its red roof.

Red Gables' cacophonous assortment of asymmetrical design elements made a singular exercise in extravagance. Dormers and cross gables receded into one another, terminating against all sides of the main hipped roof. Balconies, a porte-cochere, a tower with enclosed widow's walk—accessed by a winding stair from the third

Rear elevation, 1919 alteration, present-day view

floor—and a wraparound porch with latticework screens all were deftly cased and clad in shingles.

In the late 1890s, Lombard and Ayres, whose company had gone into receivership, sold Red Gables to renowned New York urologist Edward L. Keyes. A Yale graduate who held a medical degree from what would become New York's Cornell Medical Center, Keyes started his practice on the Lower East Side and wrote the era's definitive textbook on his specialty. After deciding to build a new, smaller house on the edge of the Art Village in Southampton, in 1909 Keyes sold Red Gables to Brooklyn shipbuilder Edward Phinley Morse. A decade later, Morse commissioned well-known Brooklyn

architect Frank Freeman to completely recast Red Gables into an estate house.

Cited in 1890 by architecture critic Montgomery Schuyler for having produced "the most artistic examples of the Richardsonian Romanesque in our domestic architecture," Frank Freeman also worked in the Queen Anne and Shingle styles in a manner consistent with the 1887 Red Gables. Consequently, there has been continued speculation that he was also the original architect for the house. Regardless, Freeman's 1919 alteration of Red Gables was a complete transmogrification. By stripping the exterior of its shingles and eccentric features, adding extensions to substantially

Staircase, present-day view

Second-floor stairhall, present-day view

Ballroom, present-day view

enlarge the building, and covering the whole with a coat of stucco, he transformed the bumptious late Victorian cottage into a stately Italian villa by the sea. A grand ballroom, added to the west, boasts a massive portico with limestone columns and Egyptian capitals. Centered in the rear facade, a second, semicircular, classical portico serves as an open-air extension of the entrance foyer. Ersatz Beaux-Arts—Tuscany meets Rome with a nod to Athens and Grecian fenestration—the building nonetheless comes off as a rather balanced edifice, a central core with end wings whose roofs are highlighted by barrel-vaulted dormers.

Inside, the dominant feature is a spectacular spiraling three-story stairwell with oak balustrades and limestone walls. Halls adjoin the landings on each floor level, providing a comfortable transition between the nine master bedrooms with eight baths and the public spaces below. Featuring an unusual amount of natural light for a building of this era, the principal rooms, except for a cozy wood-paneled library off the stairwell foyer, are oriented to the water view.

The newly formed house was renamed Grey Gables, and its owner, Edward Morse, was a Nova Scotian who came to Brooklyn at age 20 and turned a small ship-

Chapel, present-day view

smith's shop into the $20 million Morse Drydock & Repair Company. In 1929 he merged Morse with five other companies to form United Shipyards, which controlled more than 50 percent of the drydock facilities in the Port of New York. Grey Gables served as Morse's "intown" house; he also owned another house on Flying Point Beach, which remains in his family.

On August 17, 1929, Grey Gables, on 20 acres with a superintendent's home, a garage, other outbuildings, and 1,200 feet of frontage on Mecox Bay, was auctioned to Courtland Palmer of Manhattan for $100,000. Its ownership passed to Mrs. Irene Coleman, an actress, whose stage name was Ann Murdagh. Sold again for $250,000 in 1931 to the Sisters of the Order of St. Dominic of

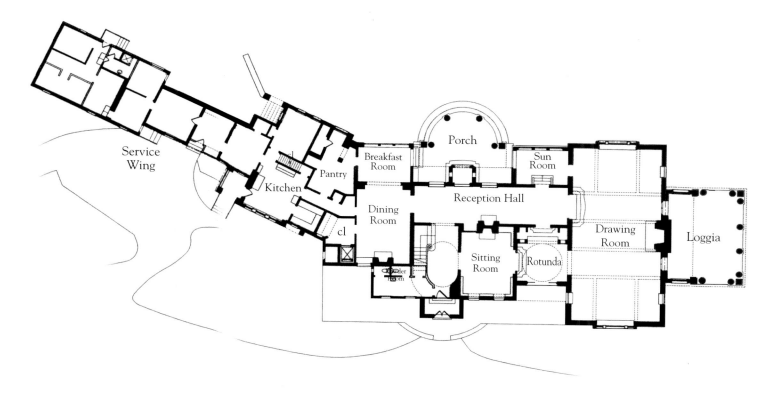

First floor plan

Amityville, it became the Villa Maria High School, a boarding institution for young women preparing for life in the sisterhood. Local girls, known as "day hops," also attended the high school. The school closed in 1953, and the property served as both an infirmary and a retirement home for senior sisters until 1985, when the Dominicans initiated an education program open to the public. The internationally recognized Siena Spirituality center, founded in 1990, offered retreats and sabbaticals under Dominican conventions which focused on New Cosmology. During the summers of 2001 and 2002, Villa Maria hosted the Hampton Designer Showcase, an event that raised money for remedial work on the facilities. These programs, however, could not provide enough income to sustain the property, and in the spring of 2005 it was once more put up for sale, with an asking price of $25 million.

The Sisters imposed two conditions on the property's purchasers. First, the 21,000-square-foot mansion could not be razed and the property was to remain basically unchanged; second, a 300-foot public view of the water had to be preserved even if other changes were made on the property. This second requirement is in keeping with the philosophy of the Sisters of St. Dominic, whose land ethic involves caring for the natural ecology and habitat of their properties.

In September 2005, the property was sold for $35 million to designers Vincent and Louise Camuto, who met all the requirements for stewardship. The Camutos were already the owners of two historic houses in Southampton, including the former Wooldon Manor pool house on Gin Lane. Their present plan is to restore Villa Maria to its former grandeur and use it for special events. For a property so physically transformed, with multiple names and many owners, it seems rather remarkable that Villa Maria will remain an oasis of permanence in a sea of development, with a viewshed for all to appreciate.

THE ART VILLAGE

1891

Studio building, present-day view

Cottage, present-day view

TO WALK down the narrow lanes in the enclave known as the Art Village is to be transported back in time to a place where intimate, miniature scale and tactile ambiance convey a richness that has nothing to do with wealth. From the plantings to the street gutters to the garden gates and enchanted cottages, the Art Village is a magical world unto itself. The effects of this inspired place can still be felt in American art and architecture more than a century later.

In 1891 the Shinnecock Summer School of Art, the first out-of-doors art school in the United States, opened to allow amateur and professional art students from all over the country to study plein air painting under the tutelage of artist William Merritt Chase. The 100 to 150 who studied there each summer boarded at the Art Club, which accommodated 30 women with a chaperone; local boardinghouses; with fishermen or farmers; or in one of the dozen cottages constructed in the Art Village compound.

At the behest of Mrs. William S. Hoyt—the daughter of Lincoln's secretary of the treasury, Salmon Chase, later a Supreme Court justice—and Mrs. Henry Kirke Porter, Samuel Parrish donated the land for the school. On February 2, 1891, a *New York World* article reported that prominent individuals such as "Mrs. Astor, Mrs. August Belmont, Mrs. Andrew Carnegie, Mrs. W. K.

Two views of the Art Village

Vanderbilt, Mrs. Ballard Smith and Mrs. Whitney" were also supporters of the school.

The choice of location for the Art Village, just beyond the western edge of Southampton Village at the flat end of Shinnecock Hills, was explained by a student: "The existence of the school there is due primarily to the fact that some rich people owned some poor land." In 1878, Ernest Ingersoll wrote in *Harper's New Monthly Magazine* that "Shinnecock Hills is a synonym of what is utterly barren and useless . . . sandy knolls densely grown with a chaparral of scrub oak and pine, alternating with swampy hollows where the moss trails far down from the skeletons of dead trees, and the imagination conjures dreadful inhabitants out of the dark tussocks."

It was on this barren, exposed landscape near the Shinnecock Indian Reservation that the Art Village cottages, grouped near the studio building, appeared like diamonds in the rough. This collection of buildings is unique in its layout of curving and angled streets, the interrelationships of these tiny residences to one another and the street front, and the avoidance of architectural statement-making. Lack of regularity, dictated by the irregular shape of the site itself, gives the complex an expansive feeling and a sense of anticipation that can come only from wondering what lies around the bend.

The cottage designs, no two alike, adhere to a unifying palette of applied elements such as unpainted shingles, rustic stone chimneys, turreted bays, subsumed porches, and low, sheltering rooflines punctuated by dormers—all characteristic of the rural regional vernacular building tradition. Antoinette de Forest Parsons, in the June 27, 1895, issue of the *St. Paul Dispatch*, described the cottages: "The outer walls, washed by rains, and polished by the sun, shine like satin. Inside the cottages are finished in wood of a dark tone, and red curtains in the diamond-paned windows, or swaying festoons of vines that clamber up to the roofs against the gray walls make almost the only spots of bright color." This self-contained subdivision was given its harmonious and cohesive identity by road gutters of cement inlaid with beach stones; primitive wooden fences between the cottages just a few inches high; and hedges with nascent landscaping, small trees called "pre-Raphaelite" by the students for their meager foliage and installed under the careful direction of Mrs. Porter.

Art Village with windmill

Several publications from the era state that prominent architects designed the cottages, and their signature detailing, possibly indicative of authorship, includes the same type of diagonal windowpanes employed in the work of architects Katharine Budd and Grosvenor Atterbury. Unpainted beaded wallboards resemble those seen in the Stanford White design of the Chase Homestead, and some fireplace surrounds with embossed swags uniquely echo the dainty Colonial theme established in The Orchard by McKim, Mead & White.

Art Village student Katharine Budd, who worked on her own cottage there, also remodeled the cottage once belonging to Mrs. Hoyt for the artist Zella de Milhau. De Milhau named her cottage Laffalot, based on the Indian name Chlioata, bestowed on her by the Shinnecocks, which meant "one who laughs a lot." Budd, also responsible for the expansion to the studio building, fused a former dormitory structure, moved from across the street, to the rustic, vertical-log studio. Dubbed Villa Artistica in Budd's personal records, the house became the private residence of Mrs. Porter in 1903 after the school closed. Many of the other cottages also had playful names, such as Half-Acre, Stepping Stones, and the Pillbox. Architect Grosvenor Atterbury's first project in the Art Village was the house he designed for himself. In 1908 he moved the house to another site in Shinnecock Hills.

Life at the Art Village consisted of hard work mixed with recreational activities. On Monday mornings, Chase conducted formal criticism in the school studio. Sketches from the previous week were placed on a 12-foot-long two-sided easel, and the students, seated on campstools, listened as more than 200 studies were critiqued in a morning's session. One student described the critiques:

This was as good as a bull-fight to the cottagers and the loungers from the hotels—the patrons were out in full force to patronize and gave parties at little expense and with great gusto to their friends, invit-

ing all they cared to invite to attend the morning criticisms. Carriages and even motor cars were at the door, the "nobility" with their lorgnettes ready, the students all sitting on little camp-stools before a large revolving easel. While Chase criticized the studies on one side a servant filled the other side with more. Thus it went round and round until hundreds of daubs had met their fate.

Another student remarked, "Isn't it perfectly heartless for them to come here and ogle through their lorgnettes, and put on the airs of connoisseurs and laugh when Mr. Chase says cutting things? I'd like to kill them all." Occasionally, Chase had to make it clear to visitors that the criticism session, intended to aid the students, was not a recreational activity.

On Tuesdays, Chase spent the entire day outside with models and criticized the work of his students while they did their plein air sketching. He was revered as a teacher, and his suggestions were tempered to meet both the needs and abilities of the students. Chase offered comments such as:

Open your sky more and paint a tree that birds could fly through . . . Try to paint the unusual: never mind if it does not meet the approval of the masses. Always remember that it is the man who paints the unusual who educates the public. I am never so disappointed in a piece of my work as when it meets with the approval of the public. . . . How much light there is in everything out of doors! Look out of a window and note how light the darkest spots in the landscape are when compared with the sash of the window . . . In painting a sandy beach try to imagine that you are walking upon it and when dealing with a round object try to feel that it is really round . . . It usually takes two to paint a good picture — one to paint and the other to stand by with an ax to kill him before he spoils it.

Plein air painting

Aside from "Chase Days" on Mondays and Tuesdays, the students worked independently outdoors on drawings and paintings during the week. Many of the social activities in the Southampton community, including the plays, dances, concerts, and "witch parties," were organized by the students of the Art Village. The most recognized event involved Chase's revival of tableaux vivants, in which models, in some cases Chase's children or pupils, were grouped in a frame as a representation of a famous painting. Among the best known were Mrs. Chase as Dagnan-Bouveret's "Madonna" and her daughter Helen as Velasquez's "Infanta."

Work from the Shinnecock Summer School of Art was exhibited in Philadelphia, in Pittsburgh, and at the New York Art School. School alumni included artists Joseph Stella, Howard Chandler Christy, Rockwell Kent, Charles W. Hawthorne, Arthur B. Frost, and Marshall Fry, and architects John Russell Pope, Grosvenor Atterbury, and Katharine Budd.

The Shinnecock Summer School of Art closed its doors when Chase resigned as headmaster after the 1902 season. Despite its brief history, the school gave expression to a distinctly new form of American landscape painting. Other plein air schools, based on the Shinnecock model, opened around the United States in places such as Cape Cod, Massachusetts; Mendota, Minnesota; and, in 1914, Carmel, California, where the Carmel School of Art again had Chase as head teacher.

Most of the buildings in the Art Village today remain relatively unaltered. Often called a toy village, it remains one of the most unique cultural landmarks in Southampton. Preparations are currently being made by the Southampton Landmarks and Historic Districts Board to have the Art Village designated a historic district.

WILLIAM MERRITT CHASE HOMESTEAD

1892

Residence of William Merritt Chase and Alice Gerson Chase

Chase house from front, c. 1908

Chase house side elevation, 1892

THE SUMMER residence of artist William Merritt Chase (1849–1916), nestled in a secluded section of Shinnecock Hills, is an architectural landmark whose importance transcends the confines of Long Island's East End. Chase, who was a student at New York's National Academy of Design, also studied in Europe before gaining acclaim through showing his work at the 1876 Centennial Exposition in Philadelphia. He later taught at the Art Students League of New York and was widely acknowledged as a gifted teacher; his pupils included Charles Demuth, Charles Sheeler, Howard Chandler Christy, and Georgia O'Keefe. Chase was considered a major painter and influential spirit in the American art scene during the late 19th and early 20th centuries, and he produced some of his most significant work at Shinnecock.

Following a tour of Europe, amateur artist Mrs. William S. Hoyt proposed the establishment of the first American out-of-doors school of art, at Shinnecock Hills. Eliciting support from Mrs. Henry Kirke Porter,

Samuel Parrish, and others to create the school, in 1890 she invited Chase to visit and asked to him to become the school's director. By the summer of 1891, the Shinnecock Summer School of Art had opened with William Merritt Chase as its head. Chase stayed at the inn associated with the Art Village complex during his first summer in residence.

Located on land donated by Samuel Parrish three miles west of the school, the Chase Homestead was completed by the summer of 1892 with McKim, Mead & White acting as architects of record. Archival documentation indicates that the house and combined studio actually had been designed in 1888, possibly for Charles L. Atterbury at a different site. Although the architect's rendering shows the house in close proximity to the water, in reality the building was situated on pastureland between Shinnecock and Peconic bays, where it once overlooked a totally undeveloped landscape. Katherine Metcalfe Root, in her book *The Life and Art of William*

Hall dining room showing stone fireplace with Augustus Saint-Gaudens's bas-relief portrait of William Merritt Chase

Merritt Chase, described the site: "Surrounded by bay, sweet fern and vivid patches of butterfly weed, Chase's house is set as it were, in the midst of one of his own landscapes, its nearest neighbor off on a distant hilltop. On one side lies the ocean in the vista; on the other Peconic Bay. The water is not near enough to be heard except in a storm; its place is decorative rather than intimate. Indeed it would seem as if house and studio must have been designed to make pictures from within, for every window and doorway framed a composition."

Fellow members of the Tile Club and the Century Association, Stanford White and Chase were friends with many interests in common. The house, designed by White pro bono, posed interesting problems from a programmatic point of view. The studio wing, which needed a certain amount of separation from the rest of the structure, was nonetheless nicely integrated within the composition by means of the massive gambrel roof that covers the entire building. From the exterior, the entrance to the house is located under a six-bay covered porch supported by fluted Doric columns with rope course capitals. The west end of the porch descends a few steps to a lower porch, this change in height denoting the articulation of the studio wing.

Inside the house, a two-story living hall serves as the locus for family activity. Iron hooks that once supported a bas-relief portrait of Chase by Augustus Saint-Gaudens remain embedded in the masonry of the room's rough stone fireplace. On the west side of the living hall, a staircase, with highly finished tooled balusters and a wooden, wound rope newel post once capped by a statue of winged Mercury, ascends to a gallery-like second-floor balcony, cantilevered on all four sides. Seven bedrooms connect to the balcony, and several others were later added in the attic as the Chase family grew.

Just under the stairwell landing is a passageway that has very low headroom and leads to a door and short stair down into the discreetly tucked-away studio. Here, Chase covered the tall walls with reproductions, many of his own paintings, objets d'art, furniture, bric-a-brac, and fishnets, creating an inner sanctum where he could paint with enthusiasm. Large north-facing windows were installed shortly after the completion of the house, and in 1902 a massive stone fireplace was added to the studio's east wall.

An arched opening on the east wall of the central living hall leads to a dining room terminated by a curved wall at its far end. The public rooms all possess a warm, rich glow and are finished in beaded boards from floor to ceiling. In the 19th century, this type of wainscoting was typically seen in modest residences. A low-budget affair pared down to a minimum of detail, the Chase house is basically devoid of decoration, but several features, both structural and decorative, imparted richness: painted trim that highlighted the massing; size modulations in the fenestration; a recessed second-floor porch on the west end; festive striped awnings adorning windows; a medallion, flanked by painted fanlights, in the living hall ceiling; a rounded dining bay; and an enormous Chinese parasol casually placed by the front door.

From the exterior, the house is layered front to back with three overlapping gambrel roofs that establish a rhythm in the massing and a resolution of volumetric connections in the interior. The gambrels reduce the scale of the two-and-a-half-story structure by one story while adding extra floor space to the second floor. Although the house appears simple, there are 5,000 square feet of space within its walls.

The Chases moved into the house with three children. They eventually added five more, and with each new arrival, a Japanese paper fish could be seen raised on a staff over the house. Archival photographs and records indicate that Chase was a devoted father who often portrayed his children in paintings such as "Hall at Shinnecock," "Morning at Canoe Place," and "The Bayberry Bush."

William Merritt Chase taught at the Shinnecock Summer School of Art through 1902, when he resigned as director. He continued to summer at his Shinnecock cottage until his death in 1916. It was then sold to a niece of Samuel Parrish. In 1983 the Chase house and studio were included on the National Register of Historic Places. Very few alterations had been made to the house over the years: the 1917 addition of two windows on the eastern gambrel wall and eyebrow windows; a rear laundry room; bathroom and porch in 1920; and a new kitchen sometime after that. The current owners continue to maintain the Chase Homestead with respect and good stewardship.

CLAVERACK

1892

~

Residence of Thomas H. Barber and Harriet Townsend Barber

Entrance elevation, present-day view

Garden elevation, present-day view

CLAVERACK, the Halsey Neck Lane property of Thomas Henry Barber, was one of the first large-scale "cottages" built in the estate section of Southampton. Designed in 1892 by notable architect Robert Henderson Robertson, a fellow summer colonist, Claverack epitomized formal living conducted with casual simplicity.

Born in England, Thomas Henry Barber (1844–1905) was raised in the United States, where he attended West Point and served in the U.S. Army until 1885. He went on to become inspector general of the National Guard of New York and in 1899 advanced to the rank of brigadier general. Barber, who was active in Southampton affairs, initiated the idea for the erection of the Soldiers and Sailors Monument in Agawam Park and oversaw its completion. He also served as a trustee of the Rogers Memorial Library. His wife, Harriet Townsend Barber (1864–942), was descended from an old Hudson Valley family, the Van Rensselaers, "Lords Directors" of the Dutch West India Company. The Van Rensselaers were one of the original Dutch families to settle in the Hudson River Valley, and their vast, 2,100-square-mile property Rensselaerwyck, near Albany, included a large stone edifice with dormers and gambrel roof, built in 1765 by Harriet's grandfather, Steven Van Rensselaer.

West facade

Harriet Barber was attached to her ancestral home and wanted her new house to replicate it as closely as possible. In 1893 the family named the house Claverack, meaning "clover field" in Dutch, which was taken from the original Rensselaerwyck house.

Claverack sits on a smooth, flat lawn behind a U-shaped driveway entered through gates framed by pairs of giant Japanese stone lanterns called *ishidoro*. Although modeled after the original manor, the new house was clad in shingles rather than stone, and its window placement and surface detailing were at variance with its Dutch colonial predecessor. Overall, Robertson's design captured the stately spirit and appearance of the 1765 house.

The main section rises two stories to a large gambrel roof with four dormers and a pedimented cross gable at its center, its added prominence owing to tall ceiling heights on the first floor. A one-story wing flanking the south end of the main structure provides a summer porch, and a complementing wing on the north encloses kitchen and service functions.

Rear garden

A Dutch door centered under a generously scaled front entry porch, supported by double Doric columns, leads into the main entrance hall. The hall, which has carved moldings and door surrounds topped by pediments, bisects the center of the house in an east-west direction and leads to the rear gardens through an arched opening under the main stairwell. This stairwell, with its lacy carved spindles and half-story landings, rises through the full three stories of the structure.

To the south of the front door is the main drawing room, with large windows overlooking the front lawn. Originally the draperies in this room were copied from a pattern used by Dolly Madison in the 1809 White House. Mrs. Barber's ancestor Mrs. Edward Livingston, a friend of Mrs. Madison, was given permission by the first lady to use the pattern at Montgomery Place, the Livingston manor house on the Hudson. Off the drawing room to the south is the summer room, used for larger parties and gatherings, and on its west side is a richly

Entrance hall

Dining room

paneled library that features a handsome fireplace and overlooks the gardens.

Across the main hall on the north side overlooking the front lawn is a large dining room, which once displayed ancestral portraits of Mrs. Barber's family, as well as Dutch furnishings—a screen, with panels of oil paintings depicting the 12th-century counts of Flanders, came from a house in Amsterdam. The remaining portion of this floor is devoted to service and staff rooms.

The second floor divides into light and airy bedroom suites off a central hall, with the southern rooms enjoying access to an outdoor terrace. The third floor contains additional guest rooms and attic space.

The 20-room house was once part of a 30-acre estate that consisted of greenhouses, garages, outbuildings, and orchards. Although reduced in size, Claverack still provides a private paradise of lush gardens and stately trees. Originally designed by the firm of Olmsted Brothers, the

Summer room

grounds featured boxwood and perennial gardens known throughout the Hamptons for their splendor. According to Louise Shelton in her 1915 book *Beautiful Gardens in America*, "Southampton, at the eastern end, in proportion to population has probably a greater number of gardens than any town in the state, almost all of them designed and developed by their owners, who have thus delightfully expressed their love of flowers." On view in the garden at Claverack was a sundial with the inscription "The hour passes, the deed remains."

Thomas Barber summered at Claverack for about 13 years before his death in 1905. His wife, one of Southampton's leading hostesses, remained at Claverack until she died in 1942. Their daughter, Ethel Barber MacLean Johnson, continued using the property until she sold it to Jesse Donahue, the former owner of Wooldon Manor. In 1973, Henry Tilford Mortimer, Claverack's fourth owner, renamed the estate Keewaydin, after his father's Tuxedo Park estate, a name derived from Henry Wadsworth Longfellow's reference in his poem "The Song of Hiawatha" to "the region of the home wind/of the Northwest Wind, Keewaydin." Appropriately, Longfellow invented Keewaydin to represent the importance of Indian culture to America, and the house that bears the name is in fact situated a mile away from the Shinnecock Nation, the oldest Indian reservation in America.

In 1988, Keewaydin served as a decorator's show house to benefit the Rogers Memorial Library in Southampton. The current owners, in 1995, embarked on a complete renovation of the house, upgrading its infrastructure, adding a sympathetically designed screened porch, and cosmetically refreshing the interiors, all while retaining the historic fabric of one of Southampton's most dignified mansions.

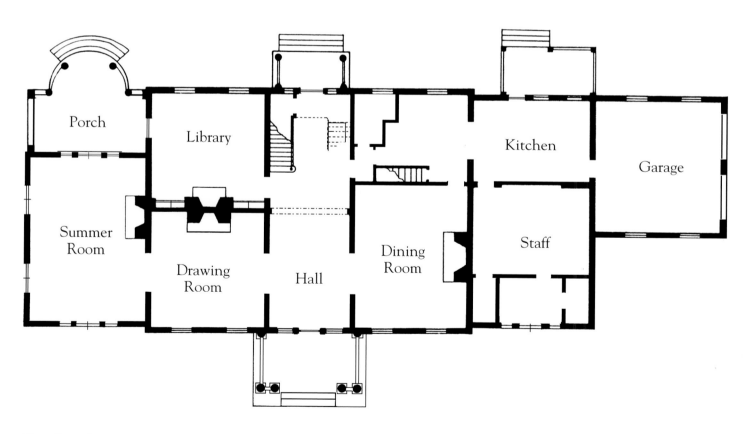

First floor plan

THE ORCHARD

c. 1895–1906

~

Residence of James Lawrence Breese and Frances Tileston Potter Breese

Front elevation

Entrance drive

THE ORCHARD, a not-so-simple house with a simple name, is one of the finest and most prominent estates in the Hamptons. Considered a masterwork of architects McKim, Mead & White, the house and its design evolved from an existing 1858 Greek Revival sea captain's house on the 30-acre Drake farm on Hill Street in Southampton.

James Lawrence Breese (1854–1934), a wealthy financier and renowned amateur photographer, bought the Drake property around 1895. Born into a socially prominent New York family that emigrated from England in the early 1700s, Breese was already a successful Wall Street broker in the firm of Breese & Smith when he married Frances Tileston Potter (1864–1917) of Newport and fathered three sons and a daughter. Despite a fortune made in finance, his real loves were art, archi-

tecture, automobiles, inventions, and photography. Breese was the leading figure in an amateur photography salon called the Carbonites, named for the carbon printing process used in photography. Other Carbonites included Breese's best friend, architect Stanford White; architects Charles McKim, William Mead, and Whitney Warren; sculptor Augustus Saint-Gaudens; and illustrator Charles Dana Gibson.

After purchasing their property, the Breeses rented for a few seasons before deciding to build. George Washington's Mount Vernon provided the model for the main section of the Breese residence. With the celebration of America's colonial past in the late 19th century, Colonial Revival homes came into vogue. The Orchard, which is noted as one of the best examples of this period, aimed to be a simple Colonial house, but its oceanic

Garden elevation

breadth of 250 feet and its 35 large rooms and vast gardens rendered it far more complex.

A long, straight formal drive lined with boxwood led to a two-and-a-half story house with eight Doric columns supporting a two-story porch with a deep overhang. Conservatories, acting as links to other wings, break up the U-shaped plan, with its primarily symmetrical facade. Recalling the plantations of the Old South, the house is clad in painted cypress shingles with overscaled exposures, its windows are framed with dark green shutters, and, à la Jefferson, its weathered gray roof is topped at the peak by a Chinese Chippendale railed piazza flanked by barreled dormers.

The interiors provide a combination of eclectic styles ranging from the colonial period to the Italian Renaissance. Through a Dutch door, the entrance hall reveals a very American display of colonial detailing,

built-up Greek Revival door frames, full-height raised-panel wainscoting, and an ornate swag-rimmed plaster ceiling medallion. On axis with the front door at the hall's end is an elliptically shaped staircase with curved inset panels terminating at the sill of a tripartite Palladian window overlooking the gardens.

East of the front hall was the original library, later converted to an Adam-style reception room, and mirrored on the west by the original music room, eventually converted to the drawing room. A breakfast room, named for its Etruscan pottery collection and neoclassical decor, adjoins the drawing room. Adjacent is the dining room, featuring an ornamental plaster ceiling, painted paneled walls, and a fireplace surrounded by Delft tiles. The kitchens, pantries, and servants' hall on the first floor, and the second-floor servants' rooms, occupy the wing north of the dining room. A spinelike

Entrance gates

Illuminated gardens

secondary hall off the entrance hall, running along the east-west axis and passing alongside the staircase, connects the end wings to the central core of the house.

At the eastern end of the hall is the conservatory, where a marble fountain trickles above a floor of Japanese tiles. Originally an open arched drive, this space served as the main entry to the house until it was enclosed in 1906. A groined vaulted, arched green trellis covered the ceiling and walls of the room, which was furnished with exotic plants, marble tables, and classical antiquities. An old Greek Revival door ensemble with a fanlight, possibly salvaged from the Drake house, is embedded in the east wall.

It is through this door that the genius of Stanford White is fully revealed. Although the parameters of scale in the rest of the house were dictated by the relationship of the original Drake house shell and limited ceiling heights, White's added music room was the largest space

on the premises and was certainly one of the most notable and spectacular rooms in the Hamptons.

Conceived by Breese and White, the music room took its present form in 1906, tripled in size from a previous small rustic studio and redecorated in the Italian Renaissance style. The room extended north and encompassed a space measuring 28 by 70 feet with 18-foot ceilings. The walls of linenfold oak paneling were partially covered with tapestries and flanked by large leaded-glass windows containing stained-glass medallions, which, according to Breese's daughter Frances Breese Miller, depicted the signers of the Magna Carta. An Aeolian pipe organ with gilded pipes filled the wall at the north end. Above is an Italian gilded, coffered ceiling with indirect lighting designed to make the entire room shimmer.

The music room served as a showcase for Breese's ever-growing collections of European art and furnishings, some 1,500 objects. Bearskin rugs, gilded chaises and consoles, oil paintings, chandeliers, torchières, mounted animal heads, commodious sofas, and various period chairs established this sumptuous room as the heart of the house.

In her autobiography, *Tanty: Encounters with the Past*, Francis Breese Miller wrote, "Although my father's taste was less flamboyant than Mr. White's, he was persuaded by him to put in ceiling-high carved gilt columns in the four corners of the room and a painted Italian ceiling. While the painting was being done, I used to enjoy watching Mr. White, his red hair en brosse, lying flat on his back on the elevated platform showing the Italian workmen how he wanted the work done." In a *Newsday* interview, Miller said, "You know for a rather formal

looking house, life was pretty informal there. . . . My father hated it when people called it a ballroom, it was our music room . . . but if we wanted to dance there, we'd just roll up the rugs." She recalled after Stanford White's shooting, "I heard the shocking news of his assassination when I saw my father rushing down the hall towards my mother's room exclaiming, 'Stan's been shot!'" The music room, one of Stanford White's final works, remains a crowning achievement in a career cut short.

East of the music room, the billiard room and squash court were subsequently converted to a library and Adam style dining room, respectively. The second floor of this wing also contained guest rooms overlooking the east lawn with a subsumed balcony behind two-story columns. Eight simply decorated master and guest

Entrance foyer with plastered ceiling

Elliptical stairwell

suites filled the second floor of the residence's central section, and the third floor contained two guest rooms and storage.

The Olmsted Brothers designed The Orchard's classically axial landscaping. In front of the house, large specimen trees, shrubbery, and orchards (these pre-existing orchards which inspired its name) surrounded a carpet of lawn. Out the back was a parterre, divided into many formal garden rooms. Roses, edged in small boxwood, formed some of these rooms, and others were filled with perennials and rhododendron. The central axis continues through lawns and hew-edged vistas, almost 700 feet from the street into an endless perspective.

The garden reached its zenith after Breese's inspirational 1905 trip to Italy, where he encountered a pergola at Capri. Afterward, Stanford White redesigned the garden to include a colonnaded 144-foot-long pergola, an extension of the residence that was constructed out of brick columns with stucco cladding, and cypress beams covered in twisted branches, to form a roof luxuriously draped with roses. A brick herringbone walk wove through the arbor and gardens, dotted with classical stat-

Top: Dining room; bottom: drawing room

Original studio

uary, urns, pots, marble herms, and antique benches. A 200-foot-long peony walk edged in boxwood, a cutting garden, a caretaker's cottage, and a garage/stable complex composed the remaining landscape. At night, the entire garden became illuminated by the new electric light provided by Breese's own power plant. In 1915, *Country Life in America* dubbed The Orchard—widely published at the time—one of "the best twelve country houses in America."

Breese and White constantly tinkered with design features throughout the property. A multi-tiered basin that constituted the central garden fountain was moved and replaced by "The Frog Boy," a small Janet Scudder sculpture of a dancing boy surrounded by three frogs.

Francis Miller in *Tanty* recounted that her father thought it looked too new and preferred the pantina of age. The statue did acquire the patina, only to lose it to an industrious child who thought he was doing a favor for Breese by scrubbing away the ravages of time.

Breese and his family were important members of Southampton society and often hosted charity events and fundraisers. In 1915 the music room was the scene of a double wedding for daughter Frances and son Robert. Breese was one of the first automobile owners in town and often was seen speeding around Southampton at a breathtaking rate of 35 miles per hour.

During the 1920s, because of fluctuating fortunes, Breese sometimes rented out The Orchard in the

Music room fireplace detail

Music room

summer. In 1926 he subdivided the estate and sold the fully furnished house on 16 acres to Charles Edward Merrill (1885–1956)—though he refused to part with the Frog Boy sculpture. Even in reduced circumstances, Breese lived in a cottage named Little Orchard on a few remaining acres and remained an active figure in Southampton society until his death at 80 in 1934.

Merrill founded the investment firm Charles E. Merrill & Company, which evolved into the world-renowned firm of Merrill Lynch & Company. He and second wife, Helen Ingram, entertained on a grand scale. In September 1932, with the house and grounds illuminated by hundreds of lanterns and lights, 1,000 guests attended daughter Doris Merrill's debutante ball. In 1935 the estate was again illuminated and swathed in flowers as 600 guests attended her wedding to Robert Magowan, the

future chairman of Safeway Stores. Merrill continued to use the estate until his death in 1956.

The contents of The Orchard, much of which came from Breese, were distributed among Merrill's three children. Daughter Doris Merrill Magowan (1914–2001) used these pieces in her many homes, including the beach house at Wooldon Manor. In a bequest to Amherst College, his alma mater, Merrill donated The Orchard, which became the Merrill Center for Economics. After the center failed in 1960, the property was sold to the Nyack Boys School. The school closed in 1972, and the deteriorating house faced potential demolition.

In 1980 the house was included on the National Register of Historic Places. A development company bought the property, converted the main house into five

Conservatory

Garden allée

condominium units, and built new townhouses along the perimeter of the estate while preserving the gardens. The Orchard, now renamed Whitefield in honor of its architect, Stanford White, remains the crown jewel of Hill Street and has frequently been cited as an excellent model for the adaptive reuse of former estate properties.

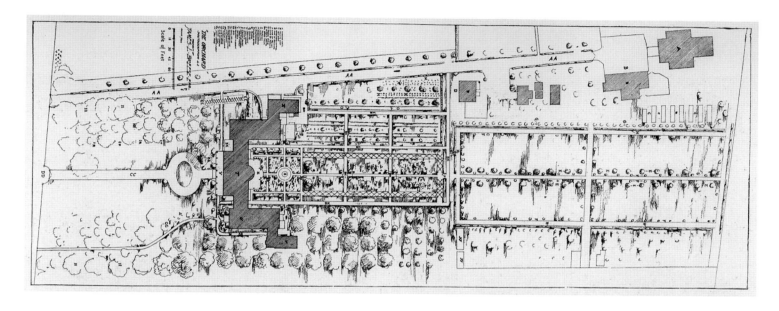

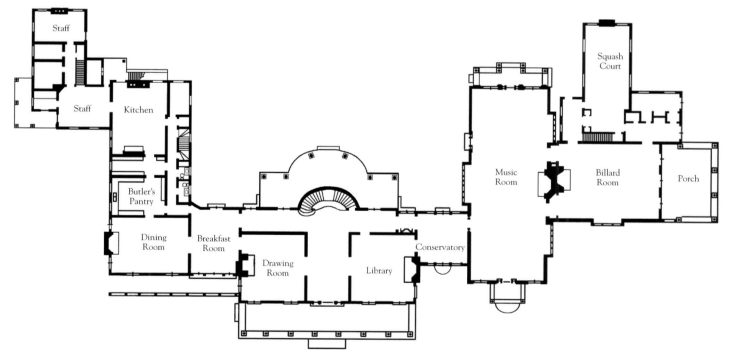

Top: Site plan; bottom: first floor plan

THE CREEKS

1899

❧

Residence of Albert Herter and Adele McGinnis Herter

Entrance facade with "The Garden of the Sun"

Georgica pond elevation

IN THE East Hampton estate of Albert Herter (1871–1950) and Adele Herter (1869–1946), imagination, individuality, and money combined to shape an atmospheric property without equal on the East End. Initially known as Près Choisis, the house was later renamed The Creeks.

Albert Herter was the son of Christian and Mary Herter. His father, famous for his highly crafted furniture and for being part of the Herter Brothers firm of New York, was a society decorator for prestigious homes such as William H. Vanderbilt's New York mansion on Fifth Avenue and rooms in the Ulysses S. Grant White House.

Herter grew up in a household dedicated to the arts. He studied painting at the Art Students' League and in Paris, where he met his future wife, Adele McGinnis, the daughter of a wealthy banker. They married in 1893 and spent their honeymoon painting in Japan and elsewhere in Asia.

When Christian Herter died in 1883, his wife, Mary, inherited an estate in excess of $10 million. In 1894 she bought Albert and Adele a wedding gift of 75 Georgica Pond acres. Inheritances from both families allowed the couple to devote their lives to their art, and each became a noted artist, he as a muralist, she as a portraitist.

The following summer, the Herters rented a house on Georgica Pond. In his recollection for *Fifty Years of the Maidstone Club*, Albert recalled his boyhood visit to Dr. and Mrs. Newton on the pond and his personal history with the neighbors:

There were no cocktails, no bridge, no all-night parties. We were happy painting in the stable and at night thinking up practical jokes on the Robert Sewells, who lived in a small cottage in the woods . . . Both Mr. and Mrs. Sewell were artists who painted classic nudes in the woods, the model being a martyred young sister-in-law who would in turn pose for Venus, or Psyche, or Calypso, and end the season burned to blistering and covered with mosquito bites. Their conservative Presbyterian neighbors across the lake at Wainscott were profoundly shocked and grieved at this Bohemian professional conduct, a disapproval which my wife and I inherited when ten years later we spent the second summer of married life in this cottage, and when we also indulged in the reprehensible habit of painting nudes out of doors.

Albert and Adele hired New York architect and lifelong summer colonist Grosvenor Atterbury to design their house, which was paid for by Mary Herter. The couple spent a year determining where to site the house and decided only after living on the property in tents during the summer as they observed the solstice and trajectory of the moon, again much to the chagrin of the neighbors.

An artist with an appreciation of color and texture, Atterbury delivered a house that engaged the landscape through the use of stucco-covered concrete walls and retaining walls. Taking full advantage of the site, wings angle off the house at 45 degrees to provide views of the creeks, of Georgica Pond, and of the spit of beach that separated it from the ocean. The angled plan also allowed Atterbury to create, for the front elevation, a

Garden terrace

Front entrance

convex face that envelops the visitor. The concave nature of the rear facade pulls the observer through the house to the water view. The color selection for the exterior reflected a bit of Sicily: salmon pink stucco, green and blue trim, and eaves awash in Pompeian red, all beneath a copper tile roof with a patina of mottled verdigris. These colors, undoubtedly chosen in consultation with the Herters, reflected the relationship of the house to the gardens and interiors. Atterbury handled the transitions beautifully in both plan and elevation. Even the chimneys play into this geometric exercise, as they pierce the roof on the diagonal and, consequently, tie together the rooflines of each wing.

Within the house, Atterbury's signature angled plan created free-flowing public spaces with interesting octagonal shapes in the living and dining rooms. The interiors related to the outside exposures, and the colors for paint, furniture accessories, and draperies had meaning that went beyond decoration. In the entrance

hall, the hangings of apricot satin mirrored a Chinese rug of similar tone. The Japanese-style balustrade in red lacquer contrasted with coppery flowers in blue pottery. In an interview Albert Herter said, "Orange and red are the colors of welcome, so that is why we place them at the doorway, but not as a note only, it should be a flood of welcoming color." Japanese prints covered the golden grasscloth walls of the light and airy living room, which also featured peacock blue pottery, golden pink moldings, and an overmantel mural by Albert. The dining room was a study in gold with green woodwork, rubbed down to a muted green finish and juxtaposed against a tabletop of lacquered gold leaf and a built-in sideboard housing jade green sake ware. A collection of Orientalia amassed during the Herter honeymoon, paintings, tapestries designed by the couple from their own looms, and antiques filled this idiosyncratic and eclectic interior. The west wing contained kitchen and support services, and the east wing

Staircase

Top: Living room; bottom: hall

Top: Dining room; bottom: garden allée

"The Garden of the Sun" detail

included the in-house studio. The second floor housed the bedrooms, all with water views.

Of all the imaginative aspects of The Creeks, the gardens drew the most attention. The sun-drenched entry side of the house, dubbed "The Garden of the Sun," contained pink, yellow, and salmon flowers that became more deeply colored near the edge of its circular form. A cacophony of flowers erupted from April through the summer, starting with tulips and crocuses; followed by yellow roses, yellow phlox, swarms of Sweet William, and dahlias; and culminating in an acre of zinnias.

The "Blue and White" garden, facing the water on the shady, cool side of the house, displayed a medley of blue and white flowers all planted in abundance. Green

and blue Persian tiles, inlaid in the concrete walls, blue pottery containers, and Sicilian oil jars held flowers and shrubs. The flowers, picked daily by a gardening staff of 30, were never allowed to go to seed. Adele broke with the American mindset that still wanted, according to a 1914 article in The Craftsman, "gardens in corsets." The Herter gardens allowed nature to bridge the gap between inside and outside with romantic individuality.

During their years at The Creeks, Albert and Adele participated in the civic, social, and artistic functions held in the East Hampton community. They opened their home to the Ladies Village Improvement Society Fair, generously supported the Library and Guild Hall, donated their time to oversee the decoration and furnish-

Albert Herter costume soirée

ing of the new Maidstone Club, and entertained friends from both the year-round and summer communities.

In the summer of 1920, Enrico Caruso rented The Creeks with his wife, the former Dorothy Benjamin, daughter of East Hampton summer resident Park Benjamin. Albert's large studio building, which contained a proscenium arch, dressing rooms, and footlights, doubled as a performance space for the famed tenor. In 1929, Herter house guest Isadora Duncan danced to "The Gift of Eternal Life," written and directed by Albert. According to Leonard Lester, who worked for Herter during Prohibition, the studio was also used to stash bootlegged whisky for his brother-in-law; vertical

storage troughs installed in the studio for Herter's large 14-foot high murals proved an ideal hiding place for contraband spirits. Adele's Sunday-afternoon teas were a tradition at The Creeks for decades. Occasionally, the Herters received their guests in Kabuki garb and placed Japanese lanterns along the two-mile-long driveway to heighten the Oriental mood.

In 1946, Adele died suddenly from a stroke. Albert died in 1950 in Santa Barbara, California, and The Creeks was left to their son, Massachusetts congressman Christian Herter, later secretary of state in the Eisenhower administration. Because he had little time to spend at his ancestral home and because his wife had no affinity for East Hampton, the estate was sold in 1952 to artist Alfonso Ossorio for $35,000. With his lifelong companion, dancer Ted Dragon, Ossorio reinvented The Creeks inside and out, stripping the interior and painting it white and the outside walls black. Adele's gardens were torn apart, replaced with modern sculptures and a $4 million conifer arboretum deemed "the Eighth Wonder of the Horticultural World" by the American Conifer Society. Ossorio's obsession with rare and exotic conifers nearly bankrupted him, for he sometimes spent $300,000 a month on it. The Creeks became a surrealis-

tic theme park—*Newsday* called it "a Disneyland for esthetes." With Ossorio presiding, it became a gathering spot in the 1950s for the major figures in Hamptons Bohemia, such as Pollock, Krasner, de Kooning, Nevelson, and Johns.

Ossorio died in 1990, and in April 1993, Dragon sold the property for $12.5 million to its current owner, the billionaire head of Revlon, Ron Perelman, who immediately discarded Ossorio's outdoor sculptures (valued at six figures each), and removed and relocated trees during a frenzied, six-week gut/renovation of the house.

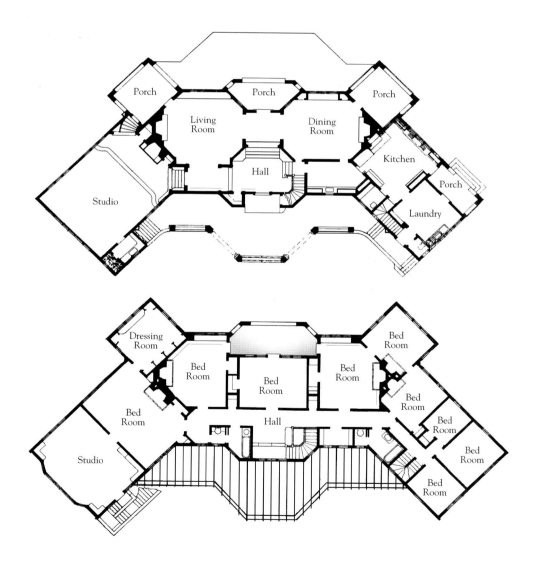

First and second floor plans

WOOLDON MANOR

1900

∽

Residences of Dr. Peter Brown Wyckoff and Cora Dillon Wyckoff &
James Paul Donahue and Jessie Woolworth Donahue

East side garden

Entrance elevation

IN 1900, Dr. Peter Wyckoff, who bought the northern end of Dr. Theodore Gaillard Thomas' property on Gin Lane at Lake Agawam, commissioned the well-known New York architectural firm of Barney & Chapman to design a 58-room half-timber English Tudor colossus for his family. A graduate of Bellevue Medical College, Dr. Wyckoff abandoned his medical practice for a highly successful career on Wall Street, which included a seat on the New York Stock Exchange.

For the Wyckoff house, Barney & Chapman created a facade composed of a masonry first floor with rambling vine-covered porches and a half-timber-and-stucco second floor, whose gables extended into a third story topped by an enormous red tile roof and eight chimneys. The estate also included stables, staff quarters, and greenhouses with extensive ornamental gardens that were frequently photographed. Hick's Nurseries of Westbury provided an infusion of large ornamental trees and plants, transforming a flat, undistinguished site into one of opulent greenery.

The approach to the mansion flowed into a circular drive through a porte cochere at the entrance. The L-shaped first-floor plan featured a paneled entrance hall with a staircase to the upper floors, a dark-paneled living hall to the east with a carved oak mantelpiece and decorative plaster ceiling, and an adjacent wainscoted

Entrance court

and wallpapered dining room also with carved wooden mantel. The kitchen, pantry, laundry, and servants' dining room completed the east wing, and to the west was a paneled library/billiard room, dominated by a huge stone mantel and spacious projecting bay leading to a covered veranda, one of many surrounding the first-floor rooms.

The second floor contained a master suite with a balcony, four guest rooms with en suite baths and views of the ocean or gardens, and an expansive terrace that overlooked the lawns. The remaining two wings were devoted to a housekeeper's room and a service wing housing the extensive staff. The third floor consisted of two large guest rooms, two baths, a studio, and more staff

quarters. The overall interior design could be characterized as "Victorian seaside," with dark wood-paneled walls and beams, elaborately colored wallpapers, ornate plaster ceilings, leaded-glass windows, and dark, heavily carved furnishings covered with velvets and pillows amid tabletops crammed with objets d'art and scattered parlor palms.

For many years the Wyckoffs, who were active members of the Southampton summer colony, provided festivities including sporting, charity, and garden parties on the estate grounds. Mrs. Wyckoff was one of the founders of the Fresh Air Home and served as its president, and she performed volunteer work with the Village Improvement Society.

Top: East elevation; bottom: ocean side elevation

Wyckoff entrance hall

In 1928, a year before his death at age 84, Dr. Wyckoff sold the house to Mrs. Jesse Woolworth Donahue, daughter of five-and-dime-store magnate F. W. Woolworth. Mrs. Donahue had just finished building her Palm Beach villa, Cielito Lindo, which was second in size only to Marjorie Merriweather Post's Mar-a-Largo, when she decided to take the plunge into Southampton society. Having purchased the house in February, she hired decorator Elsie Sloan Farley to give the house a complete renovation. According to Arts & Decoration, Mrs. Donahue stipulated a completion date of July 4, and work began immediately on the installa-

tion of new wiring and plumbing, the gutting of out-dated interiors, and the brightening of the dark wood paneling of the gloomy living room to better display new walnut and mahogany English furniture. The dining room paneling was partially removed and an Adam-style ceiling installed. Above a new marble Georgian mantel-piece, a painting by Sir Joshua Reynolds complemented new sconces, tapestries, mirrors, Chippendale furnishings, and a Waterford crystal chandelier.

With the house renovation complete, an extensive remodeling of the estate grounds was undertaken. The edge of the property, defined by a new red brick wall,

Top: Wyckoff living room; bottom: Wyckoff dining room

Wyckoff billiard room—library

exhibited an elaborate wrought-iron gate protecting the entrance to the estate. When Dr. Thomas' property was acquired to the south, the property grew to 15 acres with 610 feet of oceanfront. A broad, flat lawn replaced the demolished Thomas residence, and six gardens were added, including one laid out as a boxwood parterre, another for gladiolas and dahlias, one for blue annuals, and one for a sunken garden. A 2,000-foot gravel driveway was installed, along with expanded garages—stables, cottages, and two tennis courts.

A new Tudor-style beach house by architects Treanor & Fatio set above the dunes matched the main residence

stylistically. This pleasure pavilion included a 30-by-60-foot indoor pool, four dressing rooms with baths, a taproom, and a large living hall with a vaulted, timbered ceiling. At the time of the beach house's completion, the estate, named Wooldon Manor for the combined names of Woolworth and Donahue, was the largest and most well-appointed property in the Hamptons.

In Cleveland Amory's *The Last Resorts*, Jesse's husband, James Donahue, proudly giving a tour of his house, said at the dining room entrance, "Come on in and see it . . . All the silver's gold." Fancy flatware, however, does not ensure contentment. In 1931, James died at age 44

Top: Donahue living room; bottom: Donahue dining room

Top: Pool house, ocean side; bottom: interior of pool house

Pool house living room

Top: View of pool house from main residence; bottom: parterre with greenhouse and stable

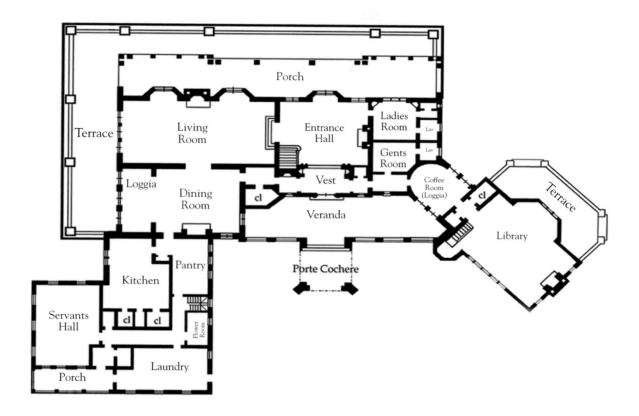

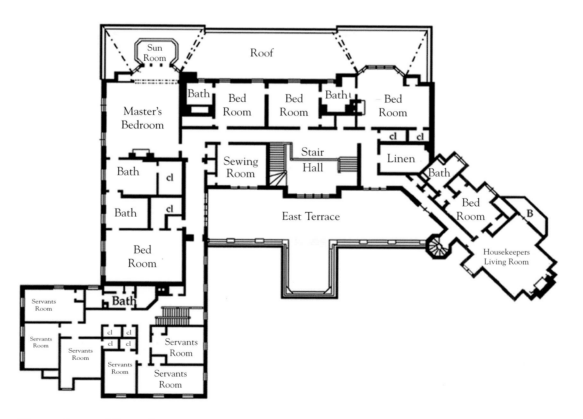

First and second floor plans

from a drug overdose. Years later, Jesse Donahue's grief continued as her flamboyant son, James Jr., succumbed to drug and alcohol abuse in his mother's luxurious Fifth Avenue apartment at the age of 51.

Mostly unused for six years, in 1937 Wooldon Manor was sold at auction for a fraction of its original price to Merrill, Lynch partner Edmund F. Lynch. Lynch, who died the following year, bought the property mainly for the beach house, which he never used. In 1940, Charles Merrill, owner of the Breese estate, purchased the beach house on five oceanfront acres from his former partner's estate. To reduce taxes, Lynch estate trustees demolished Wooldon Manor in April 1941 and then subdivided the property. The beach house was later owned by Charles Merrill's daughter, Doris, and was expanded into a residence following her marriage to Robert A. Magowan, the former CEO of Safeway Stores. The remaining garages/stables and other accessory buildings have been converted to private residences. The brick wall and the elaborate wrought-iron gate put up by James and Jesse Donahue still remain, but the site of Wooldon Manor and its elaborate gardens is now a vast green lawn. In the 1990s, new owners again enlarged the beach house. Today it might easily be mistaken for the long-lost Wooldon Manor.

Terrace

ONADUNE

1903

~

Residence of S. Fisher Johnson and Sarah Seymour Johnson

Entrance elevation

Front elevation, present-day view

ONADUNE, the summer residence of Mr. and Mrs. S. Fisher Johnson, has always been recognized as one of the grandes dames among East Hampton's cottages. Like many businessmen and industrialists who came to populate the summer colony, S. Fisher Johnson was a broker and member of the New York Stock Exchange. He died in 1904, having spent only one season in his new summer home. Onadune remained in the family for many years before it was sold to Dr. Frank Adair, a renowned cancer surgeon who also served as president of the American Cancer Society. Over the years, the house has been rented out periodically to prominent individuals such as

John D. Rockefeller Jr., who summered there in 1907, and Bianca Jagger. Bill Clinton visited Onadune when he was governor of Arkansas.

Designed by local architect John Custis Lawrence and erected by builder George Eldredge in 1903, Onadune was characterized in the *East Hampton Star* as "one of the most pleasantly located and costly residences in town, situated on a high terrace on the dunes." The cottage, continued the Star, "faces the ocean and from a broad piazza extending across the entire front, can be seen nearly the whole cottage settlement and a broad expanse of the Atlantic . . . the interior is commodious and com-

Stair hall, present-day view

fortable with large airy rooms located so as to command the best views. On the whole this is one of the coziest houses in East Hampton."

Despite its 33 rooms and 13 bedrooms, the interior does, in fact, have a modest quality. The layout follows a formal plan with a center stair hall that splits the house into two wings, one containing the dining room kitchen, sunroom, pantry, and breakfast room, the other featuring a parlor and library. Coffered ceilings, built-up moldings, and wainscoting abound throughout. The stair hall opens to the exterior loggia on one side and the stairwell on the other, lit by a series of cascading windows filled

with vertical lines of leaded glass with a circular, vine-like motif centered in the vertical leading. The total effect is that of a lacy web, both delicate and protective. The upper floors, both of which follow double-loaded corridors, contain nicely scaled bedrooms. Throughout the house, the windows are heavily cased and surrounded by back-band moldings that serve to tone down the scale of the rooms.

The exterior is a curious mix of shingled walls with half timbers and stucco in the numerous gables. At the turn of the century, houses clad in shingles proved economical to maintain, because they did not require

Library, present-day view

painting. Within two to three years, the shingled structures would turn silver gray and after many years, depending on the exposure, dark brown or black. One of the criticisms at the time was that these village houses, without paint or stain, might create a rather morbid-looking community. The antidote, practiced by a number of local builders and architects, involved integrating half timbers and stucco into the facades, resulting in a collection of villas that melded Elizabethan detailing with the Shingle style, completely in keeping with East Hampton's identification with its English heritage.

Onadune sits on what was the second set of dunes behind the ocean. Only the brave would build on the primary dune, with an exposure subject to storms and washouts. Originally one acre, the property expanded to two with the addition of a pool and pool house designed to be sympathetic with the original residence. Three stories high and perched on a terrace, Onadune is a towering structure. Such a house could never be built today, given the two-and-a-half-story, 32-foot height restriction mandated by East Hampton's zoning ordinance.

Onadune has endured successive ownerships and renovations over the past 100 years and, in its quietly elegant way, it has prevailed as a classic example of the turn-of-the-century summer colony cottage.

Top: Dining room; bottom: living room, present-day views

Garden, present-day view

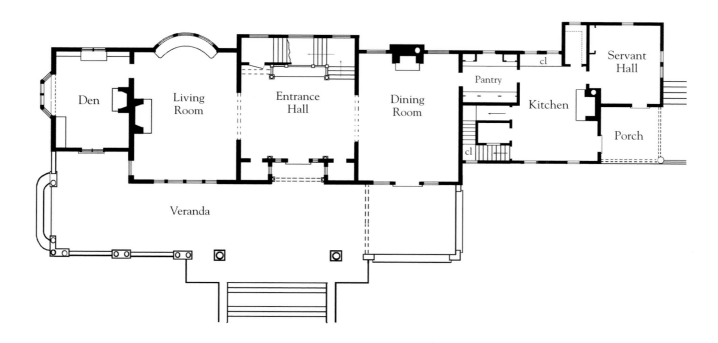

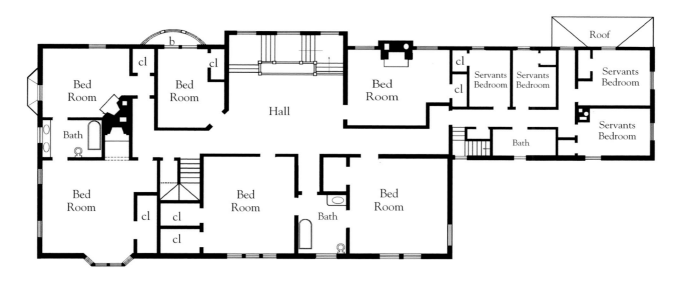

First and second floor plans

MEADOWCROFT

1904

~

Residence of Theodore Eaton Conklin and Emma Adelaide Brigham Conklin

Front elevation

Sketch of original entry

MEADOWCROFT, the 1904 gentleman's estate of Theodore Eaton Conklin, was built in the exclusive, one-square-mile enclave of Quantuck Bay, a community situated between Quogue and Westhampton Beach. Translated as "little Quogue," the name derives from the Indian name Quaquanantuck, meaning "place where the earth trembles, shaking marsh, cove, or estuary."

Theodore Conklin, whose ancestry and East End roots can be traced back to 1650s Southold, was a successful New York businessman, yachtsman, and head of the T. E. Conklin Brass and Copper Company, a firm that produced brass and copper parts for manufacturers and artists, including Conklin's friends Louis Comfort Tiffany and Philadelphia architect Wilson Eyre, who in 1903 was commissioned to plan Conklin's estate situated on a south-facing peninsula jutting into the shimmering Quantuck Bay. This stunning backdrop of land, water, and marsh provided the stage for Eyre to orchestrate the integration of the summer cottage and ancillary structures into the larger landscape. The founder of *House and Garden* magazine in 1901, Eyre was renowned for residential work that took a holistic approach to the relationship between landscape and built form.

At Meadowcroft, Eyre was charged with the task of creating a self-sustaining 100-acre farm/estate. Because the site was remotely located, a working farm was required to produce fresh food items such as meats, dairy, and produce for the estate's owners and staff. Adjacent to the farm, the 12-acre Conklin estate included a renovated guest house, a gas house, stables, and other accessory structures, as well as the main residence.

Wilson Eyre used a rational, structured plan to create a house that feels casual and inviting. The street entrance consists of a pair of brick pillars crowned with Tiffany gate lights atop stone caps with scroll supports extending downward from the light fixture. Letters announcing "Meadowcroft" in block copper awash with verdigris are embedded in the stone. Passing through another set of stuccoed pillars with scrolled iron gates, the visitor encounters a circular driveway with fountain that acts as both forecourt and outdoor room for the residence.

As in other Eyre houses, a large, open archway welcomed the visitor and punctured the otherwise linear

Rear elevation, present-day view

plan. Passing through the house to an open porch overlooking Quantuck Bay, this arch not only served to frame north and south vistas, but also established a programmatic separation of the structure by gender into a gentlemen's wing and a ladies' wing. Smoking and drinking were relegated to the western gentlemen's wing, as were a bar and billiard room. The eastern wing for the ladies contained the kitchen, dining room, and living areas. Quite aside from the unusual gender-segregation requirement, Eyre's layout for Meadowcroft responded to the kind of practical considerations he applied to each of his designs. Regarding the location of a dining room, for example, he wrote that "the dining room should be located to the east, which places the dining area on the shady side of the house in the late afternoon and avoids sun

at dinner hour, when it is hotter and slants into the room and becomes an annoyance."

As the Conklins insisted that all of Meadowcroft's bedrooms have water views, Eyre cleverly avoided potential linearity by clustering them in the obliquely angled wings flanking either end of the central hall. The ceremonial Arts and Crafts stairwell, a projecting bay on the exterior, is a focal point for the house on the interior. Composed of open arched balustrades and wainscoted walls in oak, the stairwell was crafted to retain a sense of openness despite its use of a heavy wood. In what had to be a deliberate gesture, Eyre curved the ceiling of the stairwell to bounce light into a second-floor hall that might otherwise have seemed moribund. The upstairs also featured numerous state-of-the-art bathrooms, along with back stairs connecting to each of the gender-separated wings below.

Veranda with built-in bench, present-day view

The cottage's exterior is a rather unadorned affair of rough stucco walls, shuttered double-hung windows, and red tile roof of cast terra-cotta. Eyre broke up the horizontality of the long walls by angling separate wings off either end of the central section. On the north side, facing the driveway courtyard, the angles envelop the pedestrian and, conversely, on the south side, pull the spectator into the view. Projecting bays such as the stairwell on the north side and a breakfast room on the south provide subtle rhythms and modulations in the overall massing on both elevations.

The south elevation's principal design element is a tall veranda offering shade from the summer sun. Angling with the view, the veranda features an ornate built-in bench by Eyre and a ceiling dotted with Tiffany pendant fixtures of milk glass and copper. After five gen-

erations of ownership by the Conklins, the only major change made by the current owners has been the enclosure of the arched opening with an Arts and Crafts style doorway that sits behind a new hip-roofed porch.

Although it measures roughly 9,000 square feet, Meadowcroft does not have the feeling of a large house, because of Eyre's skill in providing for the programmatic requirements of his client while employing the kind of simple detailing that brings a livable scale to a country house. In creating its look of uncalculated simplicity, Wilson Eyre endowed Meadowcroft with all of the essential elements that define a true summer cottage in the Hamptons.

Top: Living room; bottom: den with window seat, present-day view

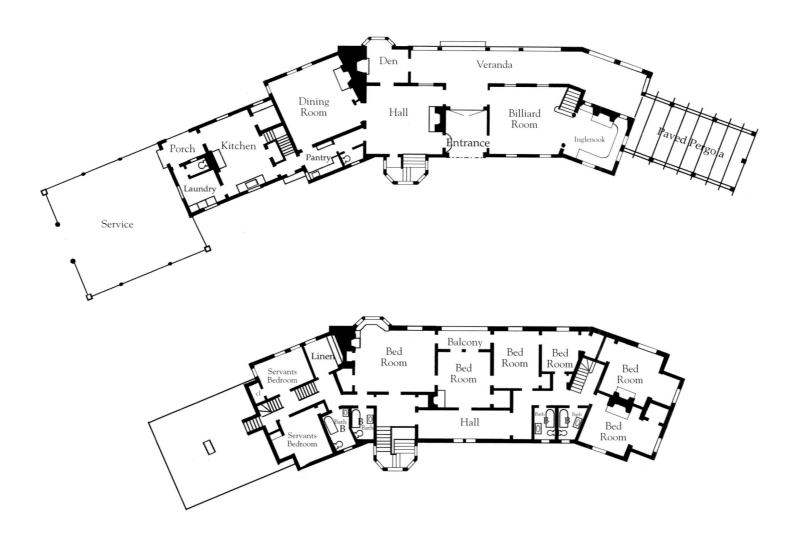

First and second floor plans

RED MAPLES

1908

Residence of Alfred William Hoyt and Rosina Elisabeth Hoyt

Aerial view looking toward ocean

Entrance elevation

RED MAPLES, the Southampton estate designed by architects Hiss & Weekes and landscape architect Ferruccio Vitale for financier Alfred William Hoyt and his mother, Rosina Elizabeth Hoyt, was modeled on the Renaissance villas of Florence and Rome. The press of its era considered Red Maples one of the finest houses in the summer colony. Completed in 1908 at a cost of $500,000, equivalent to $50 million in today's dollars, the Hoyt estate, along with the slightly later Villa Mille Fiori, introduced a new note of Mediterranean Beaux-Arts elegance to Long Island's East End. Although they had designed several residences throughout the Northeast, none of Hiss & Weekes' earlier work approached the level of opulence of this commission. For 33-year-old Vitale, Red Maples was the first entry in a distinguished roster of brilliant landscape designs.

The Hoyt fortune came from a New York City flour and grain business. When the family patriarch, Jesse Hoyt, died in 1882, he left $10 to $15 million, an enormous amount for that era. Much of Jesse Hoyt's estate went to his family, including his brother Alfred M. and nephew Alfred W., who together had established the banking firm of A. M. Hoyt & Company. During the construction of Red Maples, Alfred W. died, and the project was completed by his mother, Rosina E. Hoyt, and her daughter, Alfred's sister, Rosina Sherman Hoyt (1874–1965).

A 17-acre former cornfield, located on the corner of Ox Pasture and Halsey Neck Lane, provided the canvas for the creation of a 40-room mansion, 250 feet long by 65 feet wide, with stucco walls and a mottled green and red tile roof. Extraordinary gardens and rare specimen plantings were designed to frame the dwelling. Accessory structures included a greenhouse, a garage, a superintendent's house, stables, and a gardener's cottage.

Entrance loggia

Entrance hall

The house was approached through an ornamental gate of wrought iron and stone pillars followed by a circular drive flanked by red maple trees. The structure's imposing street-side facade presented tall, arched windows and a large porte cochere on its first story. The second story featured shorter, double-hung, elliptical windows and a broad, low-pitched hipped roof. The front entrance was recessed to form a long vestibule with semicircular sculpture niches recessed at either end. Three arched doors opened into the entrance hall, a monumental space with an Italian marble mosaic floor and walls of Caen stone, and a vaulted ceiling with mosaic tile matching the floor and inset with classical medallions. Furniture, kept to a minimum, consisted of benches, chairs, and a single center table. South of the entrance hall was an Adam-style reception room and a 30-by-40-foot main salon that overlooked a large terraced area and sunken garden. The main salon, with its oak walls, teak floor, and heavily paneled gold-trimmed ceiling constructed by Italian artisans, formed the true center of the house. South of the salon was a garden loggia, and to the north was the library. In earlier published plans, the main salon was located in the center, the library was placed west of the salon, and the reception

Entrance hall

room was in the space that later served as the library. Rosina or her daughter may have altered the original design during construction, after Alfred's death.

At the opposite end of the hall were a heavily paneled dining room with another loggia, and a light-filled grand staircase with a handrail of ornamental steel. The stairs led to seven upper-level guest and master suites, all with private baths. Two of the bedrooms facing south were laid out with sleeping porches that captured the sea breezes and provided ocean views. The rest of the house consisted of kitchens, servants' quarters, storage, and other spaces for behind-the-scenes activities.

The gardens, which surrounded the house and could be viewed from many of the rooms, provided a cool, tranquil retreat. Directly in front of the rear facade, two large 90-year-old paulownia trees framed the house. A broad marble staircase descended from the south terrace, past tubbed hydrangeas and massed shrubbery, and led to a sunken garden covering almost two acres. Beyond this were perennial and rose gardens. In the two rose gardens, each measuring 60 by 60 feet, 4,000 rare and exotic roses flourished and provided intoxicating scents. Orchards of fully mature apple trees also were planted.

Stair hall

Top: Living room; bottom: dining room

Rear elevation

A pergola, teahouse, and lily pond were installed to integrate the garden thematically with the Italian villa design of the main residence. The landscaping also incorporated fully grown trees, three thousand dwarf pines and spruces, and extensive shrubbery. Clipped hews and hedges were used freely throughout to form outdoor rooms and structures all dotted, accented, and splashed with marble statuary and terra-cotta vessels holding voluptuous masses of blooming plants.

The house was occupied by Rosina Hoyt and her daughter until Mrs. Hoyt's death in 1922. Following the daughter's marriage to socially prominent Gerard Beekman Hoppin in 1925, she used the estate less and less, and ultimately rented it to Mr. and Mrs. Edward Hutton. Mrs. Hutton, the former Marjorie Merriweather Post, entertained frequently at the estate and on the Huttons' yacht, the *Hussar*, docked in nearby Peconic Bay. Sold to oil magnate James H. Snowden in 1929, the estate changed hands again in 1932, when it was bought by John Thomas Smith, a vice president and general counsel of General Motors. Renamed Certosa and completely renovated into a streamlined Art Deco affair, the house was the scene of frequent parties, and the Smiths generously opened their famous gardens for viewing.

After Smith's death in 1947, the house was demolished and the property subdivided. The surviving former garage building has been converted into a private residence. Many of the plantings still exist and have matured to embrace newer buildings on the property. The original surviving red maples still rustle in the ocean breeze and shimmer like rubies in the sun. The magnificent Italian villa that they once so proudly framed is only a memory.

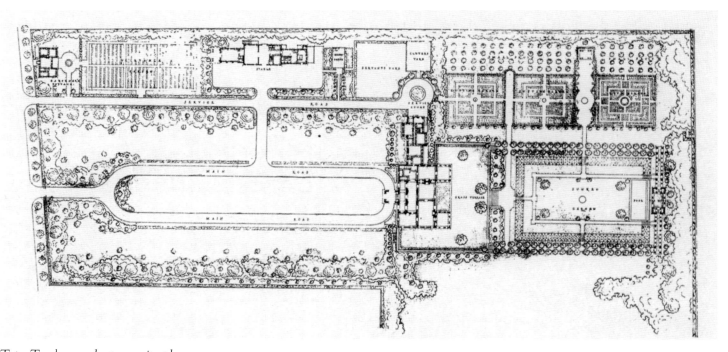

Top: Tea house; bottom: site plan

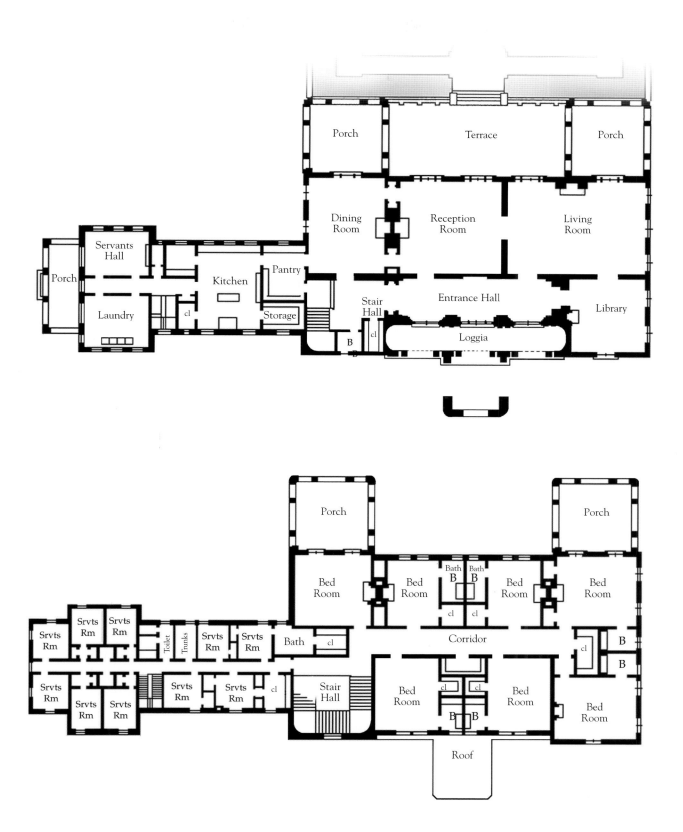

First and second floor plans

VILLA MILLE FIORI

1910

*Residence of Albert Barnes Boardman
and Georgina Gertrude Bonner Boardman*

Aerial view from Coopers Neck Lane

Front elevation

OF ALL the fantastical dwellings that have risen in the Hamptons over the years, the sumptuous Southampton estate of Albert Boardman was among the most distinctive. Known as Villa Mille Fiori, "house of a thousand flowers," it embodied everything that a summer mansion in the sand could be, a Beaux-Arts colossus in a prime, highly visabile location.

The notion that a 12-acre plot of nothing but sand, at the southwest intersection of Great Plains Road and Coopers Neck Lane, could become a millionaire's fantasy arose from the grand ambitions of attorney Albert Barnes Boardman. A partner in the prominent law firm of O'Brien, Boardman & Platt, Boardman in 1910 commissioned the architectural firm of Hill & Stout to design a lavish, palatial estate for his family. The architects, given a clean slate from which to work, created a 24-room, four-story mansion modeled after Rome's Villa de Medici. In addition, Hill & Stout were responsible for the master plan for the property, its landscape architecture, and even the design of the furnishings. Villa Mille Fiori's state-of-the-art materials—a concrete foundation, steel-reinforced concrete beams, hollow-tile terra-cotta block walls, and a clay tile roof—made the building vermin-resistant and fireproof and kept the interiors cool.

Entry detail

Door and window placement maximized cross ventilation during the short summer season.

The approach to Villa Mille Fiori was through a walled opening of engaged pillars on Coopers Neck Lane into an elliptically shaped gravel entrance court and drive with curved recesses on its sides to allow for the passage of vehicles. Directly on axis with the center of the house-in reality, the rear of the building-the long drive, lined with lampposts and flowerpots on concrete plinths, opened into a forecourt in front of the dwelling. A small opening through this wall on the right side cleverly connected to the service court on the north.

The facade presented a monumental front, its tall central section flanked by lower wings that were covered by a shallow-hipped roof of red clay tile. On the inner corners of the main section were two towers running from the ground to a fourth-story rooftop terrace. Belvederes of sorts, these towers also concealed chimneys camouflaged as columns. From the roof terrace, the viewer could survey the landscape for miles in every directions. A towering presence in its day, Boardman's villa served as a local landmark visible from far away.

Viewed from the east, Villa Mille Fiori's right wing contained servants' rooms and the kitchen, logically

Rear elevation

situated in the northeast corner of the building, where heat generated from cooking would be minimally felt in the rest of the house. The left wing consisted of a porte-cochere opening onto an entrance hall with a dazzling white reception room to the south. This entrance sequence meandered to the main hall housing the central, staircase with its marble-dusted walls that served as a visual and structural fulcrum for the entire house. Beyond, a loggia, which ran parallel to the main hall, faced the gardens to the west; this two-story space featured a barrel-vaulted ceiling painted with Italian murals, Ionic marble columns, Greek sculptures, and plaster swag lintels.

At opposite ends of the central hall were the living and dining rooms. One of the most ornate rooms in the house, the living room was lined with floral designs in satinwood, ebony, and exotic woods beneath a coffered ceiling of square panels and hexagonal rosettes with painted designs. Along the short wall above the fireplace was a frieze with "Villa Mille Fiori" and "1910," the year of the house's completion, inscribed in wood. In the dining room, the cork floors, considered to be sanitary, soundproof, and easy on the feet, blended well with a red fabric wall covering worthy of a Venetian palazzo. Walnut woodwork surrounded the room, with infill panels running full length between the ceiling beams.

Rear elevation detail

Loggia

Staircase

Living room

Rear elevation

Top: Aerial view from west; bottom: Italian garden

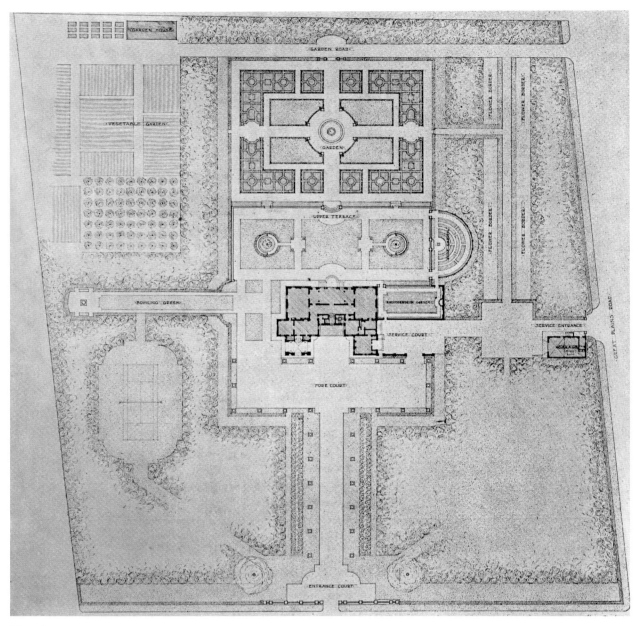

Site plan

Six master bedroom suites on the second floor all had views of the Boardmans' inspired Italian Renaissance gardens. From the second-floor balcony overlooking the rear loggia, the gardens were revealed in their totality: a 22-foot-wide fountain in the rear; lesser fountains in various quadrants; rose, rhododendron, and vegetable gardens; and, beyond, extensive lawns and a discreetly placed tennis court. Scattered throughout the gardens,

embedded in wall niches and mounted on rooftops, were numerous pieces of perfectly placed classical sculpture.

Albert Boardman owned Villa Mille Fiori until 1927, when he sold it to law partner Judge Morgan J. O'Brien, a former justice of the New York Supreme Court. O'Brien's arrival in Southampton ushered in the establishment of a prominent community of Irish Catholics. O'Brien and his family vacationed at Villa Mille Fiori

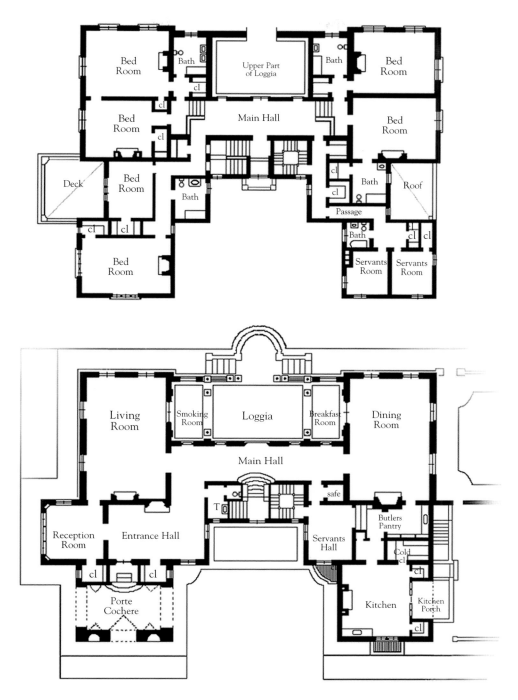

First and second floor plans

until his death at age 85 in 1937. Afterward, the estate and its furnishings were put up for auction and sold for $16,500 in July 1938. The house originally cost $250,000 to build, roughly equivalent to $25 million in 2007.

The magical Villa Mille Fiori languished for years, fell into disrepair, and was eventually demolished. All that remains today are the stucco wall that surrounds the property and the former garage, which has been converted into a private residence. The formal Italian gardens are now overgrown and long forgotten, and the site of the house awaits a new millionaire's dream.

COXWOULD

1912

*Residence of Dr. John Frederick Erdmann
and Georgina Theresa Wright Erdmann*

Front elevation from west

Front elevation from northwest

COXWOULD, the East Hampton vacation residence of Dr. John F. Erdmann, is one of the most enchanting and representative examples of English vernacular style architecture in the village. The name Coxwould is derived from the cottages of the Cotswolds in England. East Hampton, whose original settlers came from Kent, has often been cited for its Anglophilia and, to this day, maintains an affinity for all things English.

John Erdmann was a renowned general surgeon whose many prominent patients included opera tenor Enrico Caruso, New York postmaster Edward Morgan, General Motors founder William C. Durant, playwright J. Hartley Manners, and heavyweight champion James J. Corbett. Erdmann also handled special cases such as a clandestine operation, aboard a yacht on the East River, on President Grover Cleveland's cancerous mouth and

upper jaw. Additionally, he volunteered to be part of the medical team that studied the physical conditions of the returning members of Admiral Byrd's First Antarctic Expedition. In a 1926 *New Yorker* profile, the doctor, whose manner could be brisk and cryptic, was characterized as a "blunt-shaped, short-talking, efficient carpenter of life and death."

In *Fifty Years of the Maidstone Club*, Erdmann's persona was revealed in a 1931 incident regarding the repair of his front door: "This carpenter was summoned to fix it, on a Saturday morning. Just as the noon whistle blew, Dr. Erdmann came upon the mechanic packing up his tools. 'Where are you going? That door isn't finished!' 'Sorry, Doctor, it's twelve o'clock. I'll be back Monday.' The doctor looked him through and through. 'Well, all I have to say is, I hope I get you on the table someday,

Roof detail

and the noon whistle blows, and you'll have to wait until Monday to be sewed up!'"

Coxwould's architect, Harrie T. Lindeberg, proved to be another type of carpenter altogether. In 1912, when he designed Coxwould at the age of 32, Lindeberg had already developed a personal philosophy regarding domestic architecture, one that was greatly influenced by the utilitarian old farm buildings of New England and the South. Eschewing useless gables that broke up rooflines along with "unmeaning ornament or showy paint-all of which are a source of wasteful expense and depressing things to live with," Lindeberg believed the

Rear elevation, present-day view

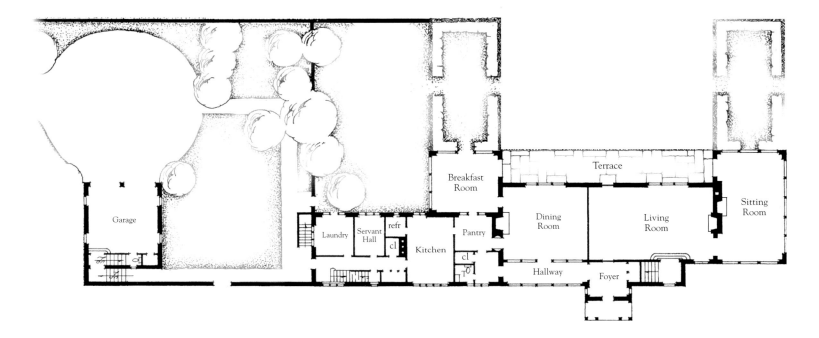

Plan

appealing roofs of English cottages maintained their allure because their surfaces were neither broken up nor varied in treatment. He also felt a country house should neither exceed two stories in height nor sit high above the ground. One step down from the living areas was enough to maintain a friendly relationship to lawn and garden.

For John Erdmann, Lindeberg designed a well-ordered, sand-finished stucco house fully integrated into a master plan. The major rooms extended into the landscaped gardens, forming a series of outdoor rooms. Public spaces were restricted to the ground floor, and the second and third floors contained bedrooms and a servants' wing. Visually, the most distinctive feature of the house is its undulating roofline of cedar shingles fashioned to resemble English thatch. Sweeping across the entire breadth of the house with curving punctuations over dormers and porch, the roof reflects not only the spirit of place and the physical undulations of the ocean's waves beyond, but also the intense perfectionism of its architect.

Inspired by Charles Follen McKim's domestic work in Lenox, Massachusetts, Lindeberg had already experimented with staggered, wavy shingle coursing on his roofs in order to create a textured effect. According to Lindeberg, constant on-site supervision was required of the architect so that the roof would not appear too extreme or too static. The "Lindeberg roof" for which the architect became famous was the direct result of hands-on involvement during construction and clearly, for Lindeberg, the design process did not end at the drawing board.

Although the house today is seen as a road-front lot with gardens in the back yard, originally the property ran from Lily Pond Lane all the way to the ocean. In the front garden, the Erdmanns created a topiary sculpture modeled after five relatives. The house was only slightly altered during the passing decades: a 1927 replacement of the original roof straightened out its coursing, the extraordinarily tall chimneys were somewhat lowered, a south-facing porch was enclosed to create a family room, and the interiors were upgraded for 21st-century living.

These changes were accomplished with a deft adherence to the spirit of the original Arts and Crafts detailing.

The current owners, Dianne Wallace and Lowell Schulman, recently had the gardens redesigned. Landscape designer Edwina von Gal worked closely with Wallace to create 15 exterior garden rooms inspired by the English gardens at Vita Sackville-West's Sissinghurst, Anthea Gibson's Westwell, and Major Lawrence Johnston's Hidcote Manor. The gardens command vistas that are interconnected by objects in the landscape, and they evidence extraordinary acumen in plant selection. Coxwould-both the house and its surrounding landscape-remains one of the most original summer colony properties in the Hamptons.

Erdmann family topiary

OLD TREES

1912

∽

Residence of Goodhue Livingston and Louisa Robb Livingston

Front elevation

Top: Rear elevation; bottom: rear elevation from Lake Agawam

Entrance detail

Entrance hall

OLD TREES, New York architect Goodhue Livingston's 1912 summer retreat for his family, possesses stature and grace befitting the pedigree of its owners. The visitor enters the estate through a large pair of white gates, then proceeds along a curving driveway through the estate past outbuildings, perennial gardens, and towering specimen trees planted in the early part of the 19th century. At the last turn in the driveway, the house rises prominently in the foreground with Lake Agawam shimmering behind it. Of the many Hamptons summer houses once surrounded by vast acreage, Old Trees is among the very few that remain intact, its mature landscaping nearly 100 years old.

A partner in the elite firm of Trowbridge & Livingston, Goodhue Livingston (1867–1951) was a member of the eminent Hudson River Valley Livingston family, proprietors of huge Colonial-era land grants. In 1686, Scots immigrant Robert Livingston (1654–1728) acquired, by royal patent, a Hudson River estate of approximately 160,000 acres, along with the title Lord of Livingston Manor. Eventually, the Livingston family holdings amounted to almost a million acres along the Hudson. Maturin and Eugene A. Livingston, along with John Jacob Astor, William Astor, William C. Schermerhorn, Alex Van Rensselaer, and others, were among the 25 original members of "the Patriarchs,"

Stair case, present-day view

families that formed the core of old New York society. The Livingstons would later become members of Mrs. Astor's Four Hundred. Socially irreproachable, the Livingstons never even gave any thought to being in society since they had always *been* society.

In 1896, Goodhue Livingston married Louisa Robb (1877–1960), the daughter of old society members James Hampden Robb and Cornelia Van Rensselaer Thayer. This coupling solidified the social powerhouse position that they were to hold wherever they lived. At Old Trees, the Livingstons entertained on a grand scale, hosting many social and charity events that included prominent local individuals and international society figures as guests.

Old Trees is a large Georgian Revival mansion clad in shingles with a symmetrical, classically formal plan. Its overall massing a rectangular volume almost 40 feet high, displays a steeply pitched hipped roof encompassing two stories that is punctuated by dormers and attic eyebrow windows. Two tall brick chimneys, devoid of

Living room

elaborate capping, anchor the roof where the hip splits from the ridge. The roof appears to drape itself over the second floor on supporting outriggers also carried across the dormers. The outrigger theme is repeated again in the trellised entry supported by two fluted Doric columns. White cottage shutters, rose-covered trellises, and fluttering striped awnings impart relaxed seaside ambiance—a harmonious collage of sight, smell, and sound with formal but not overly ornate detailing.

North of the main body of the house is a subserviently scaled but similarly detailed service wing. The east-facing lake side of the house is similarly treated, with two fluted-Doric-columned loggias resembling classical temples at its opposite ends and tall drawing room windows that open onto a rear terrace landscaped with billows of blue hydrangeas, climbing roses, and tall classical urns on plinths. The rest of the house is framed by more

hydrangeas, buddleia, day lilies, hews, roses, and ornamental trees, and privet hedges shield the service areas and enclose a cutting garden. Nearby, the recently constructed garage and pool house mimic the main residence stylistically.

Through a rectangular vestibule on the west facade, the visitor enters a long hall where ancestral family portraits were once displayed and the main stairway sweeps graciously upward alongside three narrow, ascending windows overlooking the front lawn and allée, ending at a small pool where a marble goddess reclines. The location of the stair follows the rules set forth by Edith Wharton and Ogden Codman in their book *The Decoration of Houses*: "The staircase should be close to the vestibule but not necessarily in the same room, as the staircase is generally used only by the inhabitants of the house, while the vestibule may be used by others." Decorator Lucy

Throop, author of many books on interior design, was responsible for Old Trees' original decoration.

In the formal main drawing room, three sets of French doors overlook Lake Agawam. The house situated on a berm atop a brick terrace seems to float above the lake. Next to the drawing room is the sun-filled library, a masculine-flavored room with a 14-foot ceiling decorated with reticulated Gothic plaster tracery and a matching chandelier. Oak wainscoting, terminating at eye level, reduces the scale of the room, making it a comfortable place to read, relax, and regard the lake and ocean views.

At the other end of the long entrance hall is the formal dining room, which was originally decorated in the Louis XVI style with white painted furniture. Through French doors on the lake side, mirroring the configuration of those in the library opposite, the dining room opens to a trellised loggia that occasionally served as an outdoor dining area. The main floor also contains an office, a guest bath, a butler's pantry, a kitchen, and a breakfast room.

On the second floor, which is divided by a double-loaded corridor, are the principal guest rooms, sitting rooms, and a master suite overlooking the gardens and spectacular lake views. A third floor, formerly servants' quarters, has been converted into more guest rooms, as comfortable as those on the second floor, but with even

Dining room

better views. Looking out from these rooms, it is not difficult to imagine Lake Agawam in the early 1900s as a separate enclave within the village. The lakefront owners, who each had a private dock that jutted into the water, agreed to hang lanterns with lights of different colors at the edge of the docks so that boaters could find their way home at night. Even more vivid is the image of the Betts family gliding around the lake in their gondola. After a trip to Venice, the family commissioned the construction of the boat and staffed it with a gondolier.

The Livingstons summered in Old Trees for many years until their respective deaths. In 1960 the estate was sold to the John Michael Shaheen family, who main-

tained the estate much as it was during the Livingston days. After vacationing there for almost 40 years, the Shaheens sold the property in 2000 to the current owners. The house and grounds have since been completely renovated, restored, and recast for 21st-century living without affecting their tranquil perfection or timeless simplicity. In his March 1916 *Architectural Record* review of the house, writer John Taylor Boyd observed concerning Old Trees now almost 100 years old, "Simply wrought as Mr. Livingston's house is, its very unobtrusiveness is the result of extreme care, accuracy and good taste in both house and furnishings. The more it is studied, the better will its success be appreciated."

Library, present-day view

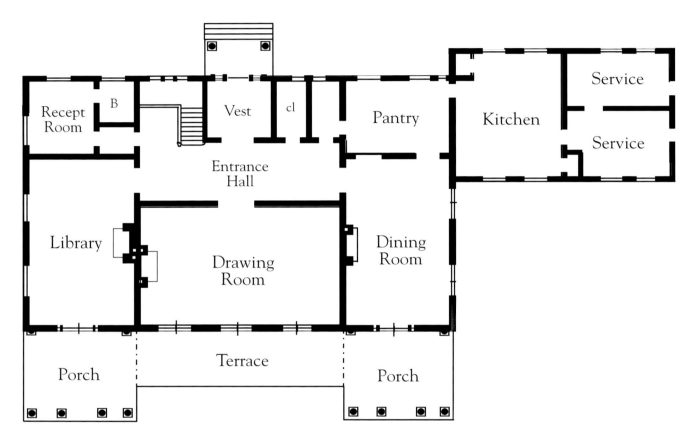

First floor plan

MINDEN

1912

❧

Residence of John E. Berwind and Katherine Murray Wood Berwind

Entrance elevation

Top: Southeast elevation fireplace; bottom: front elevation from Ocean Road in winter

South elevation under construction

WITH ITS massive tile-roof entrance and broad, sweeping facade, Minden, the 1912 Mediterranean style villa of John E. and Katherine Murray Wood Berwind, stands in stark contrast to the simple wood-framed shingle structures that line Bridgehampton's Ocean Road on its southward progress toward the sea.

A member of the prominent Berwind family of Philadelphia, John E. Berwind was vice president and partner in the Berwind-White Company, founded in 1874. One of the largest coal-mining companies in the world, Berwind-White provided much of the coal used by the U.S. Navy, as well as by American and foreign trans-Atlantic steamers. John, his brother Edward who was president of Berwind-White and three other brothers were born to Prussian immigrant parents; their father was employed as a cabinetmaker in a piano factory. By developing extensive mining operations in Pennsylvania and West Virginia, the brothers rose to become titans of the coal industry. John and Edward Berwind established offices in New York and built large country residences in the Hamptons and Newport, respectively.

Whereas Edward commissioned one of this country's most costly and renowned Beaux Arts residences, The Elms (1901), John Berwind and his wife preferred the

Top: Entrance hall fireplace; bottom: staircase

Dining room

more relaxed and informal seaside environment of Bridgehampton, where Mrs. Berwind had spent many summers as a child. Her aunt Antoinette R. Esterbrook had long lived in a large Stick style house known as Tremedden, on Ocean Road, and it was she who sold the Berwinds the 12-acre site for Minden, named for Berwind's ancestral town of Minden, Germany.

Minden is a three-story, 20,000-square-foot house attributed to New York architect and Columbia School of Mines professor Grenville Temple Snelling, who was trained at the Ecole des Beaux-Arts. A red Spanish tile roof tops the 20-room dwelling, constructed of reinforced concrete and coated with white stucco. The concrete was likely chosen by Snelling, who had practiced in Jacksonville, Florida, for its fireproofing qualities and resistance to bug infestations. Open, arched loggias, along with balconies and roofs, are supported by timber members and punctuated by eyebrow

Top: Living room; bottom: library

Reception room

windows and numerous chimneys. The house sits far back from Ocean Road, behind a sweeping lawn edged with rare specimen trees and shrubbery.

Minden's plan is basically symmetrical, with a service wing extension to the north. A prominent porte-cochere, centered on the facade, leads to a central entrance hall, which is paneled in dark wood and features a fireplace and, at its far end, a heavily carved semicircular wood staircase. Down a few steps from the hall, an ornate oak-paneled living room has a mantelpiece with a carved coat of arms, and a plaster ceiling based on one in Hampton Court Palace. This room opens onto a long loggia designed with a southern orientation to capture ocean breezes. A small paneled sitting room is also located off the hall, with a little reception room and adjacent paneled library opposite. Beyond

them are the Jacobean dining room and the service wing. The second floor has six bedroom suites, decorated in different styles, and a sleeping porch. The Bridgehampton firm of George S. De Puy is credited with Minden's interior design.

The grounds of the original 12-acre estate were luxuriant, with sunken formal rose and perennial gardens, sundials, and statuary. John Berwind also bought Sag Harbor's historic Beebe Windmill and moved it to the property. A cutting garden, a vegetable garden, pear and apple tree orchards, an eight-car garage, staff buildings, and a power plant, unique for its time, completed the estate.

Major figures in the social whirl of the Hamptons summer colony, John and Katherine Berwind entertained frequently at Minden, hosting a series of charity garden parties, musicales, and teas. Shortly after John

Porch

View of porch and garden

Berwind's death in 1928 at age 73, the Beebe Windmill was donated to the Town of Southampton as a memorial to him and moved to a property adjacent to Minden. In 1939, Katherine Berwind demolished her aunt's once grand showplace, Tremedden, which had fallen into disrepair. She continued to summer at Minden, reigning as one of the dowager hostesses of the Hamptons, and maintained the style and elegance of a bygone era until her death in 1944 at age 72.

In 1947, Minden was purchased from the Berwind estate by the Presbyterian Church for use as a retreat. Sold again in 1978, it was converted to a health spa. Minden's current owner, Leonard Riggio, chairman of the Barnes & Noble Company, purchased the estate in 1986. Except for the assemblage of modern sculptures dotting the grounds, the Berwind residence looks much as it did almost a hundred years ago.

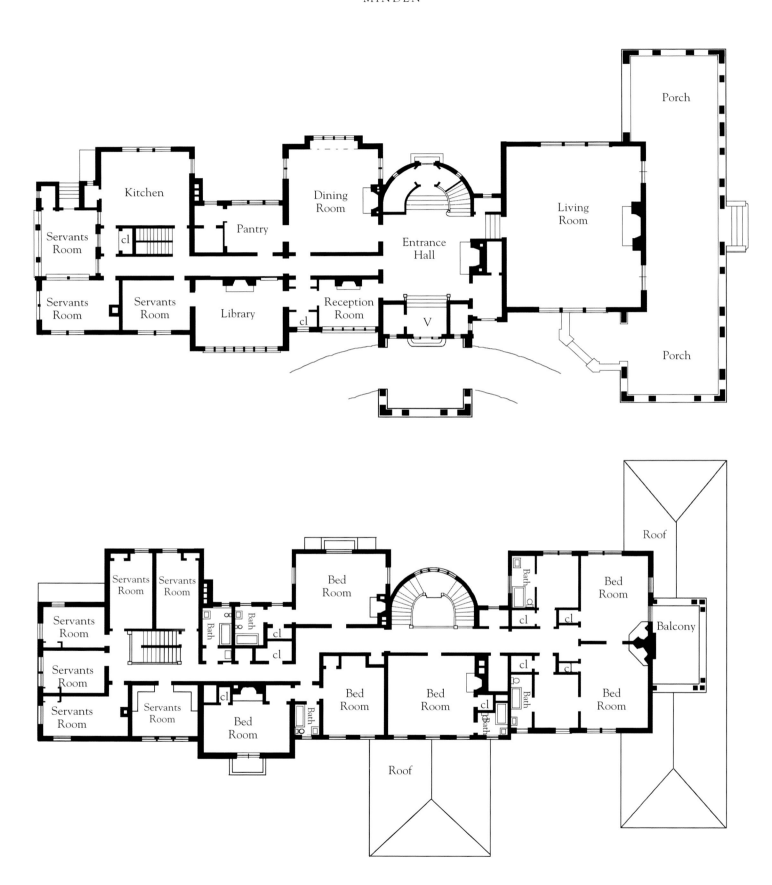

First and second floor plans

BALLYSHEAR

1913

∽

Residence of Charles Blair Macdonald and Frances Porter Macdonald

Entrance elevation

Rear elevation

BALLYSHEAR, the Southampton residence of well-known Wall Street broker and champion amateur golfer Charles Blair Macdonald (1856–1939), was created by architect F. Burrall Hoffman Jr. in 1913. The credit for Ballyshear's gardens goes jointly to landscape architect Annette Hoyt Flanders and the original garden designer, Rose Standish Nichols. Originally named for a manor and estate in Argyllshire, Scotland, the estate has had several other names, including Montrose and its current appellation, Cryptomeria, after the exotic conifers that spiral toward the sky on the south side of the residence.

C. B. Macdonald commissioned a traditional Georgian style house and had it placed on 200 acres of Shinnecock Hills landscape. He had spent five years searching the East Coast for the perfect, affordable land on which to place the National Golf Links (1911).

MacDonald was fascinated by a 1901 magazine survey of British golfers on the best golf holes in the world, and he spent a number of years visiting and documenting each of them. After returning to the United States with blueprints, he worked with surveyor Seth Raynor on a course design that emulated these great holes both physically and tactically. The result, which defined the golden era of golf course design, was a truly American course with no equal. Later, Macdonald created notable courses such as the Lido at Long Beach, the links at Piping Rock, and Bermuda's Mid Ocean Club, and he was celebrated as the father of modern golf course design.

Macdonald's master bedroom at Ballyshear overlooked the National Golf Links as well as Peconic Bay and the hummocky Shinnecock landscape of heath and moors often compared to the links at St. Andrews. In this beautiful setting, Macdonald placed Ballyshear against a backdrop of protected woods and farmland. The gentle, winding, half-mile-long approach, laid out by Raynor, recalls the English countryside in its tree plantings, rolling lawns, grazing horses, and glimpses of a pond and the grand Georgian Colonial mansion in the distance.

The rambling drive heightens the sense of anticipation. It arrives at a nicely scaled circular forecourt that frames the entry to the classically symmetrical house. Architect Hoffman's design vocabulary of well-proportioned window casings, substantial brickwork, and parapet with balustrades displays discipline and judicious use of detail rare in neo-Georgian houses of the period. Despite its four-story height, the building retains an intimate scale. Its steeply pitched, hipped roof (originally slate) combines the third story and attic space into a single unit almost equal in height to the two stories beneath it. Indiana limestone banding between the first and second floors, a stone cap along the full length of the balustraded terrace, and a double soldier course of rounded brick between the terrace floor and retaining wall below reinforce the composition's horizontal aspect. Instead of designing a brick house dripping with limestone, Hoffman employs quoins articulated in brick to neutralize the vertical elements at the corners. Again, he underplays the verticality of the structure by slightly indenting the flat-roofed end wings of the house.

On the center section of the first-floor west elevation, facing the meadow and the bay beyond, Hoffmann

Entrance hall

Top: Living room; bottom: living room, later view

Top: Library; bottom: dining room

Sun room

reached into his Beaux-Arts bag of tricks to create an elliptical bay with floor-length fenestration in the library. This Baroque-inspired technique of pulling the eye into the view not only gives the quartered-oak library a little pizzazz, but also draws the visitor into the space from the grand entrance hall to the east. Hoffman reinforced this device in the semicircular terrace stair, further compelling the viewer's eye to the vast panorama before it.

Ballyshear's well-conceived plan revolves around the entrance hall, which serves as the house's focal point of activity. High ceilings, white walls, Ionic pilasters, picture moldings, and a black and white marble checkerboard floor give character to this space, which connects to all the major public rooms. To the south, the drawing room runs east-west, its fireplace on axis to the hall. Now painted pale yellow, the room was originally clad in red birch paneling with a walnut finish.

Top: Garden; bottom: view of garden from terrace

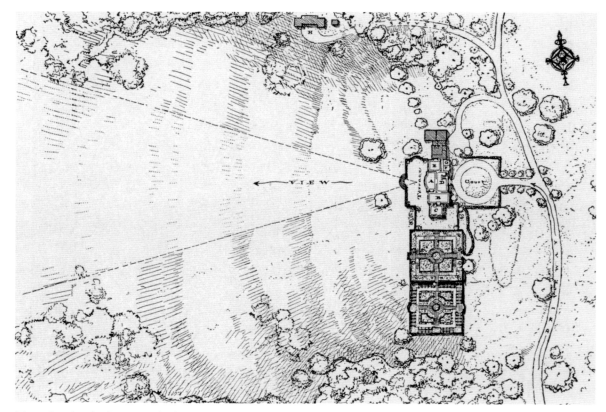

Top: Garden looking south; bottom: site plan

South of the drawing room is an airy sunroom overlooking the gardens.

North of the entrance hall, on axis with the drawing room, are a formal dining room, a butler's pantry, and kitchen and service areas. A small hall near the stairs leads to what were once reception and golf rooms. A wrought-iron stair balustrade, featuring curling waves and undulating, almost abstracted, human forms, rises up the stairwell to double-loaded corridors and six bedrooms, including the master and boudoir. The third floor contained the servants' quarters.

Except for the addition of a swimming pool below the terrace level, Ballyshear remained relatively unchanged over the years, even retaining almost all of its original bath fixtures. Recently, a sympathetic Georgian addition was added on the north side of the house, but the carriage house at the north end of the driveway remains unchanged, as do other accessory structures on the property. The formal gardens of Annette Hoyt Flanders and Rose Standish Nichols maintain a casual presence through their simple brick paths and the way they step down into the landscape. The garden closest to the

Rear terrace, present-day view

house contains the mature cryptomeria arcade, and the second garden highlights an assortment of roses and other flowering shrubs. Although they were influenced by the gardens of Europe, Flanders thought of her designs as distinctly American, created to impart a sense of "old age and intimacy." Flanders' designs have been lovingly maintained.

Because brickwork fares poorly in a salt-air environment, Ballyshear remains one of the few Georgian style residences to be built on Long Island's East End. For more than 20 years, its current owners have allowed the house to evolve to accommodate today's needs, demonstrating the kind of caring stewardship so befitting this extraordinary property.

First and second floor plans

BLACK POINT

1916

∼

Residence of Henry Huddleston Rogers Jr. and Mary Benjamin Rogers

North elevation, watercolor rendering

Aerial view

IN 1914, when Colonel Henry Huddleston Rogers Jr. commissioned Ecole des Beaux Arts-trained architects Walker & Gillette to design his oceanfront estate in Southampton, it was unlikely that he or anyone else could have imagined the transformative detailing and inspired organization that would result in an Italian-inspired villa seamlessly integrated into an American seaside landscape.

Heir to a vast fortune, Colonel Rogers began the project only a few years after the death of his robber baron father, Henry Huddleston Rogers, the famed "Hell Hound of Wall Street." A partner in the Standard Oil Trust, mastermind behind the creation of the Anaconda Copper and U.S. Steel corporations, head of a collection of railroad companies, and regarded with both fear and awe by the New York financial community, the senior H. H. Rogers was characterized by his good friend Mark Twain as "superhumanly sweet." A confirmed family man, at his death in 1909 Rogers left $16 million to each of his three daughters and his only son, Harry. The younger H. H. Rogers married the former Mary Benjamin in 1900 while still a student at Columbia University.

Entrance courtyard, watercolor rendering

Entrance hall

Entrance stair hall

Living room

The couple had two children, a son Henry and daughter Millicent, who would later become known as a great beauty and stylish trendsetter with a flair for fashion.

By the summer of 1916, the Rogers family was ensconced on their 60-acre estate at the intersection of Gin Lane and Old Town Road. It included accessory structures such as a gardener's cottage; a playhouse for the children; apartments in the "villas" for the superintendents, butcher, engineer, etc. a pump tower, and a dairy for personal use. Black Point was designed by Walker & Gillette and landscaped by the Olmsted Brothers to function so that the garden and architecture were unified. The two firms worked together on many projects over the years, and it is easy to see evidence of a collaborative process in the terracing and axial relationships established between the architecture and the landscape design.

Thematically, Black Point was all about procession and movement, from the edges of the property to the gardens and on through the villa. The approach to the villa along the west garden wall featured a view of the whole estate stretching from the stables at the north end to the house at the south end by the dunes. An entrance court, located on the southwest corner, was accessed through a pair of entry gates constructed from hand-hewn timber panels and hung on wrought-iron hinges. A marble-curbed lily pool, the centerpiece of the oblong courtyard, was surrounded by a ringed area of ground cover. Ionic

Dining room

columns, supporting a triangulated pediment, flanked the entrance door composed of heavy wooden inset panels and an arched transom. The grade-level entryway sat in the short wall of the one-story section of the asymmetrical west elevation. This facade, which contained almost no decoration, presented a large expanse of wall in grayish-pink stucco that contrasted with deep blue canvas awnings, blue-gray shutters, and a red tile roof.

The long walls of the villa faced the main garden axis on the north and the ocean on the south. A sweeping hipped roof, with overhangs supported by outriggers, ran the entire length of the structure and was deliberately constructed with a bit of an uneven sway to connote age. Whereas the exterior walls were almost Palladian in

their formality, the interior layout provided just enough offsets to alleviate the monotony of perfect symmetry. Every view, both inside and out, framed a vista that was purely experiential. Shameless borrowings from the Italian Renaissance were juxtaposed against startlingly modern details in unadorned walls, to give this seaside villa a distinctly American sensibility and scale.

The first floor of the building on the south side, elevated to be level with the top of the beach dune, allowed for the first-floor service wing, to have both light and air. By creating a terrace, which stepped down from the north side of the living room to a seemingly sunken garden, the architects were able to consistently maintain the effect of a two-story structure without revealing the steep

H.H. Roger's den

slope of the site. Consequently, the lower entrance hall became a dramatic two-story space with a stair of brick treads and risers cascading to a landing, then turning left for a few more steps up to the first-floor anteroom. Lined with potted plants along its iron railing, the stairway was lit, top and bottom, by windows containing leaded sections of 16th-century colored glass. The entrance hall was a capped by a ceiling of four crisply cut groin vaults- a flawless extension of the stucco walls.

The anteroom at the top of the stair hall opened to the den, living room, and stairwell to the second floor. The colonel's den, like the other public rooms on this floor, had a 14-foot-high ceiling of oak beams that appeared even taller because of the room's narrower dimensions. A hooded stucco overmantel in a fawn color stretched practically to the ceiling, whereas the room's walls were bluish in color. The floor was covered with red hexagonal ceramic tiles that turned into a base molding at the walls.

Breakfast loggia

Devoid of trim that would have tempered its scale, the room appeared large, as the stucco finish splayed from the walls directly to the doorjambs. Paintings were hung on the walls alongside models of Spanish galleons and streamlined yachts mounted on brackets.

Filled with light and views both from the north terrace garden side and the south porch facing the ocean, the living room continued the decorative theme of blue and fawn hues. Roughly 44 by 29 feet, it contained mul-

tiple seating areas under a coffered wood ceiling. To the east, the candlelit dining room continued the use of color and heavy old Italian furniture. The breakfast loggia to the north featured a barrel-vaulted ceiling with Florentine frescoes painted by Boston artist Robert S. Chase. Wall murals depicted historic scenes from Florence, and the ceiling displayed coats of arms from the family. Distinctive bronze Florentine pendant lamps provided light for the space.

Garden with lily pond showing windbreak wall

Six bedrooms graced the second floor, their nine-foot-high ceilings terminating in a plaster cove. Blue picture moldings circled the rooms, and door and window trims were treated with a simple flat blue band. Fireplaces, recessed into the walls, displayed only raised cement hearths, tiled surrounds, and small shelves on brackets above the openings. Painted in pale colors, these rooms provided an elegant and restrained contrast to the public rooms downstairs.

The gardens carried themes from the inside directly outdoors. The vocabulary of stucco walls with iron grill-work and hardware was used throughout the property. The primary vista, from the living room windows along the main axis of the garden, ended at a statue of an antique Minerva surrounded by columns capped with lions. Another lily pond in the center of this axis, with statuary showered by streams of water shooting from frogs' mouths, intersected a cross axis that led to east-west garden rooms. The children's playhouse, bordered by flowers and set against dense plantings, was situated beyond the inner garden wall near the driveway that connected to the service wing. The sculptures, positioned in full sun, provided contrast against a backdrop of warm-toned stucco walls. Grass-grown paving stones curved past an arbor. Contained in the high back's curve were painted Roman decorations modeled after old Italian gardens. Below the center of the terrace, a gentle stream of water emanated from a shell-backed fountain onto the tiled pavers, a

Lily pond with frog spouts

Top: Breakfast loggia overlooking garden; bottom: garden sculpture

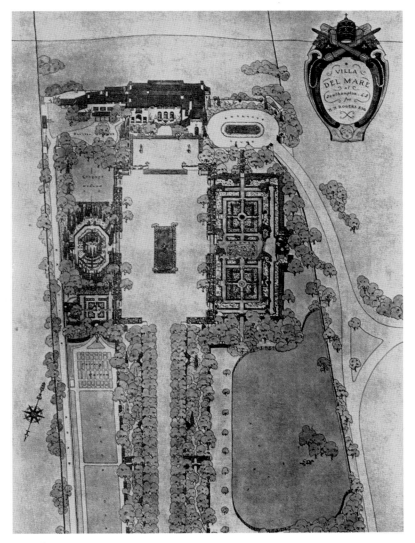

Site plan

peaceful reminder of the ocean on the opposite side of the villa. Hundreds of trees, planted by the Lewis & Valentine Company, created a garden within a short two-year period. Selective plantings, such as tall, slim trees installed directly against facade walls, amplified the effect intended by the architects. In 1922 the Rogers residence served as the centerpiece of a group of houses Walker & Gillette exhibited at the annual Architectural League of New York exhibition. That year they were awarded the gold medal for domestic architecture.

The Rogers entertained lavishly during their tenure at the villa. A dinner dance for 300, with Spanish singers, South American dancers, and a fortune-teller available for consultation, was not out of the norm. On such a night, the gardens would be filled with white and silver balloons and glowed with indirect lighting. Custom pendant lights would illuminate the south terrace, and the courtyard lily pool shone with underwater lighting while large bonfires blazed on the beach. Vibrant potted fuchsias lined the stairwell leading to the living room, which became the receiving area for the guests. A Tyrolean Bierstübe occupying one of the small gardens included costumed waiters performing songs.

H. H. Rogers died in 1935. By the late 1930s the property was broken up and the grand villa demolished, purportedly in response to high property taxes and hur-

ricane damage. All that remains today are some of the accessory structures, cottages and a white stucco wall along the estate's perimeter.

Of H.H. Rogers' grand villa, John Taylor Boyd, Jr. of *Architectural Record* wrote, "There is nothing so difficult as to be dramatic, without ever being theatrical."

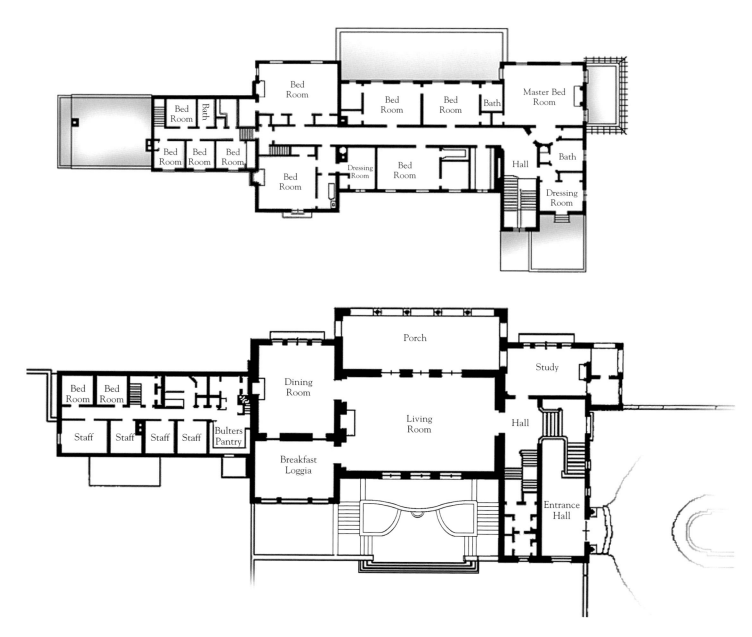

First (bottom) and second floor plans

NID DE PAPILLON

1917

Residence of Robert Appleton and Katherine Semple Jordan Appleton

Front elevation

Oceanside elevation

NID DE PAPILLON, built in 1917 by publisher Robert Appleton for his wife, the former Katherine Semple Jordan, is one of East Hampton's most inimitable structures. A little-known New York architect, Frank Eaton Newman, designed this curious and whimsical showplace for a couple firmly entrenched in the summer colony. The Appletons' oceanfront home, Nid de Papillon (meaning "butterfly's nest"), encompasses an amalgam of ideas incorporating architectural history, regional idioms, and contemporary design. And although none of this sounds particularly unique, Frank Newman's adroit compilation of these themes resulted in a strikingly original structure.

In keeping with East Hampton's contemporary village architecture and penchant for all things English, Newman fashioned a grand Elizabethan cottage in the Cotswold vein. Familiar with the vocabulary of the English manor house through his previous work, at Nid de Papillon, with its many gables, sweeping rooflines, and large rooms with rough-hewn-beamed ceilings, Newman not only restated English tradition, but pushed it over the top.

Although Newman's creation suggests he had a free hand with the design, he did provide a layout of well-proportioned rooms affording views and cross ventilation. Completed for $60,000 by builder E. M. Gay, the structure housed the typical arrangement of nicely sized rooms one would expect to find in a house from this era. A porch entry connects to a 23-by-33-foot living room with views of the ocean to the south and grassy hills to the north, and a west-side porch overlooks the Maidstone Club and golf course. Opening off the living room, the dining room also overlooks the ocean, and a stair hall, a pantry, a kitchen, and remaining service

Entrance detail

Card room

Breakfast room

functions meander off to the east from this point.

On the second floor, corridors extend from either end of the north-side stair hall, permitting almost all of the bedrooms to have south-facing ocean views. In the basement was a particularly interesting highlight, a full-size replica of an English pub, accessed through a trapdoor.

The most distinctive feature of Nid de Papillon, however, is its English "thatched" roof. Fashioned from closely spaced wood shingles, bent around the eaves, with a two-and-a-half-inch exposure to the weather by comparison, a typical shingled roof has a five-and-a-half-inch exposure. It shows Newman was clearly influenced by the shingle thatched roofs of Harrie T.

Lindeberg's Coxwould, built five years earlier and located a mile or so away. The construction documents for Nid de Papillon actually show eave details copied verbatim from Lindeberg's treatise "Thatched Roof Effects with Shingles," which appeared in *The Brickbuilder* in 1909.

The multiple jerkinhead gables and dormers and their overhangs create appealing shadow lines that further emphasize the house's silhouette. Off-white stucco walls, slight Gothic arches on window heads, and hooded lintels, especially on the stair hall fenestration, provide an idiosyncratic charm unique among Hamptons summer cottages.

Top: Garden; bottom: north lawn

Maidstoners who entertained frequently, the Robert Appletons had homes in New York, in Palm Beach, and, for many years, on the French Riviera. The couple received constant mention in the major newspapers' social notes for East Hampton and Palm Beach. *The New York Times* often reported on Nid de Papillon events, many of which had themes, such as the Gay Nineties bathing party, at which 30 guests, costumed in bathing suits with "high necks and long roomy trousers," enjoyed a swim and luncheon. Robert Appleton, who served as the president of the East Hampton Riding Club, also participated actively in the club's annual horse shows. By 1919, he amassed 100 acres surrounding Nid de Papillon, including a polo field, a horse paddock, a sunken garden, chicken coops, and 1,500 feet of oceanfront.

In January 1948, Mr. Appleton died from a fall from the sixth floor of a Palm Beach hotel; his death was deemed a "mystery" by the *Palm Beach Daily News*. Mrs. Appleton died one year later, and over time, Nid de Papillon passed to several owners. In 1983, James and Gretchen Johnson purchased the house and renovated it. During their tenure, the famous, classic roof has been replaced twice, each time matching the original shingle installation. Today, the house's character remains intact, thanks to its owners' diligence and dedication.

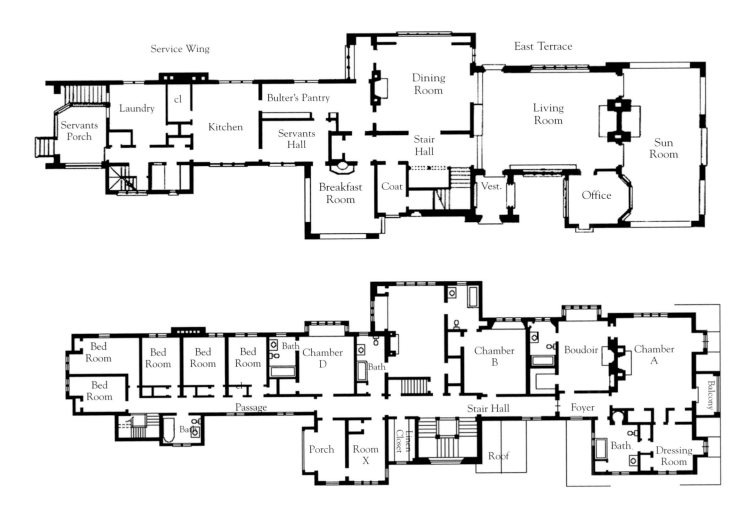

First and second floor plans

WOODHOUSE PLAYHOUSE

1917

Playhouse of Lorenzo Easton Woodhouse
and Mary Leland Kennedy Woodhouse—Marjorie Woodhouse

Front elevation

Front elevation through garden

NO SUMMER family has displayed more interest in community affairs, devoted more energy to the patronage of architecture, or had more impact on the cultural history of East Hampton than have the Woodhouse family. Lorenzo E. Woodhouse (1857–1935) and his wife, Mary Kennedy Woodhouse (1865–1961), first came to East Hampton in 1898. They visited Lorenzo's uncle and aunt, Lorenzo G. and Emma Woodhouse, at their Hunting Lane house, Greycroft, which was designed by Sayville architect Isaac H. Green Jr. By 1903, the younger Woodhouses had moved into their own new summer residence across the street. It was named The Fens and was designed by New York architect Joseph Greenleaf Thorp.

Lorenzo E. was president of the Merchants National Bank of Burlington, Vermont. He and Mary K. became active philanthropists, and the village of East Hampton was the recipient of their generosity. Mary Woodhouse was a founder of the Garden Club of East Hampton in 1911 and also served as its president. She donated her Japanese water garden and meadow to the East Hampton community for the creation of the Nature Trail and Bird Sanctuary, one of the real jewels of the village. The East Hampton Free Library, designed by architect Aymar Embury II and built in 1912, represented another financing effort on the part of the couple. In 1921 they restored Clinton Academy to its original 1784 design, and in 1931 they donated $100,000 to buy the land and finance the building of the community and art center, Guild Hall, also designed by Embury.

Over a 14-year period, the Woodhouses expanded The Fens into a fully developed estate with formal gardens

Playhouse interior (nave)

Fireplace detail

The Fens

and a 1908 addition to the house, followed by a gardener's cottage in 1911. Two bungalows, one by Embury in 1911, the other by East Hampton 'architect John Custis Lawrence, were erected in the 1910s, but the most notable addition to The Fens is the 1917 Playhouse, by New York architect F. Burrall Hoffman.

A birthday present from Mary Woodhouse to her 16-year-old arts-oriented daughter Marjorie, the Playhouse was far from a little back-yard cottage. Hoffman designed it to be an Elizabethan monument of church-like proportions, with a steeply gabled roof and a 75-foot-long great hall, 30 feet high at its peak. The grand scale of the building, its ecclesiastical character, and its Arts and Crafts-inspired design reveal the influence of Edwin Lutyens' Deanery Garden in Sonning, Berkshire, and C. F. A. Voysey's buttress-walled houses.

The exterior of the Playhouse is divided into two segments, a buttressed brick nave housing an auditorium and stage, and a half-timbered transept on the southern facade overlooking the sunken garden, filled with sunlight from leaded-glass-window sashes running from grade straight up to the gable. The roof is a composition of irregularly coursed slate shingles, thick at the eaves but tapering increasingly as they approach the ridge.

The interior features mortise-and-tenon, heavy timber trusses contrasted with a backdrop of half-timbered, stucco-filled walls. Carved wooden gargoyles performing on an accordion, cymbals, drums, and a flute decorate the bottom of the trusses where they engage the wall. Opposite the stage, at the west end of the nave, was an enormous Skinner-Aeolian pipe organ in the balcony. In

Top: Pergola connecting The Fens to the Playhouse; bottom: front garden

Mary Woodhouse

its heyday, the Playhouse was furnished with a worldly and eclectic collection of tables, furniture, Oriental rugs, and vases, all acquired by Mary Woodhouse.

In the days before the establishment of Guild Hall and its John Drew Theatre, the actor himself was a regular at the Playhouse. Drew's nephew, John Barrymore, was also said to have recited Shakespeare at the Playhouse for the Woodhouses' guests. On other occasions, the company witnessed performances by the Westminster Choir, Ruth St. Denis and her Denishawn Dancers, and Isadora Duncan. The local paper reported, "You haven't seen anything until you've been to one of Mrs. Lorenzo Woodhouse's garden parties."

The garden extends the design theme established by the Playhouse with Tudor style balustrades and a sunken-garden area to the south. Here, a pair of shrub-like wisteria flow into a reflecting pool coated with Arts and Crafts tiles. The authorship of this garden is not known, although various sources have suggested that either Hoffman or landscape architect Ruth Dean had a hand in its creation. Famed for her roses, Mary Woodhouse at one time employed at least seven gardeners to tend the arbors and plantings surrounding the Playhouse. Head gardener Maurice Collins, educated at the University College of Horticulture in Dublin, Ireland, said of the gardens in a 1950 *East Hampton Star* interview, "I love vistas—with the sun getting lower and shining through; many of the ideas on vistas worked out on the Woodhouse estate, I brought across the ocean with me. Other ideas for planting and grouping, I found in the Northwest Woods here. You can't beat Nature's work."

Cultural events at the Playhouse ceased with the death of the 32-year-old Marjorie Woodhouse in a 1933 car accident. Lorenzo Woodhouse died two years later, but his widow survived him until 1961. After Greycroft was sold and The Fens demolished because of high taxes, Mary hired local architect Richard Webb in 1953 to convert the Playhouse into a residence. Webb renovated the stage area to create a living suite and provided a servants' wing next to the kitchen. Mary Woodhouse's failing health compelled her to remain in Palm Beach until her death at age 96. She never had the opportunity to occupy the converted residence.

In 1958, David and Elizabeth Brockman bought the property and revived the tradition of providing entertainment in the Playhouse. The late Leopold Stokowski, a personal friend and regular visitor of the Brockmans, performed Bach's Toccata and Fugue on the Playhouse organ. Actors Tony Randall, Tom Poston, Eric Portman, and Claude Rains passed through the great hall at various times, as well. Still owners of the Playhouse in 2006, the Brockman family has continued the tradition of musical performance through the creation of the Playhouse Project, which offers classical music scholarships to local public high school students on the South Fork. With this endeavor, the Playhouse will continue as a reminder of East Hampton's golden era as a summer resort.

Water lily garden

BAYBERRY LAND

1918

∽

Residence of Charles Hamilton Sabin and Pauline Morton Sabin Davis

Tritoma walk

Aerial view

NO SOUTHAMPTON estate has a history as remarkable as that of Bayberry Land, the summer residence of Charles and Pauline Sabin. All the ingredients needed to create the recipe for a great American country estate existed there: owners with stature, wealth, glamor, and ambition; a renowned architectural firm capable of designing a one-of-a-kind manor house; and a pioneer landscape architect responsible for the layout of the property and the design of the gardens.

Perched on a bluff overlooking Peconic Bay, the house sat in a flat hollow at the low end of a slope. This positioning allowed the building to look as if it had been there from time immemorial, indelibly connected to its natural landscape. This interrelationship is revealed in the estate's name, taken from the bayberry shrubs so prevalent in its environs. Through a handsome wrought-iron gate in a pillared brick wall, a curving mile-long drive ran past a gatehouse, over a ridge, and down through an arched opening into a walled forecourt before the house. Facing Peconic Bay, a grass terrace, defined on one side by a retaining wall and plantings on the other, served as viewing platform and staging area for numerous social events. Surrounding the house, gardens large and small, formal and informal, acted as a series of interconnected rooms, extensions of the interior plan and exterior architecture.

Forecourt and front elevation

Bayberry Land's harmonious arrangement of design elements resulted, in large part, from the collaboration between architects Cross & Cross and landscape architect Marian Cruger Coffin. Coffin, who observed that "in any landscape scheme the designer should think as the architect, not only of his plan but also of the elevation which expresses this plan and the interrelation of the two," was deeply committed to blending house and gardens into a cohesive and complementary whole. A series of terraced, flower-saturated gardens, stepped down in three levels, is an extension of the living room to the west in a cascading ensemble to Peconic Bay and the sunsets over the water. The tritoma walk, a path of vibrant "hot" colors, pulled the eye to the water's edge. Coffin purchased the topsoil of an East End farm and had it trucked to Shinnecock Hills to enrich the gardens of Bayberry Land.

Architects John Walter Cross and Eliot Cross were established members of old New York society. The Cross brothers' residential work ran the gamut from Georgian to Colonial to Modern Picturesque. For the Sabins, their personal friends, Cross & Cross designed a manor house generally characterized as picturesque and reflected the influence of English Arts and Crafts architects Edwin Lutyens, W. R. Lethaby, M. H. Baillie Scott, and most particularly C. F. A. Voysey. Bayberry Land's very English exterior was also redolent in its use of disparate architectural elements. Contrasting with the Voysey-influenced entrance portal, for example, a small, hipped-roof balcony was set within the breakfast room gable and received eccentric support from an iron post of distinctly Spanish/Italian flavor.

The big house was designed to appear smaller than it actually was, with its massive slate roof combining two

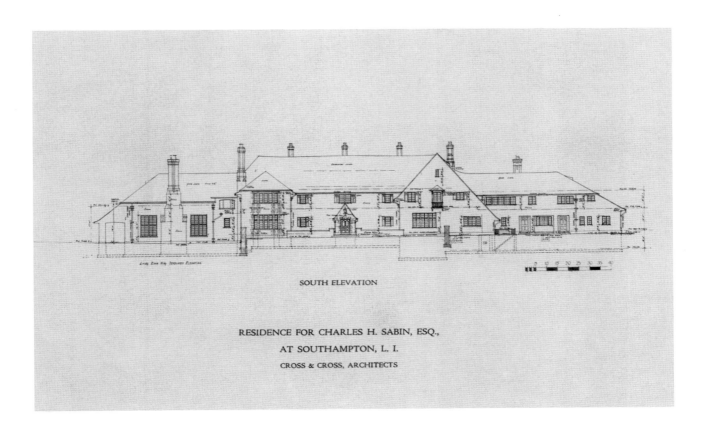

SOUTH ELEVATION

RESIDENCE FOR CHARLES H. SABIN, ESQ.,
AT SOUTHAMPTON, L. I.
CROSS & CROSS, ARCHITECTS

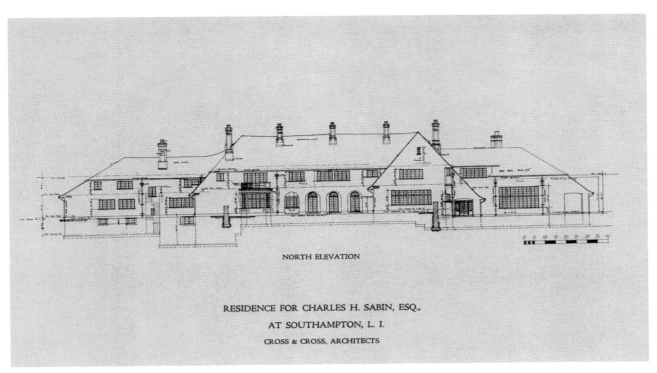

NORTH ELEVATION

RESIDENCE FOR CHARLES H. SABIN, ESQ.,
AT SOUTHAMPTON, L. I.
CROSS & CROSS, ARCHITECTS

Top: Front elevation; bottom: rear elevation

Sunken garden

stories into one and sweeping across other gable projections pulling the stone roof close to the ground. The diminished scale was also reflected in the Voysey-like entrance with its overly wide door and little stone outriggers—really no bigger than one fitted for a small cottage. Its grayish-green stucco finish, lathered over a facade of terra-cotta block, allowed the house to blend into the wild grasses of the hills. Almost an inch thick near the eaves, the individual slates that covered the roof narrowed as they approached the ridge. When the house turned a corner, the slates wove fluidly across the valley intersections as if they were a completely pliant material. The intentionally designed sags in the roof gave the building both the appearance of venerable age and a pedestrian scale. Other exterior touches included muted-red awnings for sun screening, oak shutters and window frames, leaded glass windows, chimneys of spi-

raling brick topped with clay pots and wrought-iron lantern brackets. Early photographs also showed a house "clothed" with ivy, a common practice reducing summer heat gain.

Stylistically, the interior of the manor house displayed a formality at odds with its casual exterior. The entrance led to a tiled, 50-foot-long hall with glass doors overlooking the north loggia and Peconic Bay. A glance back to the entrance revealed a double winding staircase joining in a landing over the front door and continuing up to the second floor as one stair. Samuel Yellin, America's most significant blacksmith and metalworker, created this exquisite wrought-iron masterwork in 1917. Both staircases terminated with newel posts embodying a maze of foliage, roses, and birds, capped by a planter receptacle. The equally remarkable stair rails included leaves, roses, petals, grapes, dolphins, rabbits, a squirrel nibbling on

Entrance detail

Stair hall

Library

nuts, a cockatiel with six-inch tail feathers, and other ornately sculpted birds. Yellin also produced the entry gates and other wrought-iron pieces for the estate.

East of the hall, the light-green dining room contained a Chinese red lacquer screen concealing the door to the pantry. A Bognani painting filled the overmantel in perfect alignment with the fireplace below it. Another dining room wall arrangement, in the spirit of the 18th century, featured an antique credenza centered under a gilded mirror with Sir Henry Raeburn's portrait of "Alexander, Fourth Duke of Gordon" on one side and George Romney's portrait of "Mr. Forbes," Lieutenant of the Royal Horse Guards, on the other side. The adjoining breakfast room walls were covered with lacquered Chinese wallpaper.

At the opposite end of the hall, the pine-paneled library, one of the more intimate spaces in the house, with its old Georgian doorway, overlooked the bay. Farther to the west down a few steps, a garden vestibule established a separation for the westward-skewed living room wing, which took full advantage of the garden and bay views. Measuring 30 by 40 feet, with a 17-foot ceiling height, the living room was decidedly Georgian in style, with egg and dart belt moldings, dentils, and modillions separated by gold-painted rosettes. Broken into different seating areas with couches and armchairs, the living room still retained a comfortable, livable scale. Upstairs, the bedrooms, traditionally furnished, had fireplaces. The bathroom walls, lined with panels of white glass, offered every amenity available for the era.

Living room

Completed in 1918, the manor house, main garage, gatehouse, caretaker's cottage, hunting lodge stables, secondary two-car garage with pump house, gardens, and tennis court cost the Sabins $1 million. *The Southampton Press* reported that this 314-acre estate, "among the showplaces of Southampton," led all township tax assessments at $160,000. Its July 1919 "brilliant housewarming" dinner dance, featuring separate orchestras on the front and back lawns, "held the attention of the whole summer colony." Bayberry Land was the scene of numerous social and summer colony events, dog shows, Republican gatherings, and croquet parties. It remained the epicenter for social events in the summer colony through the 1940s.

Charles Sabin and his wife came from very different backgrounds. He was a farm boy and she came from a family of wealth, privilege and social position. Charles

Hamilton Sabin (1868–1933) was born in Williamstown, Massachusetts, and educated at the Greylock Institute but could not afford to attend college. He moved to Albany and worked for a flour merchant until he pitched his way in to the banking profession. The National Commercial Bank of Albany, needing a pitcher for a decisive ballgame, hired Charlie, as he was known then, to pitch the winning game. Remaining at the bank, he rose through the ranks to become to vice president 13 years later. A protégé of politically active entrepreneur, Anthony Brady, Sabin moved to New York to become president of the Guaranty Trust Company in 1915 and chairman in 1930. So respected was he in financial circles, one statement from him could send the stock market into a tizzy.

His wife, Pauline Morton Smith Sabin Davis (1887–1955), born in Chicago, was the younger daughter

Living room door detail

Views of dining room

Top: Armillary garden; bottom: garden detail

Garden fountain

Lower garden fountain

Garage complex

of Paul and Charlotte Morton. Her grandfather, J. Sterling Morton, was a secretary of agriculture, senator, and governor of Nebraska; her father a railroad executive and secretary of the navy under Teddy Roosevelt, and her uncle, Joy Morton, from whom she would inherit millions, founded Morton Salt. In 1914, she divorced her husband, sportsman J. Hopkins Smith, and opened a profitable interior decorating business, which she abandoned in 1916 to marry a recently divorced Charles Sabin.

By today's standards the Sabins would be viewed as the ultimate power couple. He was a leader in banking and commerce with directorships in more than 30 corporations, as well as a Democratic Party activist. She was a member of the Suffolk County Republican committee, founder of the Women's National Republican Club, first woman on the Republican National Committee, and delegate to the Republican National Conventions of 1924 and 1928. Pauline Sabin was best known, however, as the founder of the Women's Organization for National Prohibition Reform (WONPR), and in that role she delivered stump speeches all over the country and testified before Congress. Mrs. Sabin's crusade landed her on the cover of *Time* magazine on July 18, 1932, with a feature article covering the activities of the

WONPR, colloquially known as "the Wet Sisterhood" and "the Sabin Women."

Charles Sabin died from a stroke in October 1933. In 1936, Pauline Sabin married Dwight Davis, who was former secretary of war, governor general of the Philippines, and the donor of tennis' famous Davis Cup. Mrs. Davis remained active in the summer colony until Dwight Davis's death in 1945. She sold Bayberry Land in 1949 to the International Brotherhood of Electrical Workers (IBEW) for use as a retreat and meeting place.

In 2001, Long Island car-leasing magnate and television station owner Michael Pascucci bought Bayberry Land from the IBEW for $45 million, then outraged preservationists, architects, and historians with the announcement of his plans to demolish the estate and build an 18-hole championship golf course on its site. Ironically, Charles Sabin was a man who loved golf, and his wife, Pauline, was one of the founders of the National Trust for Historic Preservation. After three years of negotiations with Southampton Town, and despite the protests of numerous citizens' organizations, on May 18, 2004, Bayberry Land, one of last great estates left in Southampton, was reduced to rubble within a few short hours.

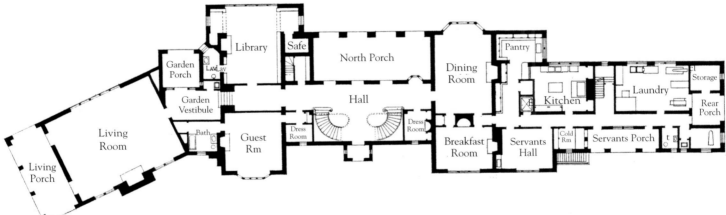

First and second floor plans

CHESTERTOWN HOUSE

1926

Residence of Henry Francis du Pont and Ruth Wales du Pont

Front elevation

Oceanside elevation

RARELY DURING an architect's career does he find a client who possesses unlimited funds, a unique idea, refined aesthetic sense, visual acuity, and unwavering attention to detail. Even more rarely do an architect and client collaborate to create a project of distinction. Chestertown House, the Southampton summer residence that architects Cross & Cross designed for Henry Francis and Ruth Wales du Pont, not only was a collaborative success, but it also realized the personal vision of its owner to create an original American house.

The great-grandson of Eleuthère Irénée du Pont de Nemours, Henry Francis du Pont was born at Winterthur, Delaware, in 1880, the only son of Colonel Henry Algernon du Pont and Mary Pauline du Pont.

Despite advantages of wealth and privilege, Henry was a terrible student at Groton, and he only barely graduated from Harvard in 1903. Upon his mother's death he assumed management responsibility for the family's Winterthur household.

In 1916, Henry du Pont married Ruth Wales, a native of Hyde Park, New York. Seven years later, in October 1923, they journeyed to Shelburne, Vermont, to visit the William Seward Webbs. They also saw the newly remodeled house of the Webbs' son and daughter-in-law, J. Watson and Electra Havemeyer Webb, the historic Brick House, with bookend additions by the architectural firm Cross & Cross. Nothing had quite prepared Harry for the visceral reaction he experienced from this

West elevation

casual visit. "I went to see this very attractive, old brick house and I was looking at the furniture. . . . I went upstairs and saw this dresser—this pine dresser. . . . It just took my breath away. I had never seen pine furniture or heard of it in fact."

Later that week, the du Ponts went to Gloucester, Massachusetts, to view Beauport, home of architect/decorator Henry Davis Sleeper, which, according to Henry du Pont, "was very attractively arranged . . . I said to my wife, 'Why don't we build an American house? Everybody has English houses and half the furniture I know they have is new. Since we're Americans, it's much more interesting to have American furniture.'"

In a two-year buying spree, du Pont amassed more than 1,900 objects, including American furniture, decorative ceramics, textiles, architectural woodwork, and other salvage items, such as hinges, nails, and locks. From houses in the Eastern Shore town of Chestertown, Maryland, he excised entire rooms of early American paneling for installation in his American house. Fittingly, he named this new Long Island residence Chestertown House.

Southampton was a natural choice for the du Ponts. Ruth Wales du Pont had spent childhood summers there at Ox Pasture, the home of her great-grandfather, former Southampton mayor Salem H. Wales, and at Mayfair,

Stair hall–gallery

the home of her uncle and aunt, the Elihu Roots. The idea of a new house, close to her family and far removed from Winterthur and her father-in-law was appealing.

In 1924, du Pont put together the team of professionals who oversaw the design of Chestertown House: architects Cross & Cross to create the house and outbuildings; Henry Davis Sleeper to advise on the interior design, finishes, color selection, and furniture arrangements; and the preeminent landscape architect Marian Coffin, a friend since childhood, to design a naturalistic landscape plan of beach grass, lowbush blueberry, and cotoneaster with Japanese and jack pines, juniper, and beach plum.

In a letter to John Cross, Henry du Pont wrote, "I should like to have the effect of the house more or less balanced. In other words, something to balance the New England woodshed effect." To meet du Pont's requirements, Cross devised an H-shaped structure similar in concept to his earlier Brick House additions. A three-wing affair, it was layered front to back, with the two long east-west wings running parallel to Meadow Lane on the north and the ocean to the south, connected by a third wing that served as a circulation spine. This connecting space doubled as galleries for display of du Pont's collection of Americana. The public rooms, also very much a stage set for du Pont's collection, combined vivid but harmonious color schemes that transitioned seamlessly.

The client-driven program for the residence was exhaustive. The 50-room house included 9 bedroom

Living room

suites, 15 servants' bedrooms, porches with stunning water views, a great hallway on each floor, living and dining rooms, a "pine" room (another living/dining area), and service facilities including a kitchen, a pantry, a laundry, and storage and mechanical rooms, which were accessed from a well-concealed exterior service court on the house's east side. A two-car garage framed one side of the front facade, and to the east a separate two-and-a-half-story six-car garage provided additional staff quarters.

From Meadow Lane, all that could be seen of Chestertown House's enormous mass was the Colonial Revival facade, its scale diminished further by the use of dainty 12-paned double-hung windows flanked by paneled shutters. On the entrance front, an overscaled front

door with scroll pediment dwarfed everything around it. Shed dormers with slate-shingled sidewalls faded into the roof mass, and the garage and bedroom walls, set back ever so slightly from the facade's central section, reduced the scale even more. Whitewashed brick lent the walls an aged appearance.

Cross & Cross had given du Pont a building "more or less balanced." Although it was perfectly symmetrical on the outside, the interior layout was eccentric in order to accommodate the period rooms du Pont collected. This irregularity was first apparent at the front door when the visitor entered peculiarly off-center, slammed tightly against a wall, in the grade-level entrance hall. According to Ruth Lord, du Pont's daughter, the ground

Pine room

floor was rarely used. Up a straight staircase, the main floor was level with the top of the dune, its public rooms facing the ocean on the south and the main guest rooms and servants' quarters facing the bay to the north.

Chestertown House's layout also revealed a strict class hierarchy. Servants had their own internal passageways and stairs separate from those used by the family and their guests. At du Pont's insistence, the family's sleeping quarters, a pink-paneled nursery and pastel green and blue bedrooms, were located in the south wing second floor, as far as possible from the servants' quarters in the north wing.

Henry du Pont was involved with every design decision, down to selecting the brand of grease trap for the kitchen. Yet the written correspondence between Cross & Cross and du Pont was always polite, congenial, and professional. After completion of the project, John Cross wrote to du Pont, "In closing this transaction I must tell you that it has been one of the most pleasant operations that I have experienced . . . The results justified what I often think—that a private house depends 90 percent on the owner and 10 percent on the architect. . . . I take my hat off to you."

In the summer of 1926, the du Ponts and their daughters moved into the house. The du Ponts entertained elegantly but on a small scale, serving dinners for eight—and occasionally for 22—with footmen behind every chair. Henry du Pont planned the menus, selected the linens,

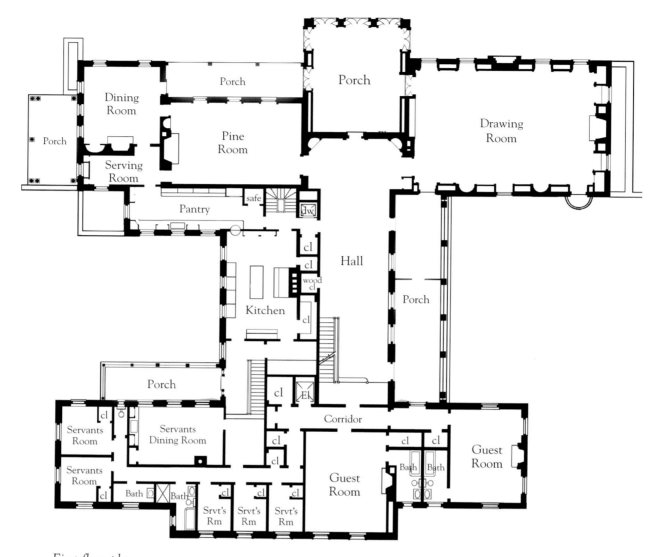

First floor plan

and ordered the flowers and food, which arrived every 10 days by refrigerated truck from the farms at Winterthur. Golf outings at Shinnecock and National were frequent, and ocean swimming was an everyday ritual.

By 1927, Henry du Pont thought of converting Chestertown House into a museum and asked John Cross to prepare plans for gallery space by gutting the servants' quarters. After realizing that his Americana assemblage contained three times as many articles as in the Metropolitan Museum of Art, du Pont decided on Winterthur as the eventual repository for his collection.

It opened to the public in 1951 as the Henry Francis du Pont Winterthur Museum. Many artifacts from Chestertown House can be found there today, such as the original entry door, the Wilhelm Schimmel carved wooden eagles from the first-floor great hallway, the spatterware collection, and the punch bowl from the entry hall table.

The family continued to use Chestertown House until Henry's death in 1969. Those contents not removed to Winterthur were auctioned in 1970, and the property was sold to actress and Andy Warhol acolyte Baby Jane

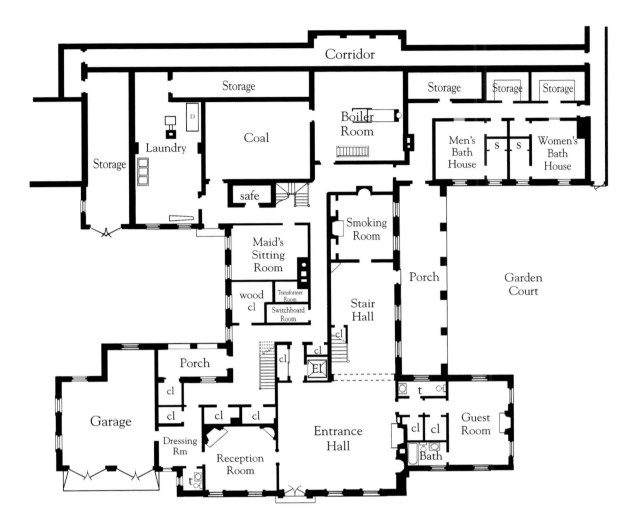

Ground floor plan

Holzer and her husband, Leonard. They defaulted on the mortgage and taxes, and removed what was left of the furnishings. The house was sold at a foreclosure auction for $310,000 to coal magnate John Samuels III.

In 1979, business entrepreneur Barry Trupin bought Chestertown House for $700,000 and renamed it Dragon's Head. Adding 20,000 square feet to the 35,000-square-foot house without the proper permits and in violation of the zoning height limitations, Trupin transformed the house into a Gothic rendition of an 18th-century Loire Valley château, complete with salt-water lagoon and Normandy pub. The turrets, dubbed the "height of hideosity" in *Newsday*, topped a house characterized as "Disneyland on LSD." Following Trupin's conviction for tax evasion, the house was sold in 1992 to WorldCom director Francesco Galesi for $2.3 million and again in 2003, to fashion designer Calvin Klein, for $29.9 million. Passersby would be hard pressed to imagine this formerly elegant structure once housed one of the most outstanding collections of decorative arts in America. Today the house is a cathedral of sheetrock, much of it gutted and altered beyond recognition.

HEATHER DUNE

1926

∽

Residence of Ellery Sedgwick James and Louise Russell Hoadley James

House and garage from road

Front elevation from across Georgica Pond

Front elevation

HEATHER DUNE, the East Hampton residence built for William Ellery Sedgwick James in 1926, at first glance appears to be just another little stucco castle by the sea. It certainly has the traits of such a building: a long, massive roof with engaged, conical turret/stairwell, lidded windows that seem to lift straight out of a roof of slate shingles and cross gables, chimneys, sand-colored walls, exposed timbered ceilings, baronial fireplaces, and a ceremonial driveway. What sets Heather Dune apart is, of all things, its lack of a recognizable style; New York architect Roger Bullard, an alumnus of Grosvenor Atterbury's office, created this residence to blend with the dunes of the East Hampton oceanfront.

When designing East Hampton's venerable Maidstone Club (1922), with its emblematic profile set against the ocean, Bullard simultaneously accepted two residential commissions on the same stretch of waterfront.

For James, Bullard presented a building conceived not as a hodgepodge from different eras, but as "pleasing, appropriate, in good taste and dignified—rather than 'Georgian' or 'French or whatnot,'" reflecting his belief that the "best results in the design of a country house are obtained when an effort is directed toward rationalizing style, or avoiding over-stylized building." Elements associated with one style could be used with elements of another, so long as the variants didn't clash.

The son of Henry Amman and Laura (Brevoort) Sedgwick James, Ellery James (1895–1932) was born in East Hampton to one of the oldest families in the summer colony. The roots of his mother's family, in fact, can be traced to the Puritans. After graduating from Groton and Yale, he married Louise Russell Hoadley, one month before shipping out to serve as a captain in World War I with the 85th Division in France and later with the Army of Occupation in Germany. He returned stateside in 1919 and joined the financial firm of Brown Brothers Harriman & Co. in New York.

Whether deliberately or coincidentally, the James family residence encompasses Puritan design elements. Its Colonial-period interiors, selected for simplicity to express the straightforward character of the house, blended with a Norman tower, Dutch fireplaces, and a peaked Gothic front door. Hand-hewn molding brackets, supporting the rough-timbered ceiling beams, reflect

Entrance detail

Oceanside garden courtyard

View through entrance hall

Entrance hall

East Hampton's enduring Anglophilia. Rough plaster walls terminate at doorways, not against casings, but rather alongside the door frames, with a bull-nosed plaster return. This reductive detail causes the rooms to appear larger and thematically unifies them.

In Bullard's attempt to relate to the local context and landscape, he subsumed the building within it; he created outdoor rooms that were not only self-contained but blended into the larger surroundings of dunes and sea. A garden off of the living room capitalized on a low wall that acted both as a windbreak and as a backdrop to plantings. A small sitting niche alongside the living room further defined this space as a grass court. The garage, with bedrooms above, sat perpendicular to the house on the east. The service court, located behind the garage to the south just behind the dune, functioned to hide the garage doors from the street, creating the effect of a purely residential compound.

From the living room, Bullard positioned windows on the north perpendicular to the main axis of the house, facing Georgica Cove and Georgica Pond, while those on the south offered views of the ocean. Heather Dune proved to be the articulation of the architect's "own aesthetic conscience" in physical form.

Top: Living room; bottom: dining room

Ellery James, died in 1932 at age 37 after a long ill-ness, having spent just a few summers in the house. His wife and three children continued to use it for many years. An addition with a low conical turret as an end wall, sensitive to the house's original design, was joined to the west terrace at a later date. The house's current owners continue to maintain Heather Dune with integrity and care.

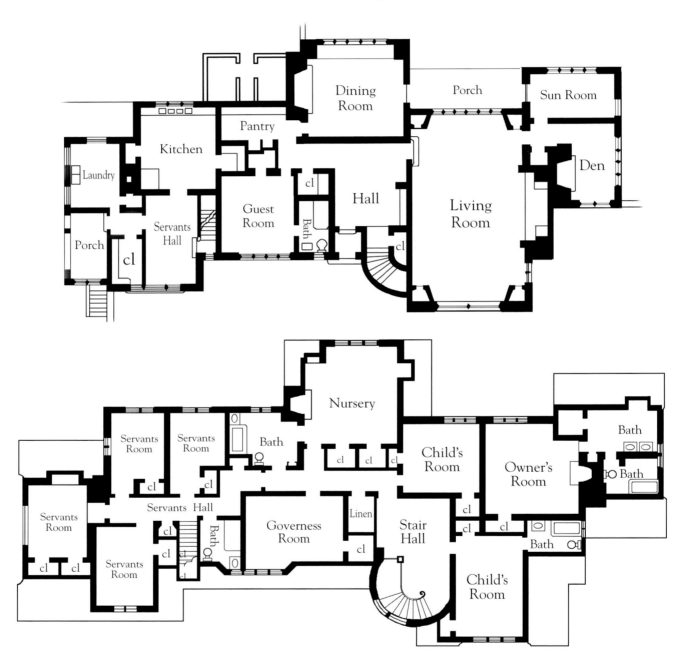

First and second floor plans

PORT OF MISSING MEN

1926–1929

⌐

Residence of Henry Huddleston Rogers Jr. and Mary Benjamin Rogers

Entrance forecourt

View of Scott cottage and house from Scallop Pond

PORT OF MISSING MEN stands on a bluff in the Cow Neck section of North Sea overlooking Scallop Pond, an oval 530-acre body of water that is part of the nationally recognized Peconic Bay Estuary. It was the Southampton vacation retreat of Colonel Henry Huddleston Rogers Jr. The Rogers compound, which originally measured more than 1,800 acres, was conceived as a self-sustaining farm and included a game preserve and a dairy. The house, referred to as a hunting box, was used by the colonel and his family as a getaway from the hustle and bustle of Southampton Village and his Gin Lane estate.

Rogers was the only son of robber baron Henry Huddleston Rogers, one of the founders of Standard Oil. Rogers Jr. was a major stockholder in that company. He inherited his father's vast Standard Oil fortune in 1909, became the owner of the Virginia Railway Company, and held directorships and positions with many other transportation concerns. The colonel, who had a life-long interest in military affairs, served in World War I with distinction. He received many citations from the United States Army for his actions and meritorious services and in 1933 received the Cross of Chevalier of the Legion of Honor from the Republic of France.

An avid yachtsman and member of the New York Yacht Club, the colonel owned the electrically driven *Fan-Kwai* and the *Charming Polly*, reputed to be the world's fastest cruiser. Colonel Rogers' generous philanthropic activities included a $30,000 donation in 1925

Top: Sketch of entry elevation; bottom: aerial view

Views of two-story great room

Top: Guest bedroom; bottom: living room of Jackomiah Scott cottage

View of library–natatorium with Scallop Pond beyond

to Southampton Hospital Nursing School, as well as gifts to numerous charities related to the world war.

An inveterate collector, the colonel amassed houses as well as antiques. For the Port of Missing Men, Rogers commissioned nationally renowned architect John Russell Pope, the creator of the National Gallery of Art and the Jefferson Memorial in Washington, D.C., to create a simple hunting retreat on lands that he had assembled over a number of years. Located just west of

Conscience Point, where the pilgrims first landed in Southampton in 1640, the property contained an existing colonial cottage dating from 1661, built for Captain Jackomiah Scott.

John Russell Pope, who had the ability to simplify and recast historical styles, reinterpreted the Colonial idiom for the design of Port of Missing Men. Pope, taking his cue from the Scott cottage and the historical fabric of the existing neighborhood, created a Colonial Revival house.

Library

This style was extremely popular in the 1920s, in part because of the popularity of Colonial Williamsburg. The house has a skewed H-shape plan, with the main section serving as a combined living/dining area and encompassing a two-story great room running north–south along the shorefront. Eccentrically attached wings at each end (one of which is the Scott cottage), placed perpendicular to the great room and flowing in an east–west direction, create an ensemble conceived to look as if layers of history were added to the main structure over time. The asymmetrical arrangement of one-and-a-half-story structures, consistent with the scale of the buildings in the surrounding neighborhood, suppresses the expansive presence of the totality.

The approach to Port of Missing Men features a pillared opening through whitewashed, brick-capped walls. The mile-long driveway, lined with trees that flower in the spring against a backdrop of rolling lawn, ascends to a forecourt of kalsomined walls in front of the house, also painted stark white. Crisply cut charcoal slates cover the roof, which gleams when the sun strikes the shingles.

The modest entry through a wide door under a small porch overhang (not part of the original design) leads to a low-headroom, wood-paneled anteroom serving as a passageway to the great room, a blown-up version of a room, installed in the American Wing of the Metropolitan Museum of Art, that was taken from the

Natatorium

1681 Old Ship Meeting House in Hingham, Massachusetts. At the south end of the room, a balcony alcove sits over a wall of books, and it overlooks a space that is framed with exposed, hand-hewn timbers supported by two massive post-and-beam trusses,. The room's east wall, backing to the forecourt, features a walk-in fireplace with a gun rack on the wall to its left. Gunshot windows in the upper half story emit natural light into a space that would otherwise be dark.

The north end of the room displays a carved eagle from an 1812 clipper ship, mounted below flags of the various army units that served under Colonel Rogers. A ship's wheel found on the property's beachfront, from the 1893 Peconic Bay shipwreck of the *Lykan Valley*, is

mounted on the wall below the eagle. Great loss of life was associated with this shipwreck, and the Port of Missing Men was named in part for the men whose lives were lost along its shoreline. Of course, the name has a double meaning, because when Colonel Rogers and his hunting friends occupied the house in the winter, they became missing men to their wives.

Nautical themes pervade the house. Rogers collected historic ship-related wallpapers, models, and paintings, many of which are overmantels. A model of the ship *Juno*, which once belonged to Admiral Jackson of the British navy and hangs from a beam in the center of the great room, was displayed for years at London's Kensington Museum.

"Aphrodite," by Edward Field Sanford

Natatorium solarium

At the end of the great room, a small corridor connects to Scott's cottage. It is here that the first clue to the colonel's sense of humor becomes apparent. Linen-covered walls include a depiction of a drunken sailor leaning against a large keg, with the caption "Like an old bold mate of Harry Rogers." The cottage, incorporating a concealed stove and sink, was renovated to function independently of the main section of the house. Adjacent to the cottage's small living room is "The Room of the Dog," which appropriately holds a collection of Bennington Pottery pooches on the mantel. "The Room of the Haunt," with its timbered ceiling and dark wood paneling surrounding dormer windows, has a commanding view of Scallop Pond. The centerpiece of the room is an early French four-poster oak bed. A Portuguese patterned rug with an antique lemon background warms the floor. "The Attic Room" exhibits another inscription, "Old Medford Rum . . . H. H. Rogers 1926."

Ship model room

The wing that projects toward the water on the opposite side of the great room contains the Rogers' bedrooms. The historic paneling of Mrs. Rogers' southwest-facing bedroom almost exactly matches that of a room in the Metropolitan Museum of Art. The original draperies for her four-poster, done in French crewelwork, were complemented by an Aubusson rug. The colonel's bedroom possesses two water-view exposures. Dubbed "The Room of the Mink," it features pull curtains behind a painted wood valance, a chintz divan, and a garden-patterned Aubusson rug. A painted profile of the mink sits on the upper stile of the raised-panel door.

Other guest rooms include "The Room of the Ruined Roman Virgins," which was usually assigned to male guests, and "The Room of the Canton," which contains Oriental antiques, Chinese rugs, paintings on glass, a sizable amount of Chinese Lowestoft, and a carved ivory scene over the daybed.

Wings adjacent to the great room have low ceilings, in keeping with the house's Colonial theme. Corridors are narrow, but even a smaller one was made interesting with a panoramic Brocq-Dufore wall covering titled "Monument of Paris."

Port of Missing Men was one of the early commissions for Eleanor Brown of McMillen, Inc., an interior designer who was fearless with regard to the intermixing of eras. The antique furniture and patterned fabrics were all authentic, right down to the trimmings. According to

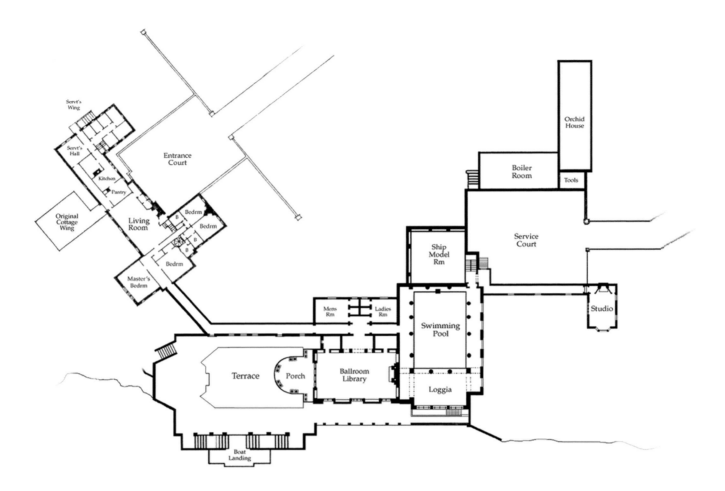

Plans

Mrs. Brown, "Colonel Rogers wouldn't come into New York to look at furniture. . . . Everything had to be trucked out to him—a considerable distance in those days. But most of it stayed."

Port of Missing Men, not lacking for eccentricity, sports an underground tunnel with a hidden door leading from the bedroom wing to a multipurpose room at the property's waterfront. Viewed from Scallop Pond, the room, built directly into the bluff wall, resembles a sculpted ship's stern, with small muntin-paned windows. Inside, several canons point at square backlit openings in the walls containing painted scenes cast against blue skies.

In 1929, construction of a Pope-designed natatorium, also connected by another tunnel bordering Mrs. Rogers' bedroom, was completed. The glass-and-steel structure, enclosing one of the largest indoor pools in the country,

included a solarium facing the pond, dressing rooms, a squash court, a room for Colonel Rogers' ship model collection, and a library. The pool house was a stylistic departure from the colonial hunting box. Here, Pope dove into the world of classicist invention and produced a Greek structure that made quite a splash. Fluted Doric columns, whose girth was directly proportional to the long spans they supported, established a rhythm for swimming in an enclosed temple for the gods.

The Rogers family also commissioned artist and muralist LeRoy Daniel MacMorris to provide the interior decoration for the pool house. Concerned that the classically Greek structure would feel too austere, particularly in the bleak winter months, the Rogers opted for MacMorris' Pompeian treatment of the interior, which he called "an artistic spree with no inhibition about invention."

Drawings, conceived as interpretations of the Pompeian decorative idiom, avoided parroting details from exhumed structures of the once buried city.

MacMorris painted a series of hunting scenes on panels that were placed on the wall spaces between column bays. To avoid the creation of a decorative flat surface, the panels were actually chiseled out of a mud mixture applied to the walls to provide the illusion of mosaic relief work. Panel scenes included Diana, centaurs, fishermen, dogs, and maidens, all capturing the warm glow of the Italian sky against a backdrop of tropical seas. Doors to the squash court and dressing rooms were hand painted in an Italian style, and a jade-colored mosaic frieze above the columns contained a golden acanthus scroll with small animals residing in the volutes. Centered on the pool across from the solarium, atop a tall pedestal, was a life-size Aphrodite, sculpted in Carrara marble by Edward Field Sanford.

The library on the northwest side facing the house had a tall, semicircular portico, accessed from a promenade along the water's edge running the length of the building and supported by pairs of slim Tuscan columns. A double set of French doors opened on the promenade overlooking Scallop Pond and Peconic Bay beyond. The walls inside the library, lined with bookshelves and dark wood paneling, dispersed sections of fluted pilasters between square columns and wall openings. A frieze, running around the entire room above the columns, contained a Greek key design capped by egg-and-dart molding. Plaster acroteria and banding relief work wove across the barrel-vaulted ceiling to octagonal coffers containing crystal chandeliers suspended from the centers of plaster medallions. The octagonal theme is repeated in the paving patterns of the bluestone on the terrace outside the library.

Colonel Rogers' ship model collection, located in a room on the northeastern side of the building, featured British "dockyard" ship models dating from the 17th, 18th, and early 19th centuries. Dockyard models derive their name from the fact that they were made simultaneously in the same dockyard as the ships they actually depict. Colonel Rogers, who acquired the models from the late 1910s to the early 1930s, owned at his death in 1935 the largest private collection in the world, and he bequeathed it to the United States Naval Academy Museum in Annapolis, Maryland.

The natatorium and library complex was demolished in the late 1940s, presumably because of concerns about maintenance costs, by the trustees of H. H. Rogers' estate.

Port of Missing Men can be seen from Great Peconic Bay, Little Peconic Bay, Scallop Pond, West Neck Creek, Little Sebonac Creek, and North Sea Road. Rogers' grandson, Peter Salm, who inherited the estate, became known for his stewardship of the wetlands surrounding Cow Neck and received praise from State Legislator Fred Thiele, who cited Salm's work as an example for all Southampton residents to follow. In recent years, 540 of 600 of acres, including the Cow Neck Farm portion of the property with its tidal and freshwater wetlands, bought from the Salm family by financier Louis Bacon, have been gifted to the Peconic Land Trust and will now be preserved in perpetuity.

Salm's widow, the former Wiltraud von Furstenberg, and her children continue to maintain Port of Missing Men, the last great estate on the south fork, with care. Antiques, fabrics, and rugs have been repaired or replaced authentically whenever possible.

Port of Missing Men hosts salt marsh cordgrass, sea lavender, and glasswort, as well as great blue herons, great egrets, black ducks, kingfishers, osprey, and omnipresent herring gulls. Owing to this dreamlike setting, its architecture, and its interiors, it remains a museum-quality property, and it occupies a special place in Southampton's history and future.

FOUR FOUNTAINS

1928

Residence of Lucian Hamilton Tyng and Ethel Hunt Tyng

Entrance forecourt

South elevation

FOUR FOUNTAINS, on Halsey Neck Lane in Southampton, was built around 1928 as a multipurpose arts center by Lucien and Ethel Tyng. Peabody, Wilson & Brown designed this unusual compound, which the Tyngs offered to the community as a venue for art exhibits, concerts, films, and fundraisers, as well as for performances by the Hamptons Players. The structure is also known as the Tyng Playhouse.

The playhouse is flanked on one side by a garage/chauffeur's quarters and by a guest cottage on the other; the three structures, lathered in creamy stucco, form a square forecourt fronted by a bronze fence of Art Deco design. The driveway, on axis with the wall's center, opens to a circle paved with outsized flagstone installed in concentric rings. The edges of this circle within a square contain lawn and plantings. Originally, each corner of the court contained a fountain propelling water into the air—hence the name Four Fountains.

The gateposts at the entrance are particularly striking. Clad in Crab Orchard sandstone blocks, they provide the base for a pair of large bronze falcons, intended to represent the Egyptian god Horus. They were replicated on a grand scale from a small bronze bird in Mrs. Tyng's collection. The stone for the gateposts, found in a range of peachy pinks, chamois yellows, and brown, is also

Entry detail

Foyer

used for the tiled roofs. Its overall effect was to reduce the scale of the buildings and provide a cottage flavor reminiscent of the English countryside.

The simple exterior of the playhouse, a windowless front with corner quoins and a hipped roof, contrasts dramatically with its decorative front doors of swirling bronze peacocks set against glass panels. Although referred to as classical Art Deco, this design really has more of the undulating quality characteristic of Art Nouveau. Beyond the doors, an entrance foyer with Crab Orchard on the floor and walls contains a small stairwell to the upstairs, a utility room, and a small kitchen. The 1,600-square-foot 40 by 40 by 20 auditorium originally had a stage at its far end. It occasionally doubled as a reception room. Its center stage on the back wall featured

a 1625 mantelpiece in slate from Genoa, and its coffered ceiling contained painted panels by Ernest Peixotto.

By 1942, the upkeep on the Four Fountains had become burdensome for the Tyngs, and they sold it at a reasonable price to its original architect, Archibald Brown, and his wife, Eleanor. Brown was president of the interior design firm McMillen, Inc. The Browns converted the playhouse into a delightful summer residence, transforming the former auditorium into a combination living/dining room. They removed two windows and added a fireplace, on axis with the windows on the opposite wall. A half wall, installed in front of the raised stage, hid the steps leading to the double-bedroom master suite and baths. Organ and projection rooms over the entrance hall were altered to create guest bedrooms

Entry doors with bronze peacock scrolls

Peacock organ grill

Auditorium showing stage

Stage with painted Italian ceiling

Main living room, present-day view

Crab orchard entry pillars with bronze falcons looking toward garage wing

and baths. Just outside the dining area windows, an allée of apple trees surrounding a manmade reflecting pool provided a serene vista.

Eleanor Brown, who liked to entertain in small groups, arranged the furnishings in the living/dining space to be intimate and flexible. Sofas and chairs had benches at hand, along with straight-back chairs that could be moved into a grouping as needed. A 9-foot by 13-foot Raoul Dufy toile, salvaged from the Browns' oceanfront studio, hung on one wall, and Wheeler Williams' figure called "Seasons" sat on the marble mantel.

In 1978, CBS chairman William Paley bought Four Fountains, and the following year the contents of the Browns' house were sold at Sotheby Parke Bernet. In his introduction to the auction catalog, designer Albert Hadley wrote that "Four Fountains was a unique architectural example of American Art Deco design." Of Eleanor Brown he said, "In her own inimitable way she created interiors of great distinction combining primarily Rococo and Neo-Classic French and Italian furniture from the 18th and 19th century, and placing it in agreeable juxtaposition to contemporary upholstery of the finest quality and richest comfort . . . the combining of beautiful, meaningful objects from the past with the best the contemporary scene has to offer was there and continues to be the design point of [Eleanor Brown]."

Bruce and Maria Bockmann, who continue to maintain the property in a way that befits the style and elegance of the previous owners, purchased Four Fountains from the Paley estate in the mid-1990s.

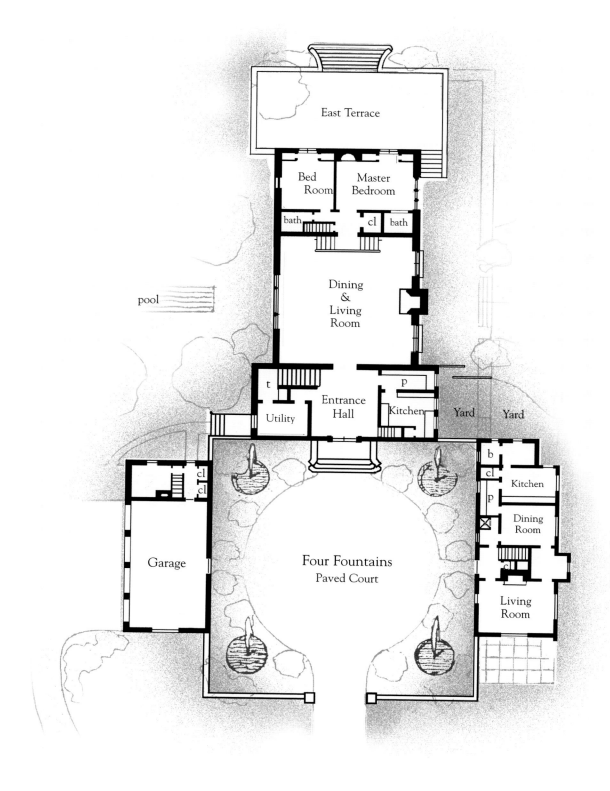

Plans, present-day layout

[278]

OCEAN CASTLE

1929

Residence of William F. Ladd and Cornelia Lee Ladd

Main entrance

Top: Southwest elevation; bottom: east elevation

Bird's-eye view rendering

LIKE A CHILD'S sandcastle set on the dunes, Ocean Castle, built in 1929 for William F. Ladd, rambles across the oceanfront as a series of twisting and turning wings. This fused-together ensemble, which could substitute for a tour of Normandy and Brittany, is an ad hoc arrangement that reflects the manner in which the design evolved.

The Ladds had commissioned architects Peabody, Wilson & Brown in 1920 to design their year-round residence, an English manor house at Lawrence, Long Island. Impressed by the studio Archibald Brown designed for his own wife on the Southampton oceanfront, the Ladds again commissioned the firm to create a similar summer retreat down the road on the Southampton dunes.

William F. Ladd, a New York Stock Exchange member, broker, and sportsman, initially asked his society architects to design a small summer getaway, but, as is often the case when money is no object, what began as a little cottage grew in scale. A house that started with one wing grew another; then a tower made an appear-

ance, followed by two more towers and a dovecote. In the middle of construction, the owners decided to raise the house on stilts to command bay and ocean views. Great mountains of sand were piled up around the house and shaped by machine into man made dunes under the direction of the architects, owners, and helpful guests. With the finishing touch of replanting the beach grass, they created an environment that was indistinguishable from the original. Through this transformation of the surrounding landmass, the house rose to four stories on the bay side and just one story on the ocean side.

A long driveway through the dunes offers the first real glimpse of the house from the entrance court. To the right, a large wing fans out to contain a series of sub-servient and descending segments with gable and hipped roofs, finally terminating along the dune at the service court. To the left of the entrance, another wing appears hinged off a round, squat dovecote. The exterior walls, conceived to look like stone, are actually concrete blocks skimmed with a parged coating resembling textured stone. French-style tiles, weaving from one roof to

View into service courtyard

Cascading stair

Living room

another, came from Denver and were rugged enough to resist the climatic variations of Southampton's weather. The plan of the house bends and undulates, very much in keeping with its man made topography. The house, which has 30 rooms and 20,000 square feet of space, stretches 350 feet—longer than a football field.

A small flight of stairs leads to the house's entrance, which is centered in a square tower with a hipped roof. French doors in the tiled entrance foyer offer a view of the ocean. To the right is a low, almost ramplike stair, with four-inch risers and long, sweeping treads connecting to the great half-timbered hall/living room. The oak timbers used throughout the house were soaked for two years at the bottom of a lake, seasoning that prevented the wood from splitting. A ship's wheel, paying homage to Ocean Castle's setting, was mounted above the carved stone mantelpiece on the ocean-side wall, with a large window opposite facing Shinnecock Bay. Adjacent to this room on the east is a crescent-shaped wood-paneled library, and on the west side, a porch

Living room bay window

with imported floor tiles and numerous windows, over-looks the ocean and the picturesque scene created by the cascading turrets and dormers of the service wing, garage, and caretaker's cottage.

The master suite, consisting of a study, a bedroom, a bath, and dressing areas, is located in the eastern wing on the first floor. A circular stair with wrought-iron rail connects to the other floors in this wing. The remaining bedrooms, all with dramatic ocean views, run along a long, twisting second-floor corridor, accessed by another sweeping stairwell terminating at the first-floor stair hall.

In 1949, William Ladd, in failing health for some time and given only a month to live, died of a self-inflicted gunshot wound. He left a note of apology to his wife for his decision. After his death, the house was sold and passed through various owners over the years.

In September 1963, Donald Leas Jr. rented Ocean Castle for use as a guesthouse for men attending the debutante ball of his stepdaughter, Fernanda Wanamaker Wetherill. Owners of the former Kiser estate, Westerly, on Ox Pasture Road, the Leas hosted one of the most lavish and expensive coming-out parties of the era, and the ball, which normally would have been covered in the society pages, made national headlines because of the "after party" that took place at Ocean Castle. The male guests swung from the chandeliers and ripped the house apart, throwing its furniture onto the beach and smashing 1,600 windowpanes by the

West sun porch overlooking ocean

time the police arrived the next morning. *Life*, *Newsweek*, *Time*, and newspapers throughout the country covered the story of the wild party at Ocean Castle.

In the 1980s, entrepreneur Barry Trupin bought Ocean Castle from theatrical producer Roy Radin and resided there while renovating the former du Pont mansion, Chestertown House. Today Ocean Castle remains in private hands, and the current owners maintain the estate with loving care.

SUNSET COURT – WESTERLY

1929

Residence of John William Kiser and Mary Peirce Kiser

Drive at entrance gates

Entrance courtyard

South elevation

SITUATED IN the western part of Southampton's estate section, at the intersection of Ox Pasture Road and Captains Neck Lane, Westerly is one of the Hamptons' rare but distinctive Georgian Revival mansions. Designed by the firm of Hiss & Weekes, it was built in 1929 for industrialist John W. Kiser Jr. and his family. The Kisers likely commissioned the firm after renting Red Maples, another Southampton house the architects designed. Initially the Kisers christened their new home Sunset Court, but they later changed the name to Westerly.

Constructed of red antique brick with a slate roof, the 25-room Westerly originally sat on 30 acres with 170 feet of frontage on Heady Creek. From Ox Pasture Road, the visitor approaches the house through a white picket entrance gate opening onto a long, tree-lined allée that terminates in a formal forecourt enclosed by rhododendron bushes. The gargantuan house is rendered far less

Top: Dining room; bottom: library

Living room—Ballroom

Top: Sunroom; bottom: master bedroom

West elevation

formidable by being broken into three separate wings similar to those of the Breese house, The Orchard. The elongated U-shaped plan runs east to west for about 180 feet. The main body of the house contains the formal entertaining rooms, and the eastern mass holds the service wing. The wing to the west is devoted to a living room/ballroom and a sunroom overlooking the gardens. Westerly's symmetrical facade, with evenly spaced windows framed by white shutters, is reminiscent of the great houses of the Virginia hunt country and Long Island's North Shore. A semicircular marble stair with iron railings leads to the elaborate front entrance, offering just a hint of the refined interiors.

Entering the house beneath a sweeping iron-railed staircase, the visitor ascends a few steps into a black-and-white marble-tiled foyer that continues through to the rear terrace and contains deep, shell-topped niches for floral arrangements. From this point, the library and dining room are accessed through an oblong, transverse-vaulted hall that acts as a spine for the main floor between the easterly service wing and a marble foyer adjacent to the living room/ballroom to the west. A small reception room, a powder room, closets, and a flower-arranging room line the front of the house.

Prominent society decorator Elsie Sloan Farley originally designed the interiors. In the library she used

Garden pool with swan sculptures

Swedish knotty pine and installed a black and gold marble mantelpiece, over which hung a portrait of Mrs. Kiser by artist Howard Chandler Christy. In the dining room, Farley cast the walls in a pale lemon yellow, chose an antique crystal chandelier and wall sconces, designed recessed niches to hold collections of porcelain, and selected a mixture of Adam and Sheraton furnishings. The major room in the house is the living room at the far west end. Originally, its walls were painted gray-green and the room furnished with 18th-century French and English pieces, an Adam style mantelpiece, and an iron-and-crystal chandelier. The enormous ballroom provided the staging area for the Kisers' entertainment of members of Southampton and Palm Beach society. The second-floor master bedroom and family suites were all elegantly and comfortably decorated with chintzes and soft colors. A massive third floor held overflow guests and service and storage rooms.

On Westerly's southern exterior, a covered terrace leading to the gardens and rolling lawns could be accessed from the dining room, entrance hall, and library. Annette Hoyt Flanders, creator of many significant estate landscapes and gardens in the Hamptons, devised a scheme of dense privet hedges, mature trees, and specimen plantings with a sunken garden and lily pond approached by a curved staircase off the west-wing sunroom.

The Kiser family sold the estate in the late 1950s, and it was eventually purchased by the Leas family of Philadelphia. In August 1963, one of the most infamous parties ever given in the Hamptons took place at Westerly. Eight hundred guests attended a debutante party the Leas gave for their daughter Fernanda Wanamaker Wetherill. For the occasion, the grounds were transformed into a rendition of Versailles by the sea.

Today Westerly, still in private hands, is as well maintained as when it was first built.

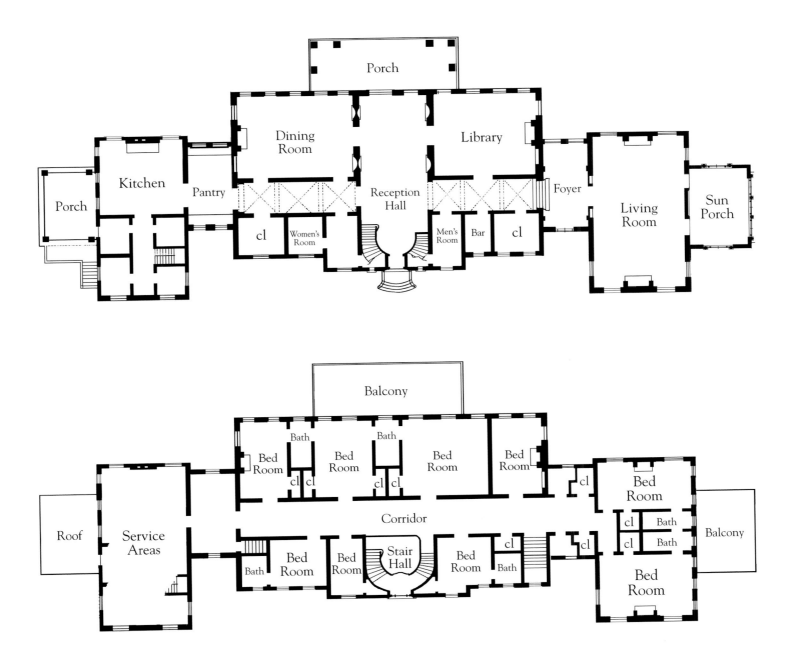

First and second floor plans

THE BOUWERIE

1930

∽

Residence of Wesley Creveling Bowers and Gladys Seward Bowers

Southeastern oceanside elevation

Meadow Lane elevation

TUCKED DEEP into the dunes along Meadow Lane in Southampton, with only a glimpse of protruding chimneys and a Spanish tile roof visible to passersby, is the Wesley C. Bowers estate. Engulfed by surrounding dunes, the house appears to have been buried for years with shifting sands only recently exposing the aged villa.

Dr. Wesley Creveling Bowers, who was a leading physician in otolaryngology at New York's St. Luke's Hospital, and his wife, Gladys Seward Bowers, were active members of the summer colony. Mrs. Bowers' charitable interests included Southampton Hospital, the Southampton Fresh Air Home, and the Southampton Chapter of the Garden Club of America.

In 1930, after summering in Southampton for many years, the Bowers commissioned New York architect Leroy P. Ward to design a house in the dunes. The imaginative Ward had already designed four substantial houses on Long Island, all in different styles. For the Bowers, he created a three-and-a-half-story Mediterranean-style villa overlooking both the Atlantic Ocean and Shinnecock Bay. According to local lore, the inspiration for the house came from a villa the couple saw on their honeymoon in the south of France. "The Bouwerie," a play on the family name, also alluded to the idea of a quaint cottage.

From the time it was built, The Bouwerie was conceived to seem antedated, its exterior massing resembling a collection of additions that accrued over time. Low-pitched gable and hipped roofs descend and spill onto smaller hipped roofs alongside a projecting bay and entry. Shutters and carved wooden balconies exposed to the elements, antique tiles, time-worn timbers, mottled stucco, and ancient hardware contribute to the aged appearance. A small, square garden pavilion with stucco columns and a hipped roof of red Spanish tiles sits just to the south. The house is pure American Riviera, antiquated yet engaging, with a European pedigree applied to a picturesque, vernacular Revival style immensely popular in the 1920s and 1930s.

The long, episodic plan of this house was conceived to take advantage of the views and simultaneously fill

Westside fountain and patio

Front entrance

Living room

the building with light and air. The living room, placed at an angle to main body of the house, offers views of sunsets over Shinnecock Bay and the ocean to the south. The terrace beside the living room overlooks both the garden and pool. An exterior stair, snaking up around the circular tower facing the ocean, provides bathers with direct access to second-story baths and bedrooms. The dining room is finished with coarse gray/beige plaster between rough-hewn beams on walls and ceiling. Throughout the house, flooring, made from wide-plank adzed pine boards, is laid on the diagonal.

A major feature of the house is the two-story stair hall with an elliptically arched French casement window directly above the main entrance. It is supposedly a replica of a 200-year-old stair, with delicate wrought-iron railing that contrasts sharply with its pine steps and hefty ceiling beams. Composed of wavy balusters separated by straight ones, all capped with a scrolled handrail, the design echoes the curling ocean waves in the distance. Thus the stair balustrade combines with the function of the staircase to present a metaphor for movement.

The original Provençal furnishings and interior detailing were consistent with the overall theme of the house. Bluish tones in the walls were carried over into fabric selections for the furniture, and the general ambiance of the interior was warm and gracious.

The erection of the Bowers residence in 1930 coincided with building expansion into Southampton's barrier

Dining room

Second-floor stair well

beach. Remotely located from Southampton Village, the barrier beach is a thin, vulnerable strip of land separating the Atlantic Ocean from Shinnecock Bay. Because of its isolation, the barrier beach was one of the last portions of Southampton Village to be developed.

The Bowers residence is now part of the Beach Road Historic District, which contains architect-designed mansions in the popular styles of the period, including Tudor, Colonial, and Spanish Colonial Revival. Built at a time when some of the wealthiest and most socially prominent families in the country—the du Ponts, Mellons, and Woolworth/Donahues—were establishing summer residences on Southampton's oceanfront, The Bouwerie is a significant example of a type of summer mansion found not only in Southampton, but also in other waterfront resorts frequented by the nation's elite. The house is currently owned by the Kulukundis family and is undergoing extensive renovation.

First and second floor plans

THE SHALLOWS

1931

❧

Residence of Lucien Hamilton Tyng and Ethel Hunt Tyng

Entry elevation

Heady Creek elevation

THE SHALLOWS is one of the first houses, not only on the East End but also in the whole of America, to break with tradition and embrace International Style Modernism. Built in 1931 for Lucien and Ethel Tyng on Halsey Neck Lane in Southampton, the house replaced a wood-framed edifice destroyed in 1930 by a disastrous fire. The Tyngs, along with three guests, were injured as they jumped for their lives from the second floor.

Architects Peabody, Wilson & Brown designed the new, modern house requested by the Tyngs; it was one of the seven houses the firm submitted to the Architectural League of New York in 1931 to win the prestigious Silver Medal. The Shallows was an appropriate home for a socially prominent couple known for their soirées, philanthropic activities, and patronage of the arts. Lucien

Tyng, who owned half the land that composed the Shinnecock Hills Golf Club, was a financier and public utilities executive. His wife, Ethel Tyng, an accomplished painter, was also recognized for her studios in New York and Southampton, as well as for her fundraising efforts to aid destitute artists during the Great Depression.

Situated north of Dune Road and fronting Taylor Creek, the house drapes north–south across the property, oriented to take advantage of panoramic water views of Shinnecock Bay to the west and the ocean to the south and east. The Shallows is a linear structure, built on the existing foundation of the first house and constructed out of masonry for fireproofing reasons. Clad in off-white cement stucco, appearing to be influenced by the work of Le Corbusier and Robert Mallet-Stevens, its exterior

South elevation

is a study in punctuated rectilinearity. It features numerous balconies that project outward, as well as balconettes that erode into the structure—all conceived to provide egress and safe haven in the event of a fire. Corner casement windows open at 90-degree angles to expose entire rooms to the outdoors. The three-story, flat-roofed house resembles an ocean liner, complete with a top-floor penthouse suite surrounded by an open-roof deck.

Notwithstanding the asymmetry of its progressive exterior, the plan for the interior of The Shallows offers a traditional but comfortable arrangement of rooms with details and finishes that are streamlined and modern. Public rooms are on the first floor, with the bedrooms and servants' wing on the second. Entry is through a

gracious center hall whose eight-foot openings are clad with Art Deco casings, scalloped across their lintels, and tapering geometrically at the ends to connect with vertical fluting running to the floor. The rear lawn and Taylor Creek are straight ahead, a large living room is to the left, and to the right are openings to the stairwell and dining room, which in turn meander into the library, kitchen, elevator, and service rooms.

Cascading through the three stories, the switchback Art Deco stairwell has landings at each half-flight level, with a balustrade of three metal rails running parallel to the shoe rail connected to slim support posts every few feet. At the landings these rails angle downward to create V-shaped decorative panels. The entire ensemble is

West elevation detail

Foyer, present-day view

Living room, present-day view

Stair hall, present-day view

Stair from second floor landing, present-day view

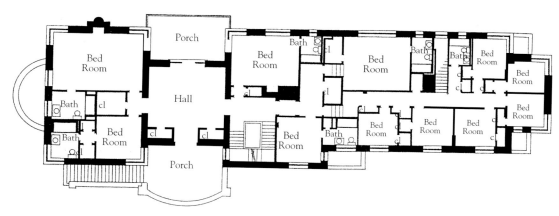

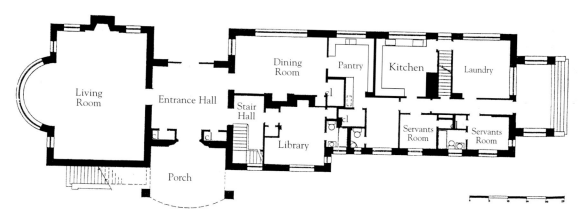

Top: Dancing on the terrace; below: first and second floor plans

capped with a thin brass rail that winds unbroken through the three levels, terminating at the first floor by curving right into the base of the stair.

The Tyngs later sold the house to General John Pershing's son F. Warren Pershing, who commissioned designer Billy Baldwin to redecorate its interiors. After 75 years, the exterior of The Shallows remains relatively unchanged. A few windows have been removed, and the east balcony above the entrance has been enclosed to become part of the master bedroom suite. For the past 30 years, it has been owned by Harry and Gail Theodoracopulos.

The Shallows stands between two eras. In its plan it is resolutely Beaux-Arts, and yet its exterior represents International Style Modernism. Today, engulfed in ivy, it marks the end of the Hamptons' Golden Age and embodies the transition from one period to another.

Garden terrace

PORTFOLIO OF HOUSES

TREMEDDEN, 1878, Bridgehampton. Residence of Richard Esterbrook, Jr. Carlos C. Buck, architect. Demolished.

1884, East Hampton. Residence of Thomas Moran. Thomas Moran, designer. Owned by Guild Hall Museum.

LENOIR/LINDEN, 1886/1915, Southampton. Residence of Grange Sard and Rufus Lenoir Patterson. Architect unknown; Grosvenor Atterbury, Private residence.

WYNDCOTE, 1887, Southampton. Residence of Robert Henderson Robertson. Robert Henderson Robertson, architect. Private residence.

ANDELMANS, 1889, Sag Harbor. Residence of Joseph Fahys. Montrose W. Morris, architect. Status unknown.

1891, East Hampton. Residence of Charles Henry Adams. William B. Tuthill, architect. Private residence.

1891, East Hampton. Residence of Henry A. James. Architect unknown; Joseph Greenleaf Thorp, additions. Demolished.

1891, East Hampton. Residence of William E. Wheelock. Isaac H. Green, Jr., architect. Private residence.

CLENCH-WARTON, 1892, Sag Harbor. Residence of Henry F. Cook and Lena M. Fahys Cook. Montrose W. Morris, architect. Status unknown.

DUNES, 1895, East Hampton. Residence of Frank Bestow Wiborg. Grosvenor Atterbury, architect. Demolished by fire, 1941.

HEATHERMERE, 1896, Southampton. Residence of Arthur B. Claflin. Grosvenor Atterbury, architect. Southampton College Administration Building.

1896, Southampton. Residence of Georgiana and Abby Howland. Katharine Budd, architect. Private residence.

GREY GARDENS, 1897, East Hampton. Residence of Mrs. Stanhope Phillips and Mrs. Robert Carmen Hill. Joseph Greenleaf Thorp, architect. Private residence.

MAYFAIR, 1896, Southampton. Residence of Elihu Root. Carrère & Hastings, architects. Private residence.

BY THE WAY, c. 1897, Southampton. Residence of Dr. George A. Dixon, Henry B. Barnes, and Dr. Henry Rogers Benjamin. Architect unknown. Private residence.

OVERLEA, 1897, East Hampton. Residence of C.W. Eidlitz. C.W. Eidlitz, architect. Private residence.

1898, East Hampton. Residence of Schuyler Quakenbush. C.W. Eidlitz, architect. Private residence.

1899, East Hampton. Residence of C.C. Rice and D.W. McCord. Grosvenor Atterbury, architect. Demolished.

WILLISTON HOUSE, 1899, Southampton. Residence of Judge Horace Russell and William R. Simonds. Bruce Price, architect. Private residence.

WEST LAWN, c. 1900, Southampton. Residence of Charles H. Lee and Edward Tiffany Dyer. F. Burrall Hoffman, Jr., architect. Private residence.

ELYRIA, c. 1900, Southampton Residence of Dr. Albert H. Ely. Grosvenor Atterbury, architect. Private residence.

GARDENSIDE, c. 1900, Southampton. Residence of Francis L. Wellman, Frederick A. Snow, and Mrs. Jacques Balsan, nee Consuelo Vanderbilt. Architect unknown.

1901, East Hampton Residence of John Drew. James Brown Lord, architect. Demolished.

LITTLE BURLEES, 1905, East Hampton. Residence of Edward T. Cockcroft. Albro & Lindeberg, architects. Private residence.

1905, Sag Harbor. Residence of Frank Colton Havens. Adolph F. Leicht, architect. Cormaria Retreat House.

BROUWER'S CASTLE, 1906, Westhampton Residence of Theophilus A. Brouwer, Jr. Theophilus A. Brouwer, Jr., designer. Casa Basso Restaurant.

ANDROS HILLS, 1906, Shinnecock. Residence of Thomas Gerald Condon. Grosvenor Atterbury, architect. Private residence.

1908, Devon. Residence of Richmond Levering. Rudolph, Tietig & Walter Lee, architects. Private residence.

WEST BANKS, 1910, North Haven. Residence of Reginald Barclay. Guy Lowell, architect. Private residence.

MEADOWMERE, 1910, Southampton. Residence of Henry G. Trevor. Grosvenor Atterbury, architect. Demolished.

WINDBREAK, 1911, Southampton. Residence of Josiah Copley Thaw. Architect unknown. Demolished.

1915, East Hampton. Residence of Clarence F. Alcott. Harrie T. Lindeberg/Albro & Lindeberg, architect. Private residence

SOLTERRA, 1915, Southampton Residence of Mrs. Frederick Baker and Elizabeth M. Horne. Hiss & Weekes, architects. Demolished.

FURTHERLANE, 1915, Amagansett Residence of Edward E. Bartlett, Jr. William Lawrence Bottomley, architect. Status unknown.

1915, Southampton. Residence of Mrs. Peter Fenelon Collier. Warren & Clark, architects. Status unknown.

1916, East Hampton. Residence of William H. Woodin. Grosvenor Atterbury, attributed architect. Private residence.

LITTLE CLOSE, 1917, East Hampton. Residence of William Sherman Jenney. Polhemus & Coffin, architects. Private residence.

FORT HILL, 1918, Shinnecock. Residence of Dr. Albert H. Ely. Grosvenor Atterbury, architect. Demolished.

VILLA MARIA, 1919, Southampton. Residence of Edward Purcell and Ethel Humphrey Mellon. Edward Purcell Mellon, architect. Private residence.

TEN ACRE, 1921, Southampton. Residence of Joseph Palmer Knapp. John Russell Pope, architect. Private residence.

ARCHITECTS' BIOGRAPHIES

ALBRO & LINDEBERG
Lewis Colt Albro (1876–1924) was born in Paris, France, to American parents. He was raised and educated in Pittsfield, Massachusetts, and then went to New York City to study architecture. He enrolled at the Metropolitan Art School and as a student went to work for McKim, Mead & White, rapidly becoming one of the firm's top designers. Albro eventually opened his own practice. From 1906 to 1914 he was in partnership with Harrie T. Lindeberg, and after this partnership ended, he practiced alone again until his death on March 1, 1924, at home in New York City at the age of 48.

Harrie Thomas Lindeberg (1880–1959) was born in Bergen Point, New York, where he resided until going to New York City to study architecture. He found work at the firm of McKim, Mead & White, where, like Albro, he quickly rose in position. The future partners met while working at the firm. After the partnership ended, Lindeberg continued in private practice in the city and later at his home in Locust Valley, New York. He died on January 10, 1959, at home on Long Island at the age of 78.

The firm of Albro & Lindeberg designed many notable American country estates for socially prominent families. Many of their projects favored the Arts & Crafts movement and English Cotswold look.

ALBRO, LEWIS COLT.
See Albro & Lindeberg

ATTERBURY, GROSVENOR
Grosvenor Atterbury (1869–1956) was born in Detroit, Michigan, in 1869 to Charles Larned Atterbury and Katherine Mitchell Dow. His father was a socially prominent corporation attorney in New York City, and the family spent their summers in the Shinnecock Hills at Southampton, New York. Atterbury's early education was at the Berkley School in New York City. He went on to Yale University, where he received a BA in 1891. He

next studied at the Columbia School of Architecture at Columbia University in 1892 and then went to Paris, where he attended the Ecole des Beaux-Arts in 1894. In the summers between 1889 and 1893, Atterbury studied painting with William Merritt Chase in the Hamptons, which introduced him to the area's natural beauty.

Before starting his own practice, Atterbury was with the firm of McKim, Mead & White. He worked in a traditional style but was at the forefront of technological invention in the use of new and economical building techniques. Although Atterbury is best known for his country house commissions, town houses, private clubs, and commercial buildings, he executed many moderate-income housing projects. He designed and built the model town Forest Hills Gardens, Forest Hills, New York, backed by the Russell Sage Foundation. This was one of his best-known works, and in it he first developed the use of prefab mass production to provide low-cost unit housing.

Grosvenor Atterbury was a fellow of the American Institute of Architects (AIA) and served as chairman of the committee on civic design for its New York chapter. In 1953 he received the AIA's medal of honor. Some of his other professional affiliations were the National Institute of Social Sciences, the Society of Beaux-Arts Architects, the Society of Columbia Architects, and the Architectural League of New York.

With his wife, the former Dorothy A. Johnstone, Atterbury lived in a house called Little Sugar Loaf, which he designed himself in Shinnecock Hills. Toward the end of his life he had a stroke, and he died on October 18, 1956, at the age of 87 in Southampton, New York. He desired to be remembered for his work for low-cost housing.

BARNEY & CHAPMAN
John Stewart Barney (1869–1925) was born in New York City, where he was raised and educated. After graduating from

Columbia University in 1890, he attended the Ecole des Beaux-Arts in Paris. Around the late 1890s, he formed a partnership with architect Henry Otis Chapman in New York City. The partnership lasted only until 1908, after which Barney had a solo practice. After 1915 he gave less time to architecture and devoted the rest of his life to landscape painting. John Stewart Barney died November 22, 1925, at the age of 57 after an operation for an illness.

Henry Otis Chapman (1862–1929) was born in Otisville, New York. In 1890 he graduated from Cornell University and then studied in Europe for a year. He practiced architecture in New York City by himself when he returned until forming a partnership with John Stewart Barney in the late 1890s. After the partnership ended, Chapman continued to practice architecture and worked with his son Henry Jr. at their firm, Henry Otis Chapman & Son. At the time of his death on July 27, 1929, at the age of 66, he resided at Woodmere, Long Island, New York.

The firm of Barney & Chapman was noted for the design of commercial buildings, hotels, churches, and residences.

BARNEY, JOHN STEWART.
See Barney & Chapman

BROWN, ARCHIBALD MANNING.
See Peabody, Wilson & Brown

BUDD, KATHARINE COTHEAL
Katharine Cotheal Budd (1860–1951) was born in Clinton, Iowa. Her father, Eli Budd, was a world traveler and owner of international clipper ships, and she grew up with every advantage. Known as "KCB," she began her career as an artist in New York, where she helped found the Art Students League. She later became an architect, one of the few women to successfully practice in the early 20th century. A student of William Merritt Chase in New York and at his Shinnecock Summer School of Art at the Art Village, Budd entered the architectural field in 1895.

Budd attended an architectural class at the Modern Museum of Art (part of Columbia University in New York), where she won an award for the best work in class at the end of the semester. The juror, Grenville Temple Snelling, her former professor, offered her a job in his office. After Budd designed the Howland residence in Shinnecock Hills for Art Village classmates Georgiana and Abby Roberta Howland in 1896, she continued her architectural education at the Atelier de Monclos, Ecole des Beaux-Arts.

Upon her return to New York she worked for architect Grosvenor Atterbury, another Shinnecock Summer School classmate. KCB's art world connections, traveling excursions,

education, and privileged background provided her with an elite clientele when she opened her own practice on Madison Avenue. She was commissioned to design the Anne Brown Music School overlooking the Hudson River in Yonkers, as well as a five-bedroom prototype house for Mrs. John D. Rockefeller Jr., conceived to serve as a model for lower-middle-class housing. The Y.W.C.A. commissioned her to design 96 Hostess houses built between 1917 and 1919 to provide temporary shelter for women visiting enlisted family members during World War I. In 1924, she became the first female member of the New York chapter of the AIA. She also wrote numerous articles for different professional publications on domestic science.

In the 1930s she went to Europe and learned copper plate etching in the studio of Edouard Léon and in 1934 won the prestigious Medaille de Bronze from the Salon des Artistes Francais, Paris. Her artwork was exhibited in the Metropolitan Museum of Art in New York, the Salon d'Automne, and the Charpentier Gallery, in Paris, as well as in the U.S. National Museum, Smithsonian Institute, Washington, D.C., and the Tucson Center for Arts and Crafts.

She died on July10, 1951, at the age of 91 in Tucson, Arizona.

BULLARD, ROGER HARRINGTON
Roger H. Bullard (1884–1935) was born in New York City, went to public schools, and attended Columbia University for architecture. Upon graduating from Columbia in 1907, he went to work at the office of Grosvenor Atterbury, and then in 1917 he joined the firm of Phillip Goodwin and Heathcote Woolsey and became a partner. He was with the firm of Goodwin, Bullard & Woolsey until 1921, when he broke away to establish a solo practice.

Bullard was known especially for his country house architecture and clubhouses along the East Coast done in the English Tudor style, but in 1933 he won the American Institute of Architects (AIA) gold medal for his design of "America's Little House" in a competition sponsored by Better Homes in America. Bullard was a member of the executive committee of the New York chapter of the AIA and of the Architectural League of New York. He died early in his career at age 50 from pneumonia on March 2, 1935, at his Long Island home.

CHAPMAN, HENRY OTIS.
See Barney & Chapman

COFFIN, MARIAN CRUGER
Marian Cruger Coffin (1876–1957) was born in Scarborough, New York, in 1876. She received her early education at home with private tutors, and in 1901 she attended the Massachusetts Institute of Technology to study landscape architecture. After

graduation, she moved with her mother moved to New York City and lived at the National Arts Club on Gramercy Park. Marian Coffin's career got off to a slow start because most architecture firms would not hire women. Work gradually came in, however, and with the recommendations of her childhood friend Henry Francis du Pont, her commissions became bigger and more frequent.

Marian Coffin's professional work was mainly private estate landscaping and gardens. Her projects were in many of the most fashionable suburbs and resorts along the East Coast. She also worked with Henry du Pont on the development of his estate and gardens at Winterthur, in Wilmington, Delaware. Other commissions besides estate work included serving as landscape architect for Delaware College, at Newark, Delaware, and restoring the early gardens at Fort Ticonderoga, New York.

Coffin was a fellow of the American Society of Landscape Architects. She served on the Horticultural Committee of the New York Botanical Garden and received the gold medal of honor from the Architectural League of New York. She died at age 81 on February 2, 1957, at her home in New Haven, Connecticut.

CROSS & CROSS
John Walter Cross (1878-1951) and his brother, Eliot (1884-1949), the sons of Richard J. and Matilda Redmond Cross, were born in South Orange, New Jersey and raised in New York City on Washington Square North. John Walter, after receiving an A.B. degree from Yale in 1900, attended the Columbia School of Mines for two years before choosing architecture as his profession. Upon graduating from the Ecole des Beaux-Arts in Paris in 1907, he returned to New York and began the firm of Cross and Cross with his brother Eliot, who had attended Groton and graduated from Harvard in 1906.

Together, the Cross brothers created a portfolio of diverse residential and commercial structures mostly in the northeast. As members of "Old New York Society" the architects created elegant and sophisticated residential works in addition to some of New York City's most significant buildings. John was considered the designer of the firm while Eliot pursued real estate interests. He established the development company of Webb and Knapp in 1922, which attracted clients for the firm. But it was Cross brothers' social connections and club–based (Knickerbocker, Links, Racquet, Brook, National Golf, The Hanger, River and Tennis and Coffee House) associations that allowed them to develop a select and choice client base.

Whether the design was Colonial Revival, Georgian Revival, Tudor Revival or English Arts and Crafts, their residential designs displayed a subtle and tasteful signature. Among the better-known commercial structures are two of New York's most dazzling Art Deco skyscrapers, the RCA Tower (now the General Electric Building) and the City Bank Farmers Trust Company Building. They also designed the Guaranty Trust Company buildings both in New York and Paris. Cross & Cross, in association with Rosario Candela, created the Neo-Georgian apartment building 1 Sutton Place and in 1941, the moderne, Art Deco/Greek Revival styled Tiffany & Company Building.

Elected to the National Institute of Arts and Letters in 1947, John Walter Cross was also a member of the Société des Architectes Diplomé par le Gouvernment. He died at age 73 in Hot Springs, Virginia. Eliot was a former director of the New York Chapter of the Red Cross as well as the First and Fifth Avenue Associations. He died in Princeton, New Jersey after a long illness. When John Walter's son, H. Page Cross, returned from World War II, the firm continued under the name of Cross & Son.

EYRE, WILSON
Wilson Eyre (1858–1944) was born in Florence, Italy, to American parents and lived there until age 11. Upon returning to the United States, he attended schools in Newport, Rhode Island, and in Canada. Eyre spent two years at the Massachusetts Institute of Technology before going to work for the architectural firm of James Peacock Sims in 1877 in Philadelphia, Pennsylvania. After the death of Sims in 1881, he took over the firm and practiced by himself until 1912, when he went into partnership with John Gilbert McIlvaine. Eyre & McIlvaine became an important firm specializing in large residential projects along the East Coast. From 1900 to 1915, the firm had a branch in New York City and lasted until McIlvaine's death in 1939. The firm was known for its interpretations of the Queen Anne and Shingle styles.

Wilson Eyre was well known for his beautiful pen-and-ink perspectives and renderings, and in 1901 he founded *House & Garden* magazine, serving as its editor until 1905. Eyre was a fellow of the American Institute of Architects, a founder of the T-Square Club in Philadelphia, a teacher, and a musician. He was active in many architecture societies, as well as in arts and civics organizations. He died at age 86 on October 23, 1944, at his Philadelphia home.

FARRAND, BEATRIX JONES

Beatrix Jones Farrand (1872–1959) was born in New York City. Her father, Frederic Rhinelander Jones, was a member of the Jones family of New York, a clan that included famed novelist Edith (Newbold Jones) Wharton. Beatrix Jones Farrand did not attend any institutions for the study of landscape design. She spent two years being tutored by horticulturalist Charles Sprague Sargent at the Arnold Arboretum, Harvard University, and then went abroad to study the great gardens of England, France, and Italy. Upon her return to the United States she opened an office in 1895 and steadily built a flourishing business. She worked with many prominent architects on the numerous landscape and garden design projects of America's Gilded Age.

In 1912 she married Max Farrand, a professor of history at Yale University. One of her most extensive residential projects was for the Robert Bliss estate, Dumbarton Oaks, in Washington, D.C. Beatrix Farrand's work also involved institutional commissions. She worked on the landscape designs for Princeton University, Yale University, the University of Chicago, and the California Institute of Technology. Farrand was a fellow and charter member of the American Society of Landscape Architects. She received many awards during her career and in 1940 was made an honorary member of the American Institute of Architects. She also received the Garden Club of America Achievement Medal, the Massachusetts Horticultural Society gold medal, and the New York Botanical Garden Distinguished Service Award. She died at age 86 on February 28, 1959, at her Bar Harbor, Maine, home.

FATIO, MAURICE.
See Treanor & Fatio

FLANDERS, ANNETTE HOYT

Annette Hoyt Flanders (1887–1946) was born in Milwaukee, Wisconsin. She received her early education at Smith College, from which she graduated in 1910, and studied landscape architecture at the University of Illinois and attended the Marquette University School of Engineering. After that she went to Europe and spent some time at the Sorbonne in Paris. She worked with the prominent landscaping firm of Vitale, Brinckerhoff & Geiffert until 1922, when she left to practice on her own, and she became one of the most important American landscape architects of the period. She had an office in New York City for many years until returning to Milwaukee, where she practiced until her death.

Annette Hoyt Flanders worked on many of the new American country estates being created for the social elite in the early 20th century. She also had commissions in Europe and Canada. She

received numerous awards; in 1932 she won the gold medal of the Architectural League of New York, for the French garden she designed for Helena Woolworth McCann in Oyster Bay. She also designed a garden in the "classic modern" style for the 1933 Chicago World's Fair. She was a mentor to many young women landscape architects and a prolific writer for garden magazines and in books on gardening. She was a fellow of the American Society of Landscape Architects. She died at the age of 59 in Milwaukee on June 7, 1946.

FREEMAN, FRANK

Frank Freeman (1861–1949) was born in Hamilton, Ontario. He had no formal education in architecture but learned while working under architects. In 1887 he opened his own firm in New York. Although he did a great deal of work and is often referred to as "Brooklyn's Greatest Architect," little biographical information is available on Freeman. He died at age 88 on October 14, 1949.

GILLETTE, LEON NARCISSE.
See Walker & Gillette

GREEN, ISAAC HENRY JR.

Isaac Henry Green Jr. (1858–1937) was a noted Long Island architect. Raised in Sayville, Green (called Jr. after his namesake and uncle) was the son of lumberyard owner Samuel Willett Green and his wife Henrietta Vail. The Greens' ancestry dated back to the New England Puritans, and the family's origins could be traced to Sayville and Riverhead.

Little is known regarding Green's architectural education, but various accounts indicate that he apprenticed with self-taught architect/builder George Skidmore of Riverhead, remotely related to his mother's family. Known as Ike, he eventually took over his father's lumberyard in 1881 and designed houses for its customers. From 1879 to 1917, his career, which was centered in Sayville, encompassed the design of churches, the Oysterman's Bank, three Sayville business blocks, a firehouse, and the Sayville Town Hall and Opera house.

Noted for residential commissions, his work could be seen from Babylon to Montauk, in the North Shore towns of Nissequogue, St. James, and Setauket, and the far reaches including Seale Harbor, Maine. With large land holdings, Green family members were prominent employers and members of the Sayville community. Among Green's Sayville summer cottage clients were W.K. Vanderbilt, Frank S. Jones, William Bayard Cutting, Robert "Bert" Roosevelt and Bon Ami King, Eversly Child. His success on the East End began with Dr. Everett Herrick's residence, Pudding Hill, in East Hampton and continued with Dr. George Munroe's residence, the First and Second Maidstone Clubhouses, and Lorenzo G. Woodhouse's Greycroft among others.

Green, known primarily for his high-end residential work, not only incorporated the idioms of the East End's regional vernacular architecture into the Shingle style but also into his interpretations of Colonial Revival, Tudor, and Beaux-Arts styles.

In declining health, Green retired from active practice at age 64 in 1922.

HILL & STOUT

Frederick Parsell Hill (1862–1957) attended Rutgers Preparatory School and graduated from Rutgers College in 1883. From 1887 to about 1900 he worked as a draftsman in the office of McKim, Mead & White. After serving in the U.S. Navy during and after the Spanish-American War, he went into partnership with Edmund Coffin Stout (1863–1937) as Hill & Stout. The association lasted until 1917 when he opened his own firm. He later practiced in Bermuda (Pembroke, 1919–1923), Somerset Bridge, New Jersey (1923–1935), and on Nantucket.

Edmund Stout was educated at the Columbia School of Mines where he studied engineering and architecture. He and his wife, Aletta, a civic and political activist in New Jersey, were socially prominent both in New York and on Long Island. After his partnership with Frederick Hill ended, Stout worked on low-cost housing in Newark for the Prudential Insurance Company of America. The firm of Hill & Stout designed buildings predominantly located in the New York City area.

HISS & WEEKES

Philip Hiss (1857–1940) was born in Baltimore, Maryland. He started his architectural education with private tutors, traveled to Paris to complete his studies, and in 1889 went to New York to begin his architectural career. In 1899 he went into partnership with H. Hobart Weekes. His was chairman of the housing committee of the National Civic Federation (1926), general chairman of the Art-in-Trades Club of New York, and a member of the American Institute of Architects. Philip Hiss and family were active members of New York, Newport, Palm Beach, and Southampton society. Hiss died in New York City on December 15, 1940, at age 83.

H. Hobart Weekes (1867–1950) was born in New York City. His initial education was at the Trinity Church School, and he continued with studies in architecture and sculpture in the United States and Europe. He worked at the firm of McKim, Mead & White before going into partnership with Philip Hiss. He became a fellow of the American Institute of Architects and also held a membership in the Sons of the American Revolution. H. Hobart Weekes died on December 13, 1950, in New York City.

The firm of Hiss & Weekes was noted for working in the Beaux-Arts style. Their commissions included many country estates, town houses, hotels, apartment houses, office buildings, and churches. The Gotham Hotel on New York's Fifth Avenue is considered one of their best works.

HISS, PHILIP.
See Hiss & Weekes

HOFFMAN, FRANCIS BURRALL, JR.

Francis Burrall Hoffman Jr. (1882–1980) was born in New Orleans in 1882. He was descended from an old New York family and was raised among members of New York's Gilded Age society. He started his professional education at Harvard University, graduating in 1903, and then attended the Ecole des Beaux-Arts in Paris. In 1907 he joined the New York firm of Carrère & Hastings, which had designed the family's town house at 58 East 79th Street. In 1910 he opened his own practice in New York.

Francis Burrall Hoffman Jr. practiced as a gentleman architect in the Beaux-Arts tradition and is well known for his work on country estates and town houses, mostly along the East Coast. Vizcaya, the Deering residence in Miami, Florida, is considered a masterpiece by many historians and is listed on the National Register of Historic Places. Hoffman also designed luxury apartment buildings and theaters. He belonged to many clubs and organizations. He died at the age of 98 on November 27, 1980, at his Hobe Sound, Florida, home.

LAWRENCE, JOHN CUSTIS

John Custis Lawrence (1867–1944) was born in Montauk, New York, and at the age of 14 went to sea working on yachts and fishing ships. He later returned to Long Island and was hired as a carpenter for the builder George A. Eldredge in East Hampton. Eldredge was the principal builder for many of the summer cottages at the time, and although Lawrence had no formal education in architecture, he must have acquired much of his knowledge while working on these residences. He was hired by other local builders and spent some time in Connecticut as a staircase builder. In 1920 he became a registered architect.

John Custis Lawrence became one of East Hampton's prominent architects and designed numerous houses for members of the summer colony. He was an active member in local social and charity events. He died at the age of 76 on August 26, 1944, at his East Hampton home.

LINDEBERG, HARRIE T.
See Albro & Lindeberg

LINDSEY, EDWARD DELANO
Edward Delano Lindsey (1841–1915) was born in New Bedford, Massachusetts. He was educated at Harvard and then went to Paris, where he studied at the Ecole des Beaux-Arts. In 1867 he came to New York City to practice architecture.

Lindsey was one of the first architects to design fireproof buildings in New York City and gained renown for these projects, which included the French Theatre and the Drexel Building. He also handled many residential projects throughout his career, and many of the techniques he used in commercial structures were also applied, for example, in the James Herman Aldrich residence, Maycroft, at Sag Harbor, New York. He was also considered a scholar—he taught for a time at Princeton University—and promoted the importance of art and knowledge in his profession. He died at age 74 from paralysis on April 30, 1915, at his Flushing, Long Island, home.

LIVINGSTON, GOODHUE.
See Trowbridge & Livingston

MCKIM, CHARLES FOLLEN.
See McKim, Mead & White

MCKIM, MEAD & WHITE
Charles Follen McKim (1847–1909) was born in Isabella Furnace, Pennsylvania. After attending Harvard and the Ecole des Beaux-Arts, he went to work for the firm of Gambrill & Richardson in New York. Within a few years he opened his own practice, eventually forming partnerships with William R. Mead, William Bigelow, and Stanford White. He was a president of the American Institute of Architects (AIA), founder of the American Academy in Rome, and recipient of numerous awards, including the gold medal award of the Royal Institute of British Architects and the AIA gold medal. He belonged to several gentlemen's clubs and knew many of his clients socially and as friends. He died on September 9, 1909, at St. James, Long Island, New York, at age 62.

William Rutherford Mead (1846–1928) was born in Brattleboro, Vermont. He graduated with a BA from Amherst College in 1867 and then went to New York City to apprentice in the office of Russell Sturgis. He left in 1871 to go abroad to study European architecture. After returning to New York, he went into practice with Charles McKim. Mead was a fellow of the American Institute of Architects, and he was involved with the Academy of Arts and Letters, the National Academy of Design, and the American Academy in Rome, serving as its president. He

received many awards for his excellence in architecture, including one given to him by King Victor Emanuel of Italy. He died while vacationing in Paris on June 6, 1928, at the age of 82.

Stanford White (1853–1906) was born in New York City, where he was raised in an artistic family that exposed him to art and artists at an early age. He never received any formal education in architecture, but in 1872 he went to work as an apprentice for the architecture firm of Gambrill & Richardson. There he worked closely with Henry Hobson Richardson on many of Richardson's early works. White toured Europe in 1878, and upon returning to America in 1879 he went into partnership with Charles McKim, whom he had known through family, and William Rutherford Mead, to form McKim, Mead & White. White was very active in New York society of the Gilded Age, and his social connections led to important commissions for the firm. Stanford White died at the age of 53 on June 25, 1906, after being shot by Pittsburgh millionaire Harry K. Thaw while watching a performance in the roof garden of one of his greatest works, Madison Square Garden.

The firm of McKim, Mead & White was the most prolific architecture office of its day, and each partner offered an expertise. McKim was the lead designer, Mead was the organizer who managed the office and got things done, and White brought great artistic flair and sophistication. They designed many of the largest and most significant buildings in New York City and throughout the United States, including houses, private clubs, office buildings, flagship stores, university campuses, train stations, and every other prime commission an architect could desire. The firm's office was also a training ground for many of the era's important architects; John Carrère, Thomas Hastings, Cass Gilbert, Harrie T. Lindeberg, and Grosvenor Atterbury were just a few who got their start there and went on to form their own prestigious offices. McKim, Mead & White was noted for its grand monumental public buildings that often referred to ancient Greece and Rome. In its private works, the Shingle and Colonial Revival styles were employed and French châteaux and Georgian palaces served as inspiration.

MEAD, WILLIAM RUTHERFORD.
See McKim, Mead & White

NEWMAN, FRANK EATON

NICHOLS, ROSE STANDISH
Rose Standish Nichols (1872–1960) was born in Boston, Massachusetts, grew up there, and spent her summers with her family at Cornish, New Hampshire. A niece of sculptor Augustus Saint-Gaudens, she was part of the "Cornish Colony," where she

mingled with the great architects, artists, and aesthetes of the Gilded Age. She pursued a career as a landscape architect after studying with architect Charles Platt, being taught by Thomas Hastings at the Massachusetts Institute of Technology, attending the Ecole des Beaux-Arts in Paris, and traveling extensively. Like other women landscape architects of her time—Marian Coffin, Ellen Shipman, Beatrix Farrand, and Annette Hoyt Flanders—Nichols worked with many prominent architects, such as Charles Platt, David Adler, and Howard Van Doren Shaw, on projects in Lake Forest, Illinois, and across the country.

Nichols was especially well known for her writings on garden design. She authored numerous articles and three books, *English Pleasure Gardens* (1902), *Spanish and Portuguese Pleasure Gardens* (1924), and *Italian Pleasure Gardens* (1928). She was a suffragette, active in women's rights, and a pacifist, and always involved with social issues. In her Beacon Hill home, her salons and Sunday teas were not to be missed. In a 1915 article in the *Boston Traveler* she wrote, "Many gardens have 'arrived' because a man's brawn has been directed by a woman's brain." Nichols was associated with the U.S. Women's Peace Party and the Women's International League for Peace and Freedom. She presented lectures and was a talented embroiderer and woodcarver. She died at the age of 88 on January 27, 1960, at her Boston home.

FREDERICK LAW OLMSTED; OLMSTED BROTHERS
Frederick Law Olmsted is considered the father of American landscape architecture, and Olmsted Brothers was viewed as the premier landscaping firm of the late 19th and early 20th centuries. Frederick Law Olmsted (1822–1903) was born in Hartford, Connecticut, into a wealthy merchant family and did not plan on becoming a landscape architect. When he came of age he left home, going first to New York City to study scientific farming, then to Europe for a tour with his brother. He only briefly attended a university for advanced study and spent most of his youth at various unrelated jobs. One of these jobs, as a columnist, somehow led him in 1857 to land a position as the superintendent of Central Park in New York City; he was 35 years old. Olmsted met Calvert Vaux, who was working on the design of the park, and the two men teamed up to develop the winning concept and proceeded to complete it. After a few years on his own in other ventures, Olmsted returned to New York to work with Vaux on the design of Prospect Park and other projects. In 1874 he also worked on the design of the landscape surrounding the U.S. capitol building at Washington, D.C.

In 1883 Olmsted left New York and established his business in Brookline, Massachusetts. During this time he worked on the Boston park system's "Emerald Necklace" and the 1893 World's Fair in Chicago. One of the last great commissions of his career was the 125,000-acre park and forest surrounding the newly constructed George Washington Vanderbilt estate, Biltmore, at Asheville, North Carolina. Olmsted gradually turned the operations of the firm over to his two sons, Frederick Law Olmsted Jr. (1870–1957), a Harvard graduate, and John Charles Olmsted (1852–1920), a Yale graduate; his sons guided the firm into the next century and oversaw some of its most renowned work. Frederick Law Olmsted died August 28, 1903, at the age of 81 while in the McLean Hospital at Waverley, Massachusetts.

The Olmsted Brothers continued for almost another 75 years. They completed more than 5,000 commissions throughout the country, including parks, institutions, college and university campuses, zoos, arboretums, and numerous private estates, many on Long Island.

PEABODY, JULIAN.
See Peabody, Wilson & Brown

PEABODY, WILSON & BROWN
Julian L. Peabody (1881–1935) was born in New York City. He graduated from Harvard University in 1903 and then went to the Ecole des Beaux-Arts in Paris to study architecture. Upon his return to New York, he went to work for various architects, including Grosvenor Atterbury. Peabody was a talented watercolorist and often exhibited his paintings in gallery showings. He practiced architecture in New York City until his death at age 54 in 1935 when the steamship *Mohawk*, which he was on with his wife, struck another ship in the fog on the off the New Jersey coast and sank, killing them and 31 others.

Albert E. Wilson (1879–1955) was born in New York City. He graduated in 1904 from Columbia University. Wilson worked as an architect in New York and in 1911 entered into a competition with Julian Peabody to design a town hall at Huntington, New York. Upon winning this commission, they began their careers together. After the death of Peabody and the dissolving of the firm, Wilson continued to practice with a partner in the firm of Wilson & Rahm. Albert E. Wilson died on June 16, 1955, at his home in Mamaroneck, New York, at the age of 76.

Archibald Manning Brown (1881–1956) was born in New York, graduated in 1903 from Harvard University, and in 1905 went to study architecture at the Ecole des Beaux-Arts in Paris. He returned to New York and practiced architecture alone until he joined in partnership with Julian Peabody and Albert Wilson. After 1935 he continued to practice on his own and eventually formed the firm of Brown, Lawford & Forbes. He died on November 29, 1956, at age 75 at his home in New York City.

The firm of Peabody, Wilson & Brown was founded in 1911 and was well versed in the country house genre. They designed houses and estates all along the East Coast and in other parts of the country, but much of their work was done on Long Island's North Shore and in the Hamptons. Although they worked in many of the Beaux-Arts styles of day, on Long Island they favored incorporating old farmhouse buildings into much larger and grander additions. In the Hamptons they employed French Riviera and Italian Mediterranean styles and were at the forefront of International Modernism.

POPE, JOHN RUSSELL

John Russell Pope (1874–1937), one of America's supreme classical architects, was born on April 7, 1874, in New York City to artistic parents and was raised in a home of painting, music, and drawing. He received his early education at the College of the City of New York before going on to graduate in 1894 from Columbia University, where his skill in drafting and rendering won him great acclaim. He pursued his studies at the American Academy in Rome and continued at the Ecole des Beaux-Arts in Paris. On his return to the State, he worked for architect Bruce Price, primarily on large country house commissions. During this period he nurtured relationships with Price's clients, and they later became his own.

In 1905 Pope established his own office and taught concurrently with Charles Follen McKim in one of McKim's ateliers at Columbia University. Pope shared a love of classicism with McKim and viewed him as his mentor. Some of Pope's first commissions were large country houses done in eclectic historical styles. In 1909, architect Otto R. Eggers, who was known for his exceptional renderings and presentation techniques, became a member of Pope's firm, as did Daniel P. Higgins shortly thereafter. Lacking formal training in architecture, Higgins was hired as an accountant and eventually attended night school at New York University's School of Architecture. With his outgoing personality, he became an asset to the firm in terms of sales, public relations, and management. John Russell Pope never made either of these men full partners, but they were compensated in profit sharing and given high-level responsibilities.

In 1912 John Russell Pope met and married Sadie Jones, who was 20 years his junior and a daughter of wealthy industrialist Pembroke Jones. Although it may not have been Pope's goal to acquire a rich wife, his marriage gave him easier access to the new Gilded Age elite and provided a comfortable lifestyle that put him on par with his clientele.

The firm of John Russell Pope flourished for many years until Pope's death. Their work encompassed several popular historical styles, such as neoclassical, Georgian, Tudor Elizabethan, Colonial Revival, Shingle, and Beaux-Arts, all interpreted in clean, non-ornate orchestrations. The firm's country-house designs could be somewhat austere. This quality was even more notable in museum, memorial, and mausoleum commissions. The firm designed office buildings, railroad stations, and institutional and public buildings such as city halls, universities, churches, and banks. These commercial projects, however, were not as plentiful or well known as their residential commissions in the Hamptons; Long Island's North Shore; Tuxedo Park, New York; Newport, Rhode Island; and Washington, D.C. Pope also designed clubhouses, as well as some of the United States' most magnificent and beloved monuments, such as the Jefferson Memorial, the National Gallery of Art, and the redesign of the Washington Mall, all in Washington, D.C.

John Russell Pope received much acclaim and press during his career. He received awards from bodies including the American Institute of Architects, the Architectural League of New York, the Jean LeClaire Institute of France, and the Royal Institute of British Architects. He served as president of the American Academy in Rome in 1933. With the rise of modernism, Pope's work, no longer considered avant-garde, became irrelevant, and he fell into obscurity. In the last years of his life, he withdrew from his office because of personal tragedies and illness, choosing to work on just a few key jobs. He resided in Newport, Rhode Island, on the cliffs in a dramatic house called The Waves, which he designed for his family. Pope died in his New York City home on August 27, 1937, at the age of 63. After his death, Joseph Hudnut, in a 1941 *Magazine of Art* article on the building of the National Gallery of Art, called him "the Last of The Romans."

ROBERT H. ROBERTSON

Robert Henderson Robertson (1849–1919) was born in Philadelphia, Pennsylvania, on April 29, 1849. He studied architecture in Scotland and received a degree from Rutgers College in 1869. Robertson worked briefly in the office of Philadelphia architect Henry Sims, then moved on to the New York office of George B. Post. He started his own firm in 1871, and from 1875 to 1881 he formed a partnership with William A. Potter, and they designed many college buildings and churches.

After 1881 Robertson practiced on his own and initially specialized in ecclesiastical commissions, favoring the Romanesque style. He later moved into commercial, public, and residential work in which he designed in diverse styles, including Victorian Queen Anne, Gothic, Shingle, American Colonial Revival, and Japanese Rustic as demonstrated in Camp Santanoni in the Adirondacks. Robertson's firm was recognized for its Gothic churches and railroad stations and early skyscrapers, most notably the Park Row Building near city hall in New York City.

Robertson came from an old distinguished family and moved in East Coast high society. He had homes in New York and Southampton, where he was an active member of the summer colony. In Southampton he designed the original Rogers Memorial Library on Job's Lane; the Thomas Barber estate, Claverack, on Halsey Neck Lane; and his own house, Wyndcote, on South Main Street. Wyndcote was later owned by his son, architect Thomas Markoe Robertson.

He died at the age of 70 on June 5, 1919, in the Adirondacks while visiting old friend Seward Webb at his camp Forest Lodge.

STOUT, EDMUND COFFIN.
See Hill & Stout

TREANOR & FATIO
William A. Treanor (1878–1946) was born in Yonkers, New York, received his education at Pratt and Columbia universities, and started his career working in the offices of first William Welles Bosworth and then Harrie T. Lindeberg. In 1921, Treanor and Maurice Fatio, whom he met while at Lindeberg's office, formed a partnership. William A. Treanor died on August 30, 1946, at his home in Katonah, New York, at the age of 58.

Maurice Fatio (1897–1943) was born in Geneva, Switzerland, to a prominent aristocratic banking family. He attended the Ecole des Beaux-Arts and the University of Zurich, where the renowned Swiss architect Karl Moser was one his professors. In 1920 Fatio came to the United States to practice architecture and started at the office of Harrie T. Lindeberg. Maurice Fatio died on December 3, 1943, at age 46.

During their partnership, Treanor & Fatio successfully designed houses for members of American and European high society. Fatio, with his aristocratic background, charm, and good looks, was easily accepted into the highest circles of society and brought the firm most of its stellar commissions. Many projects were located along the East Coast, from Long Island to Palm Beach, where their works are most revered. In 1925 they opened an office in Palm Beach, which Fatio ran, and designed numerous houses and villas in the Spanish, Italianate, neo-Georgian, and Regency styles. In 1938 Treanor & Fatio won a gold medal from the French government for works exhibited at the United States Pavilion at the Paris International Exposition.

TREANOR, WILLIAM A.
See Treanor & Fatio

TROWBRIDGE & LIVINGSTON
Samuel Breck Parkman Trowbridge (1862–1925) was born in New York City to General William Petit Trowbridge and Lucy Parkman Trowbridge. He received his education at Trinity College, graduating in 1881, studied architecture at Columbia University, then went to Athens, Greece, to supervise the building of the American School of Classical Studies. He finished his education at the Ecole des Beaux-Arts in Paris. In New York he first worked at the architectural offices of George B. Post. In 1901 he formed the firm of Trowbridge & Livingston with fellow architect Goodhue Livingston.

Throughout his career, Trowbridge devoted himself to architectural and arts groups. President Roosevelt appointed him chairman of the National Council of Fine Arts, and Trowbridge also served as president of both the Architectural League of New York and the Society of Beaux-Arts Architects. He died on January 29, 1925, of pneumonia at age 63 in his New York City home.

Goodhue Livingston (1867–1951) was born into the socially prominent Livingston family of New York. His father was Robert Edward Livingston, and his mother was Susan de Peyster Livingston. He received his architectural education from Columbia University and went to work for the architect George B. Post. In Post's office he met Samuel Trowbridge, and after a few years they left to establish their own firm. Livingston was an active member of New York society and belonged to many architectural, arts, and social clubs. He was a fellow of the American Institute of Architects, a member of the Architectural League of New York, and a founder of the National Golf Links of America at Southampton, New York. He died on June 3, 1951, in Southampton, at the age of 84.

The firm of Trowbridge & Livingston received many important commissions and was considered one of the finest of its time. Its work included commercial and residential buildings along the East Coast, in California, and in Japan.

TROWBRIDGE, SAMUEL BRECK PARKMAN.
See Trowbridge & Livingston

VITALE, FERRUCCIO
Ferruccio Vitale (1875–1933) was born in Florence, Italy, where he was raised and educated. In 1904 he came to the United States to practice landscape architecture. Although his primary work was estates and gardens, he also created plans for the towns of Scarsdale and Pleasantville, New York. Later in his career he

was appointed by President Calvin Coolidge to assist in the planning of Washington, D.C.'s landscapes.

Vitale first worked with the firm of Parsons & Pentecost, and then from 1908 to 1915 he practiced alone. After a short venture with Clarence Fowler he went into partnership with two staff members, Arthur Brinckerhoff and Alfred Geiffert Jr. Geiffert, with his Beaux-Arts background, primarily ran the design and production part of the office, and Vitale dealt with the clients and provided the initial design concepts. In 1924, after Arthur Brinckerhoff left the firm, Vitale and Geiffert continued to join forces as Vitale & Geiffert.

Vitale was very active in promoting landscape architecture and wrote books and articles on the subject. He founded, with Frederick Law Olmsted Jr., the Landscape Architecture Department at the American Academy in Rome, where he was a trustee and cofounded the Rome Prize in Landscape Architecture. He was also a fellow of the American Society of Landscape Architects, a member of the Architectural League of New York, and an honorary member of the American Institute of Architects. In 1920 he won the gold medal of the Architectural League of New York. He was also a member of New York's Coffee House Club, the Union Club, and the Century Association, all organizations in which he made many contacts with architects and future clients. At the time of his death he was on the architectural commission of the Chicago World's Fair. He died on February 26, 1933, at home in New York City, from pneumonia at the age of 58.

The great skill of Vitale and his firm was in how they could take the formal landscape plantings around a main residence and gradually let them fade out into the estate to become naturalized wilderness. Unlike many other firms of their time, they did not replicate landscapes and gardens of previous eras, but used the past as an inspiration in their work.

They received numerous commissions throughout the United States and became known as some of the foremost landscape architects of their time. They were integral to the planning and design of many estates of America's country house era, working with such architects as Harrie T. Lindeberg, Charles Platt, David Adler, Delano & Aldrich, and Hiss & Weekes.

WALKER, ALEXANDER STEWART.
See Walker & Gillette

WALKER & GILLETTE
Alexander Stewart Walker (1876–1952) was born in Jersey City, New Jersey. His younger years were spent at St. Paul's School in Concord, New Hampshire, and he went on to graduate with a BS

from Harvard University. In 1901 he was working at the architectural firm of Warren & Wetmore, where he met Leon Narcisse Gillette, and the two formed their own practice in 1906. A member of New York high society, Walker belonged to many of the city's prestigious clubs. His professional memberships included the Beaux-Arts Institute of Design. He died at the age of 72 in New York City on June 10, 1952.

Leon Narcisse Gillette (1878–1945) was born in Malden, Massachusetts. After studying at the University of Minnesota, he worked at the Minneapolis, Minnesota, firm of Bertrand & Keith, architects. In 1899 he received his certificate of architecture from the University of Pennsylvania and then went to New York City, where he worked in the architectural offices of Howell & Stokes, then Schickel & Ditmars, and then for architects Babb, Cook & Willard. In 1901 Gillette went to Paris to study at the Ecole des Beaux-Arts, and upon receiving his diploma in 1903 he returned to New York, where he next worked with the architectural offices of Warren & Wetmore. In 1906, with Alexander Stewart Walker, he founded the firm of Walker & Gillette. Gillette was a fellow of the American Institute of Architects and president of the New York Society of Beaux-Arts Architects. After a long illness, he died in New York City on May 3, 1945, at the age of 67.

Walker & Gillette became one of the preeminent architectural firms of its time. Commissions covered all building types and especially included great estates and town houses for prominent members of American high society. The firm also worked with many prominent landscape architects, such as the Olmsted Brothers of Brookline, Massachusetts. Walker & Gillette received numerous awards, including the American Institute of Architects medal (1910) for apartment house design, the gold medal of the Architectural League of New York (1922), and the gold medal of the American Institute of Architects (1925).

WARD, LEROY P.
Leroy P. Ward (1889–?) was born in Burlington, Vermont, and educated at Cornell. After completing his studies he went to work for various architects, establishing his own firm in 1928. In 1948 he went into partnership with Harry J. Kerrigan.

Ward's early work was mostly residential and noted for its use of wall planes and fenestration. During Ward's partnership with Kerrigan, the firm did hospitals, health-care buildings, and apartment buildings.

BIBLIOGRAPHY

BOOKS AND ARTICLES

Adams, James Truslow. *Memorials of Old Bridgehampton*. Port Washington, New York: Ira J. Friedman, 1962; orig. publ. 1916.

Albright, Barbara, and Carolyn Halsey, eds. *Sagaponack: Then and Now*. Sagaponack, New York: Sally Peterson Memorial Scholarship Fund, 2006.

Amory, Cleveland. *The Last Resorts*. New York: Harper & Brothers, 1948.

———. *Who Killed Society?* New York: Harper & Brothers, 1960.

Andrews, Jack. *Samuel Yellin, Metalworker*. Ocean Pines, Md.: Skipjack Press, 2000.

Andrews, Marietta Minnigerode. *Memoirs of a Poor Relation*. New York: E. P. Dutton, 1927.

Andrews, Wayne. *Architecture, Ambition, and Americans: A Social History of American Architecture*. New York: Free Press, 1978.

Aslet, Clive. *The American Country House*. New Haven, Conn.: Yale University Press, 1990.

Bahto, George. *The Evangelist of Golf: The Story of Charles Blair MacDonald*. Chelsea, Mich.: Clock Tower Press, 2002

Baker, John Cordis, ed. *American Country Homes and Their Gardens*. Philadelphia: John C. Winston, 1906.

Baker, Paul. *Stanny: The Gilded Life of Stanford White*. New York: Free Press, 1989.

Baldwin, Charles C. *Stanford White*. New York: Da Capo Press, 1976.

Bedford, Steven McLeod. *John Russell Pope: Architect of Empire*. New York: Rizzoli, 1998.

Beebe, Lucius. *The Big Spenders*. New York: Doubleday, 1966.

Beveridge, Charles E., and Paul Rocheleau. *Frederick Law Olmsted: Designing the American Landscape*. New York: Rizzoli, 1995.

Birmingham, Stephen. *America's Secret Aristocracy*. Boston: Little, Brown, 1987.

———. *The Golden Dream: Suburbia in the Seventies*. New York: Harper & Row, 1978.

———. *The Grandes Dames*. New York: Simon and Schuster, 1982.

———. *Real Lace: America's Irish Rich*. New York: Harper & Row, 1973.

Birnbaum, Charles A., and Robin Karson, eds. *Pioneers of American Landscape Design*. New York: McGraw Hill, 2000.

Brandt, Clare. *An American Aristocracy: The Livingstons*. Garden City, New York: Doubleday, 1986.

Brough, James. *Consuelo: Portrait of an American Heiress*. New York: Coward, McCann & Geoghegan, 1976.

———. *The Woolworths*. New York: McGraw Hill, 1982.

Brown, Jane. *Beatrix: The Gardening Life of Beatrix Jones Farrand, 1872–1959*. New York: Viking, 1995.

Brown, Erica. *Sixty Years of Interior Design: The World of McMillen*. New York: Viking Press, 1982.

Bryant, William Cullen. *Picturesque America*. New York: D. Appleton, 1872–74.

Cable, Mary. *Top Drawer: American High Society from the Gilded Age to the Roaring Twenties*. New York: Atheneum, 1984.

Cantor, Jay. *Winterthur*. New York: Harry N. Abrams, 1997.

Chapney, Elizabeth W. *Witch Winnie at Shinnecock*. New York: Dodd, Mead, 1894.

Churchill, Allen. *The Splendor Seekers: An Informal Glimpse of America's Multimillionaire Spenders—Members of the $50,000,000 Club*. New York: Grosset & Dunlap, 1974.

———. *The Upper Crust: An Informal History of New York's Highest Society*. Englewood Cliffs, N.J.: Prentice-Hall, 1970.

Coffin, Marian Cruger. *Trees and Shrubs for Landscape Effects*. New York: Charles Scribner's Sons, 1953.

Collier, Richard. *The Rainbow People: A Gaudy World of the Very Rich and Those Who Served Them*. New York: Dodd, Mead, 1984.

Comstock, Helen. *100 Most Beautiful Rooms in America*. New York: Studio Publications, 1958.

Corry, John. *Golden Clan: The Murrays, the McDonnells, and the Irish American Aristocracy*. Boston: Houghton Mifflin, 1977.

Cowles, Virginia. *The Astors*. New York: Knopf, 1979.

Craig, Theresa. *Edith Wharton: A House Full of Rooms—Architecture, Interiors, and Gardens*. New York: Monacelli Press, 1996.

Craven, Wayne. *Stanford White: Decorator in Opulence and Dealer in Antiquities*. New York: Columbia University Press, 2005.

Cummings, Mary. *Hurricane in the Hamptons, 1938: Images of America*. Portsmouth, N.H.: Arcadia, 2006.

Cummings, Mary. *Southampton: Images of America*. Dover, N.H.: Arcadia, 1996.

Curtis, Charlotte. *The Rich and Other Atrocities*. New York: Harper & Row, 1976.

Curts, Paul H., ed. *Bridgehampton's Three Hundred Years*. Bridgehampton, New York: The Hampton Press, 1956.

Davis, William. *The Rich: A Study of the Species*. New York: Franklin Watts, 1982.

Donnelly, Honoria Murphy, with Richard N. Billings. *Sara & Gerald: Villa America and After*. New York: Times Books, 1982.

Dulles, F. R. *The American Red Cross: A History*. New York: Harper & Brothers, 1950; repr. Portsmouth, N.H.: Greenwood-Heinemann, 1971.

Dwight, Eleanor. *The Gilded Age: Edith Wharton and Her Contemporaries*. New York: Universe, 1996.

Elwood, P. H., Jr. *American Landscape Architecture*. New York: Architectural Book Publishing, 1924.

Engel, Robert, Howard Kirshenbaum, and Paul Malo. *Santanoni*. Keeseville, New York: Adirondack Architectural Heritage, 2000.

Esten, John. *Hampton Style: Houses, Gardens, Artists*. Boston: Little, Brown, 1993.

———. *Hamptons Gardens: A 350-Year Legacy*. New York: Rizzoli, 2004.

Fatio, Alexandra, ed. *Maurice Fatio, Architect*. Stuart, Fla.: Southeastern Printing, 1992.

Fearon, Peter. *Hamptons Babylon: Life among the Super Rich on America's Riviera*. Secaucus, N.J.: Carol Publishing, 1998.

Ferree, Barr. *American Estates and Gardens*. New York: Munn, 1904.

Fishman, David, Thomas Mellins, and Robert A. M. Stern. *New York 1880: Architecture and Urbanism in the Gilded Age*. New York: Monacelli Press, 1999.

Fleetwood, Stephanie, with Marianna Woodward. *Devon*. United States: Anne S. Green, 1995.

Fleming, Geoffrey K. *Bridgehampton: Images of America*. Dover, N.H.: Arcadia, 2003.

Fleming, Nancy. *Money, Manure & Maintenance: Ingredients for Successful Gardens of Marian Coffin, Pioneer Landscape Architect, 1876–1957*. Weston, Mass.: Country Place Books, 1995.

Gaines, Steven. *Philistines at the Hedgerow: Passion and Property in the Hamptons*. Boston: Little, Brown, 1998.

Gallati, Barbara. *William Merritt Chase*. New York: Harry N. Abrams, in association with The National Museum of American Art, Smithsonian Institution, 1995.

Garrison, James B. *Mastering Tradition: The Residential Architecture of John Russell Pope*. New York: Acanthus Press, 2004.

Gilborn, Craig. *Adirondack Camps: Homes Away from Home, 1850–1950*. Syracuse, New York: The Adirondack Museum/Syracuse University Press, 2000.

Gillespie, Kate, and Bruce Weber. *Chase Inside and Out: The Aesthetic Interiors of William Merritt Chase*. New York: Berry-Hill Galleries, 2004.

Gilmartin, Gregory, John Massengale, and Robert A. M. Stern. *New York 1900: Metropolitan Architecture and Urbanism, 1890–1915*. New York: Rizzoli, 1983.

Gilmartin, Gregory, Thomas Mellins, and Robert A. M. Stern. *New York 1930: Architecture and Urbanism between the Two World Wars*. New York: Rizzoli, 1987.

Grafton, David. *The Sisters: The Life and Times of the Fabulous Cushing Sisters*. New York: Villard Books, 1992.

Griswold, Mac, and Eleanor Weller. *The Golden Age of American Gardens*. New York: Harry N. Abrams, 1991.

Harwood, Kathryn Chapman. *The Lives of Vizcaya: Annals of a Great House*. Miami, Fla.: Banyan Books, 1985.

Herman, Stewart H. *God's Summer Cottage*. Shelter Island, New York: Shelter Island Historical Society, 1980.

Hewitt, Mark Allan. *The Architect & the American Country House*. New Haven, Conn.: Yale University Press, 1990.

Heymann, C. David. *Poor Little Rich Girl*. New York: Random House, 1983.

History of Berwind. Philadelphia: Berwind Group, 1993.

Hoffstot, Barbara D. *Landmark Architecture of Palm Beach*. Pittsburgh: Ober Park, 1974.

Homberger, Eric. *Mrs. Astor's New York*. New Haven, Conn.: Yale University Press, 2002.

Howe, Samuel. *American Country Houses of To-Day*. New York: Architectural Book Publishing, 1915.

Hudson Nurseries, Inc. New York: Hudson Nurseries, 1929.

Johnston, Shirley. *Palm Beach Houses*. New York: Rizzoli, 1991.

Kathrens, Michael C. *Great Houses of New York, 1880–1930*. New York: Acanthus Press, 2005.

Koskoff, David E. *The Mellons: The Chronicle of America's Richest Family*. New York: Thomas Y. Crowell, 1978.

Kyvig, David. *Repealing National Prohibition*. Chicago: University of Chicago Press, 1979.

Landscape Planting and Engineering. New York: Lewis & Valentine, 1922.

Lehr, Elizabeth Drexel. *"King Lehr" and the Gilded Age*. London: J. B. Lippincott, 1935.

Lewis, R. W. B. *Edith Wharton: A Biography*. New York: Fromm, 1985.

Lindeberg, H. T. *Domestic Architecture of H. T. Lindeberg*. New York: William Helburn, 1940; repr. New York: Acanthus Press, 1996.

Lord, Ruth. *Henry F. du Pont and Winterthur*. New Haven, Conn.: Yale University Press, 1999.

Lowe, David Garrard. *Stanford White's New York*. New York: Doubleday, 1992.

MacDonald, Charles Blair. *Scotland's Gift: How America Discovered Golf*. London: Tatra Press, 2003.

Maher, James T. *The Twilight of Splendor*. Boston: Little, Brown, 1975.

Martin, Frederick Townsend. *The Leisure Class in America: Things I Remember*. New York: Arno Press, 1975.

McAllister, Ward. *Society as I Have Found It*. New York: Cassell, 1890.

McKenzie, Michael. *Meadowcroft: A Century of Elegance in the Hamptons*. New York: American Image Books, 2004.

McKim, Mead & White, 1879–1915. Repr. ed. New York: Arno Press, 1977.

Mellon, Paul. *Reflections in a Silver Spoon*. New York: William Morrow, 1992.

Miller, Frances. *More about "Tanty": A Second Growing Up*. Sag Harbor, New York: Sandbox Press, 1980.

————. *"Tanty": Encounters with the Past*. Sag Harbor, New York: Sandbox Press, 1979.

————. *"Tanty": The Daring Decades*. Sag Harbor, New York: Sandbox Press, 1981.

Miller, Ken. *The Hamptons: Long Island's East End*. New York: Rizzoli, 1993.

Mooney, Michael MacDonald. *Evelyn Nesbit and Stanford White: Love and Death in the Gilded Age*. New York: William Morrow, 1976.

Morrison, William. *The Main Line: Country Houses of Philadelphia's Storied Suburb, 1870–1930*. New York: Acanthus Press, 2002.

Murray, Meredith. *Steamed Crabs and Cranberries: The Story of Quantuck Beach*. Yaphank, New York: Searles Graphics, 2000.

Nichols, Charles Wilbur de Lyon. *The Leisure Class in America: The Ultra-Fashionable Peerage of America*. New York: George Harjes, 1904.

Noffsinger, James Philip. *The Influence of the Ecole des Beaux-Arts on the Architects of the United States*. Washington, D.C.: Catholic University of America Press, 1955.

Packard, Vance. *The Ultra Rich: How Much Is Too Much?* Boston: Little, Brown, 1989.

Patterson, Augusta Owen. *American Homes of To-day: Their Architectural Style, Their Environment, Their Characteristics*. New York: Macmillan, 1924.

Patterson, Jerry E. *The First Four Hundred: Mrs. Astor's New York in the Gilded Age*. New York: Rizzoli, 2000.

Perkins, Edwin J. *Wall Street to Main Street: Charles Merrill and Middle-Class Investors*. Cambridge: Cambridge University Press, 1999.

Petrow, Steven, with Richard Barons. *The Lost Hamptons*. Portsmouth, N.H.: Arcadia, 2004.

Pisano, Ronald. *Long Island Landscape Painting, 1820–1920*. Boston: Little, Brown, 1985.

———. *The Tile Club and the Aesthetic Movement in America*. New York: Harry N. Abrams, in association with the Museums at Stony Brook, 1999.

Pulitzer, Ralph. *New York Society on Parade*. New York: Harper & Brothers, 1910.

Rae, John W., and East Hampton Library. *East Hampton: Images of America*. Charleston, S.C.: Arcadia, 2000.

Rattray, Jeannette Edwards. *Fifty Years of the Maidstone Club, 1891–1941*. East Hampton, New York: The Maidstone Club, 1941.

Samuels, Ellen R., et al. *East Hampton Invents the Culture of Summer: The Legacy of the Woodhouse Family of Huntting Lane*. East Hampton, New York: East Hampton Historical Society, 1994.

Sandford, Ann. *Grandfather Lived Here The Transformation of Bridgehampton, New York, 1870–1970*. Sagaponack, New York: Poxabogue, 2006.

Schnadelbach, R. Terry. *Ferruccio Vitale: Landscape Architect of the Country Place Era*. New York: Princeton Architectural Press, 2001.

Sclare, Lisa, and Donald Sclare. *Beaux-Arts Estates: A Guide to the Architecture of Long Island*. New York: Viking, 1979.

Scully, Vincent J., Jr. *The Shingle Style and the Stick Style: Architectural Theory and Design from Downing to the Origins of Wright*. New Haven, Conn.: Yale University Press, 1955 (rev. 1971).

———. *The Shingle Style Today; or the Historian's Revenge*. New York: George Braziller, 1974.

Seabury, Samuel. *Two Hundred and Seventy-five Years of East Hampton*. East Hampton, New York: N.p., 1926.

Searing, Helen, ed. *In Search of Modern Architecture: A Tribute to Henry-Russell Hitchcock*. Cambridge, Mass.: MIT Press, 1982.

Shelton, Louise. *Beautiful Gardens in America*. New York: Charles Scribner's Sons, 1924.

Smith, Sally Bedell. *In All His Glory: The Life of William S. Paley*. New York: Simon and Schuster, 1990.

Thorndike, Joseph J., Jr. *The Very Rich: A History of Wealth*. New York: All Heritage, 1976.

Thorne, Martha, ed. *David Adler, Architect: The Elements of Style*. New Haven, Conn.: Yale University Press, in association with The Art Institute of Chicago, 2002.

Throop, Lucy Abbot. *Furnishing the Home of Good Taste*. New York: Robert M. McBride, 1920.

Torre, Susana, ed. *Women in American Architecture: A Historic and Contemporary Perspective*. New York: Whitney Library of Design, 1977.

Townsend, Reginald T. *God Packed My Picnic Basket: Reminiscences of the Golden Age*. New York: Hastings House, 1970.

Van Rensselaer, Mrs. John King. *Newport: Our Social Capital*. Philadelphia: J. B. Lippincott, 1905.

———. *The Social Ladder*. New York: Henry Holt, 1924.

Watermill: Celebrating Community: The History of a Long Island Hamlet. Mattituck, New York: N.p., 1996.

Wecter, Dixon. *The Saga of American Society: A Record of Social Aspiration, 1607–1937*. New York: Charles Scribner's Sons, 1970.

Wetterau, Helen. *Shinnecock Hills Long Ago*. East Patchogue, New York: Searles Graphics, 1991.

Wharton, Edith, and Ogden Codman Jr. *The Decoration of Houses*. New York: Norton, 1978.

White, Samuel G. *The Houses of McKim, Mead & White*. New York: Rizzoli, 1998.

Wilson, Christopher. *Dancing with the Devil: The Windsors and Jimmy Donahue*. New York: St. Martin's Press, 2000.

Winokur, Jon. *The Rich Are Different*. New York: Random House, 1996.

Zaitzevsky, Cynthia. *Noted Women Landscape Architects*. New York: Norton, 2004.

Zaykowski, Dorothy Ingersoll. *Sag Harbor: The Story of an American Beauty*. Sag Harbor, New York: Sag Harbor Historical Society, 1991.

CATALOGS

Christie's New York.

Parke-Bernet Galleries, Inc.

Previews Incorporated.

Sotheby's Realty.

PAMPHLETS AND REPORTS

"Bayberry Land Approximately 314 Acres," *Guaranty Trust Company of New York*. Real Estate Brochure.

"Built by Women." New York: The Alliance of Women in Architecture, 1981.

Division for Historic Preservation, New York State Parks and Recreation, Historic and National Districts Inventory Form. "Beach Road Historic District." Southampton Village, Southampton, New York, August 20, 1986.

Greenman-Pedersen, Inc. *Final Environmental Impact Statement (FEIS), The Bayberry Project.* November 14, 2003.

Heatley, Rose. "History of North Haven in Celebration of Our Country's Bicentennial, 1776-1976."

Reed, Henry Hope. "The Elms." Pamphlet, Preservation Society of Newport County.

Institute for Long Island Archaeology. "Bayberry Land, Rest and Refuge in Southampton." New York: Institute for Long Island Archeology, Stony Brook University, May 2004.

Institute for Long Island Archaeology. *Architectural Documentation and Recordation of Four Buildings at Bayberry Land, the Country Estate of Charles H. and Pauline Morton Sabin.* A Report Prepared for the Town of Southampton, May 2004. New York: Stony Brook University.

Sag Harbor: In the Land of the Sunrise Trail, 1707–1927. Sag Harbor, N.Y.: Sag Harbor Village Trustees, 1927.

Town of Southampton. "Historic Site Designation Application Form for Bayberry Land." November 26, 2003.

U.S. Department of the Interior, National Park Service, National Register of Historic Places Inventory, Nomination Form. "Southampton Village Multiple Resource Area, Beach Road Historic District." August, 20, 1986.

Willey, Nancy Boyd. *The Story of Sag Harbor.* Sag Harbor, N.Y.: The Long Island Herald House, 1949.

UNPUBLISHED MATERIALS

Keene, Robert. Unpublished history of the "De Bost House" (Southampton Town Historian Collection).

Nolty, Sister Honora. Unpublished history of the Siena Spirituality Center at Villa Maria.

Opperman, Victoria Budd. *Katharine Cotheal Budd (1860–1951), One of America's Early Women Architects* (master's thesis, University of the State of New York at Buffalo, 1983).

Rose, Rev. Henry T. *The Story of Rosemary Lodge.* Handwritten manuscript including newspaper articles and period photographs. In the possession of owners R. A. Cordingley, E. A. King, and Therese Bernbach.

GENERAL REFERENCE

The American Institute of Architects, Long Island Chapter, and the Society for the Preservation of Long Island Antiquities. *AIA Architectural Guide to Nassau and Suffolk Counties, Long Island.* Mineola, New York: Dover, 1992.

The Blue Book of the Hamptons. Southampton, N.Y.: The Blue Book of the Hamptons.

Dictionary of American Biography. New York: Scribner Book Company, 1965.

East Hampton Star Obituary Index. East Hampton, New York.

Hefner, Robert J., ed. *East Hampton's Heritage.* New York: Norton, in association with the East Hampton Ladies Village Improvement Society, 1982.

Long Island Society Register. Brooklyn, N.Y.: Rugby Press, 1929.

MacKay, Robert B., ed. *Long Island Country Houses and Their Architects, 1860–1940.* New York: Norton, 1997.

Macmillan Encyclopedia of Architects. Volumes 1–4. New York: The Free Press, 1982 .

National Cyclopaedia of American Biography. New York: 1899–1946.

The New York Times Obituary Index, New York 1857–2006.

Sicherman, Barbara, and Carol Green, eds. *Notable American Women: The Modern Period—A Biographical Dictionary.* Reprint ed. Cambridge, Massachusetts: Belknap Press, 1983.

Shettleworth, Earle, G., ed. *A Biographical Dictionary of Architects in Maine.* Vol. 7. Maine Citizens for Historic Preservation, 1995.

Social Directory of Southampton. 1926.

Social Directory of the Hamptons, Southampton New York: The Social Directory of the Hamptons.

Social Register. New York: The Social Register Association.

Southampton Press. "Among the Cottagers" (weekly column).

Weisburg, Henry, and Lisa Donneson. *Guide to Sag Harbor.* Sag Harbor, N.Y.: The John Street Press, 1975.

White, Norval, and Elliot Willensky. *AIA Guide to New York City*. New York: Three Rivers Press, 2000.

Withey, Henry F., and Elsie Rathburn Withey. *Biographical Dictionary of American Architects (Deceased)*. Los Angeles: Hennessey & Ingalls, 1970.

Wodehouse, Lawrence. *American Architects from the Civil War to the First World War*. Detroit: Gale Research, 1976.

———. *American Architects from the First World War to the Present*. Detroit: Gale Research, 1977.

PERIODICALS AND NEWSPAPERS

Antiques Magazine

American Architect

American Architect and Building News

Architectural Digest

Architectural Forum

Architectural League of New York

Architectural Record

Architectural Review

Architecture

Art World

Arts and Decoration

Brooklyn Daily Eagle

Boston Herald

The Brickbuilder

Country Magazine

Country Life in America

The Craftsman

Dan's Papers

East Hampton Star

Hampton Chronicle

Hamptons Magazine

House and Garden

House Beautiful

The International Studio

Landscape Architecture

Long Island Forum

New York Architect

New York Herald Tribune

The New York Times

The New York Times Obituary

Palm Beach Daily News

Progressive Architecture

Sag Harbor Express

Scientific American, Architects and Builders Edition

Southampton Press

Spur

Syracuse Herald

Town and Country

Vogue

PERIODICALS AND ARTICLES

The Architect. "Port of Missing Men." November 1929.

The Architect. "Pompeian Swimming Pool of Colonel H. H. Rogers, Southampton, L.I." August, 1930.

The Architect. "Playhouse for Lucien M. Tyng, Southampton, L.I." March, 1931.

American Architect. "The House of Ellery S. James." June 5, 1929.

Architectural Record. "The Work of Barney & Chapman." September 1904.

Architectural Record. "Hunting Box and Swimming Pool Group for H. H. Rogers." 1929.

The Architectural Review. "Residence for Charles H. Sabin, Esq., at Southampton, L.I." November 1919.

Architectural Record. "House of Lucien N. Tyng." November 1931.

Architecture. "Villa Mille Fiori, Southampton, L.I. Hill and Stout Architects." October 15, 1913.

Arts and Decoration. "Interiors in the Long Island Home of Mr. J.E. Berwind." November 15, 1930.

Arts and Decoration. "The Garden of Charles H. Sabin at Southampton, L.I." February 1922.

Arts and Decoration. "Fine Detail in Beautiful Gardens." {date?}

Arts and Decoration. "From the Windswept Dunes." March 1933.

Atterbury, Grosvenor. "Personality in Architecture." *Arts and Decoration*, April 1930.

Auchincloss, Louis. "Home Furnishings." *The New York Times*, April 11, 1999.

Aurichio, Andrea. "A Mansion's Fate Awaits Zone Ruling." *The New York Times*, January 14, 1979.

Aurichio, Andrea. "Elegance Returning to Old Mansion." *The New York Times*, October 14, 1979.

Barrington, Amy. "A Fielde of Delite." *The House Beautiful* 45, April 1919.

Beekman, Barclay. "Social Set." *New York Daily Mirror*, August 29, 1939.

Behrens, David. "In a Grand Manor." *Newsday*, July 23, 1981.

Brenner, Marie. "Mr. Trupin Builds His Dream House." *New York Magazine*, June 18, 1984.

Boyd, John Taylor, Jr. "The Country House of H. H. Rogers, Esq." *Architectural Record*, January 1916.

———. "Two Country Houses at Southampton Long Island." *Architectural Record*, March 1916.

Boyle, Hal. "Trouble Bares Itself in This Paradise." *Stevens Point Daily Journal*, August 28, 1954.

Brooklyn Daily Eagle. "Boom in Southampton." June 22, 1890.

Brooklyn Daily Eagle. "Art at Shinnecock Hills." August 8, 1892.

Brooklyn Daily Eagle. "A School in the Sands." October 14, 1894.

Brooklyn Daily Eagle. "Summer Visitors at the Hamptons." July 28, 1895.

Brooklyn Daily Eagle. "Shinnecock Art School." July 28, 1900.

Bullard, Roger. "A House Especially Designed for the Dunes of East Hampton." *Arts and Decoration*, October 1929.

Cameron, Katharine T. "East Hampton: A 19th-Century Artists' Paradise." *East Hampton Star*, December 17, 1998.

Carpenter, Erin. "Rally Held by AIA to Preserve Bayberry Land." *Suffolk Life*, January 28, 2004.

Chappell, George S. "LeRoy Daniel MacMorris, Designer of Screens." *The Architect*, April 1930.

Chester, Marjorie.

———. "An Arts and Crafts Astonishment." *East Hampton Star*, August 14, 2003.

———. "Design: Restoration at Its Very Best." *East Hampton Star*, August 12, 1999.

———. "Rare Trees, Rare Collectors." *The New York Times*, August 23, 1992.

Cikovsky, Nicolai, Jr. "William Merritt Chase at Shinnecock Hills." *Antiques Magazine*, August 1987.

Colello, Michael. "Activists Fight to Save Mansion." *Independent*, January 28, 2004.

———. "Bayberry: 'Haves vs. Have Nots'." *Independent*, February 2004.

Cooper, Rebecca. "Wrecking Ball Claims Manor." *Southampton Press*, May 20, 2004.

Cooper, Wendy. "H. F. du Pont's Fondness for Furniture: A Collecting Odyssey." *Antiques*, January 2002.

Country Life. "An Interview with Harrie T. Lindeberg." July 1927.

Country Life in America. "Certosa." November 1934.

Country Life in America. "Country House of Mr. Charles H. Sabin Southampton, L.I." April 1927.

The Craftsman. "Three Sicilian Gardeners: What They Have Accomplished with the Help of Two Artists and Nature." June 1914.

Cummings, Mary. "Adaptive Reuse in Three Acts." www.hamptonsview.com

———. "Bayberry Land." www.hamptonsview.com

———. "The History of the Bayberry Land Estate Is Quite Telling." *Southampton Press*, May 19, 2005.

———. "A Hundred Years of Comfort and Charm: Meadowcroft Is Still Grand after a Century." *Southampton Press*, October 9, 2003.

———. "Montauk's Monuments to a Creative Collaboration." *The Sun*, July 15, 1982.

———. "Saving Great Estates: The Options Dwindle." *The New York Times*, January 10, 1982.

———. "The Things That Remain the Same." www.hamptons.com

Currie, Constance Gibson. "Isaac H. Green, Long Island Architect and His Brookside." *Long Island Forum* Summer 2000.

Davis-Goff, Annabel. "Cotswold Revival." *House and Garden*, December 1998.

De Forest Parsons, Antoinette. "Summer Art Life at Shinnecock and Mendota." *St. Paul Dispatch*, June 27, 1898.

De Kay, Charles. "East Hampton the Restful." *The New York Times*, October 30, 1898.

————. "Eastern Long Island: Its Architecture and Art Settlements." *American Architect*, April 1, 1908.

————. "Summer Homes at East Hampton, L.I." *Architectural Record*, January 1908.

————. "Villas All Concrete." *Architectural Record*, February 1905.

Dunn, Richard. "A Dubious Lineage." *East Hampton Star*, November 1, 1998.

Eames, Alexandra. "The Cottage of J. Harper Poor." *East Hampton Star*, March 28, 1996.

East Hampton Star. "Dr. John Erdmann, Surgeon, Is Dead at the Age of 90." April 29, 1954.

East Hampton Star. "Robert Appleton Dies in a Fall at Palm Beach." January 8, 1948.

East Hampton Star. "Mrs. Adele Herter, Noted Artist, Dies Suddenly Tuesday." October 3, 1946.

Edwards, Julie Eldridge. "The Brick House: The Vermont Country House of Electra Havemeyer Webb." *Antiques*, January 2003.

Eicks, Margaret Follin. "A Fabled House by the Shore." *New York World Telegram*, August 16, 1941.

Eversmann, Pauline K. "Life at Winterthur: Henry Francis du Pont's American Country Estate." *Antiques and the Arts Online*.

Farley, Elsie Sloan. "Decorating and Furnishing a Palatial Home." *Arts and Decoration*, March 1929.

Fielding, Leslie. "Red Maples: The Home of Mrs. Alfred M. Hoyt." *Town and Country*, May 9, 1914.

Forbes, A. H. "The Work of Albro and Lindeberg." *Architecture*, November 15, 1912.

Foster, N. Sherrill. "Boarders to Builders: The Beginnings of Resort Architecture in East Hampton, 1870–1894." *East Hampton Star*, March 8, 15, 22, 29, 1979.

Frank Leslie's Weekly. "The Shinnecock Art School." September 29, 1892.

Frazer, Amanda Star. "Nuns Sue Episcopal Diocese." *East Hampton Star*, April 11, 2002.

Freedman, Mitchell. "Battle for Southampton 'Legacy.'" *Newsday*, January 29, 2004.

————. "Golf Course Plan Gets Hole in One." *Newsday*, February 11, 2004.

————. "Group Rallies to Save Southampton Mansion." *Newsday*, January 25, 2004.

Gade, John A. "Long Island Country Places—'The Orchard' at Southampton." *House and Garden*, March 1903.

Garrison, Virginia. "Old Times at the Grandview." *East Hampton Star*, April 20, 2006.

Gatewood, Dallas. "Historic Listing for Southampton Manor." *Newsday*, July 13, 1980.

Gill, Brendan. "F. Burrall Hoffman, Jr.: A Gentleman Architect in the Beaux Arts Tradition." *Architectural Digest*, July 1993.

Gillespie, Harriet. "A Southampton House." *The House Beautiful*, September 1913.

Greene, Mel. "Mansion and Estate Going Condo." *Daily News*, July 27, 1980.

Goldberger, Paul. "East Hampton Architecture: Plain and Fancy." *East Hampton Star*, August 6, 1998.

————. "The Once and Future Montauk." *The New York Times*, September 15, 1994.

Gordon, Alastair. "An Artfully Planned Village." *East Hampton Star*, Spring 1988.

————. "Stanford White at Montauk." *East Hampton Star*, August 1985.

Graybeal, Jay A., and Peter M. Kenney. "The William Efner Wheelock Collection at the East Hampton Historical Society." *Antiques*, August 1987.

Green, Baylis. "Maycroft: Hurry Up and Wait." *East Hampton Star*, July 29, 2004.

————. "A Tattered Glory Lingers at the Maycroft Estate." *East Hampton Star*, March 18, 2004.

Hardin, Taylor Scott. "Potentialities of Dunes for Buildings." *Home and Field*, July 1930.

Heacock, Caren. "Southampton's 'La Belle Epoque.'" *Resort Life*, November 1985.

Helena Daily Independent. "Charles Sabin, Noted New York Banker, Dies." October 12, 1933.

Herter, Albert. "The Value of 'Clean' Color in Decoration and Its Effect upon Emotion." *The Craftsman*, May 1916.

Hewitt, Janis. "Historic Cavett House Destroyed by Blaze." *East Hampton Star*, March 20, 1997.

House and Garden. "In the Gardens of Miss Rosina Hoyt." June 1919.

Hoyt, J. R. C. "Shinnecock Art School." *Collier's Weekly*, April 22, 1897.

Hunting, Mary Anne. "Living with Antiques: Rosemary Lodge in Water Mill, New York." *Antiques Magazine*, July 2000.

Johnson, Margaret. "Touring Homes, Hamptons Style." *House Magazine*, July/August 2005.

Keating, Raymond J. "Politics Shouldn't Block New LI Golf Courses." *Newsday*, February 10, 2004.

Klemesrud, Judith. "A Health Spa in the Hamptons Gets Itself in Shape." *The New York Times*, March 7, 1978.

Kotz, Stephen J. "Bayberry Plan Teed Up." *Southampton Press*, May 2, 2002.

Larmoth, Jeanine. "The Substance of Grace: Reconsidering Painter William Merritt Chase's Summer House in Southampton." *Architectural Digest*, May 2005.

Larson, Hilary L. "Bayberry Is Now Named Sebonack." *Southampton Press*, May 13, 2003.

———. "Bayberry's 'Benefit' Debated by Board." *Southampton Press*, July 10, 2003.

Lay, Chas Downing. "Style and Expression in Landscape Architecture." *The Architectural Forum*, July 1924.

Lindeberg, Harrie T. "A Return of Reason in Architecture." *Architectural Record*, October 1933.

———. "Thatched Roof Effects with Shingles." *Brickbuilder*, July 1909.

Mayne, Sheila. "The Miraculous Beauty of the Herter Garden." *Arts and Decoration*, July 1925.

McAdam, Thomas. "A Garden That Charms Both Night and Day." *Country Life in America*, May 1908.

Menu, Gavin. "North Haven Estate to Be Relocated." *Southampton Press*, May 5, 2005.

Miller, Wilhelm. "Successful American Gardens: The Breese Estate at Southampton, Long Island, Illustrating an American Type of Country Life, Architecture and Gardening." *Country Life in America*, May 1910.

Moeran, Edward Henry. "Southampton's First Vacationists." *Long Island Forum*, April–May 1943.

Morice, John H. "The First Out-of-Door Art School in the United States." *Southampton Press*, November 15, 22, 1945.

Morris, Tom. "Glamour amid the Dunes." *Newsday*, Summer–Fall, 2000.

Moses, Lionel. "Some Principles of Good Planning." *Art World*, July 1917.

The New Country Life 32, No 1 (May 1917): 36–37.

New York Herald. "And Now the Game Is Golf." August 30, 1891.

The New York Times. "Albert Herter, 78, Noted as Muralist." February 16, 1950.

The New York Times. "All After Poor Reynard." August 30, 1885.

The New York Times. "A Busy Southampton Season." June 6, 1926.

The New York Times. "Buys Southampton Beach Plot." December 15, 1940.

The New York Times. "Byrd Aides' Health Is Rigidly Tested." July 29, 1928.

The New York Times. "C. B. Macdonald, 83, Ex-Golf Star, Dies." April 22, 1939.

The New York Times. "Col. H. H. Rogers, Long Ill, Dies at 55." July 26, 1935.

The New York Times. "Col. Rogers Is Host at Brilliant Ball." August 26, 1934.

The New York Times. "East Hampton Golf Club." November 21, 1994.

The New York Times. "Easthampton Society: Hotels Open and Crowds of Summer Residents Pour In." June 19, 1904.

The New York Times. "F. H. Markoe Honors Two Young Artists." August 11, 1932.

The New York Times. "Famous Mansion to Be Torn Down." April 30, 1941.

The New York Times. "Francis B. Hoffman, 98, Architect." November 28, 1980.

The New York Times. "Gay Nineties Party at East Hampton." September 4, 1933.

The New York Times. "Harrie T. Lindeberg, Architect, Dead: Former State Department Consultant." January 11, 1959.

The New York Times. "In the Hamptons, Gentility Regained." June 30, 1988.

The New York Times. "Life Stories of Painters Reversed by Albert Herter." August 7, 1904.

The New York Times. "Literary Colony at East Hampton." July 27, 1902.

The New York Times. "Long Island Estate Offered at Auction." April 25, 1937.

The New York Times. "Long Island Thief Gets $30,000 Gems." September 18, 1941.

The New York Times. "Marking a Milestone in Medical College Merger." December 8, 1948.

The New York Times. "Miss Doris Merrill Presented in Debut." August 28, 1932.

The New York Times. "Miss Ladd Honored at Southampton." August 9, 1929.

The New York Times. "Mrs. N. J. Van Vleck Married at Home." January 11, 1937.

The New York Times. "Mrs. Robert Appleton." March 3, 1949.

The New York Times. "O'Brien Estate Auction Today." July 23, 1938.

The New York Times. "O'Brien Estate Is Sold." July 24, 1938.

The New York Times. "Parents of L.I. Debutante Urge That Mansion Vandals Be Tried." October 30, 1963.

The New York Times. "Picturesque Southampton." August 15, 1897.

The New York Times. "Rain Sweeps City; Aids Water Supply." April 2, 1931.

The New York Times. "Retired Broker Is Shot." April 19, 1949.

The New York Times. "Robert Appleton." March 3, 1949.

The New York Times. "Robert Appletons Give Dinner Party" August 22, 1934.

The New York Times. "S. Fisher Johnson." June 2, 1904.

The New York Times, "Theodore B. Conklin Dies; Long Island Yachtsman, 75." March 11, 1966.

The New York Times. "Throng at Recital at Southampton." August 23, 1933.

The New York Times. "Van Vlecks Hosts at Novel Party." August 4, 1928.

The New York Times. "William F. Ladd Dies of Bullet Wounds." June 2, 1949.

New Yorker. "Pandora and the Doctor." December 4, 1926.

Palm Beach Daily News. "Appleton Death Called Mystery." January 5, 1948.

Palm Beach Daily News. "Funeral Services for Mrs. Appleton to Be Held Today." March 3, 1949.

Patterson, Augusta Owen. "Colonel H. H. Rogers 'Port of Missing Men.' " *Town and Country,* July 1930.

———. "House That Ambles over the Dunes." *Town and Country,* January 1, 1930.

———. "A Private Beach House and Swimming Pool." *Town and Country,* November 15, 1929.

Peconic Land Trust Newsletter. "Trust Receives Largest Conservation Gift in Its History." August 11, 2003.

Price, C. Matlack. "The Recent Work of Albro and Lindberg." *Architecture,* January 1915.

———. "Thought and Thinking in Architecture: Compliments on the Work of Harrie T. Lindeberg." *International Studio,* October 1915.

Rattiner, Dan. "History on the Line." *Dan's Papers,* April 2, 2004.

Rattiner, Dan, and Robin E Smith. "Protest: Citizens Brave Bitter Cold to Try to Save Bayberry Land." *Dan's Papers,* January 30, 2004.

Rist, Curtis. "East Hampton Restoration Drama: Renewing an 1887 Shingle Style Manor." *Architectural Digest,* February 2000.

Roberts, Mary Fanton. "Southampton Home of Varied Beauty." *Arts and Decoration,* January 1930.

Ruff, Joshua, and William Ayres. "H. F. du Pont's Chestertown House, Southampton, New York." *Antiques,* July 2001.

Sag Harbor Express. "An Appreciation of James Herman Aldrich." January 18, 1917.

Sag Harbor Express. "James Herman Aldrich Dies Suddenly." January 4, 1917.

Saylor, Henry H. "The Twelve Best Country Houses in America: 'The Orchard, The Home of James L. Breese, at Southampton, Long Island, New York' " *Country Life in America,* March 1915.

Schaer, Sidney C. "A House Divided, A Mansion Saved." *Newsday,* August 4, 1980.

Southampton Magazine. "Ballyshear." Autumn and Winter 1913.

Southampton Magazine. "Claverack." Summer 1912.

Southampton Magazine. "Laffalot." Autumn 1912.

Southampton Magazine. "Villa Mille Fiori." Spring 1912.

Southampton Press. "Bayberry Is Now Named Sebonack." May 13, 2004.

Southampton Press. "Country Home of Mr. Henry H. Rogers on the Dunes at Southampton." February 10, 1916.

Southampton Press. "Indict 14 Socialites in House Wrecking." November 7, 1963.

Southampton Press. "Mr. and Mrs. Sabin Have Brilliant Housewarming." July 7, 1919.

Southampton Press. "Republicans Meet at Bayberry Land." July 22, 1920.

Southampton Press. "Super Dance for Miss Doris Merrill." September 1, 1932.

Speed, John Gilmer. "An Artist's Summer Vacation." *Harper's New Monthly Magazine*, June 1893.

Spur. "The Summer Home of Miss Rosina S. Hoyt at Southampton, Long Island." September 15, 1915.

Stipe, Mary. "Meadowcroft: Jewel of Quantuck Bay." *Distinction*, August/September 2004.

Strickland, Carol. "East Hampton Showplace on the Block." *The New York Times*, July 21, 1991.

Surchin, Anne. "Why Save Bayberry Land? It's Our History." *Southampton Press*, December 11, 2003.

Sutton, Bill. "Bayberry Owners Offering a Trade." *Southampton Press*, December 4, 2003.

———. "Board Closes In on Bayberry Vote." *Southampton Press*, January 15, 2004.

———. "Opponents Prepare Last Push to Save Manor House." *Southampton Press*, January 22, 2004.

———. "Tribe Joins Bayberry Opponents." *Southampton Press*, January 29, 2004.

———. "Zone Change in Place, Golf Course Is Coming." *Southampton Press*, February 12, 2004.

Syracuse Herald. "Chas. H. Sabin, World Banker, Is Dead at 65." October 11, 1933.

Syracuse Herald. "Estate of C. H. Sabin Valued at $2,943,456 in Surrogate's Court." December 4, 1938.

Tabor, Grace. "The Colorful Garden of An Artist: The Home of Mr. Albert Herter at East Hampton, L.I.—Where Color Comes into Its Own." *Country Life in America*, February 1916.

Time. "Ladies at Roslyn." July 18, 1932.

Town and Country. "Lake Agawam Idyll." July 1987.

Town and Country. "A Roman Pool on a Long Island Estate." July 1, 1930.

Town and Country. "Tennis in Southampton." July 22, 1911.

Toy, Vivian. "Supporters Try to Save 1919 Manor." *The New York Times*, July 20, 2003.

Vail, Marci. "Restoration at Pudding Hill." *The Independent*, January 20, 1999.

Walker, Grant H. "The Henry Huddleston Rogers Collection of Ship Models at the U.S. Naval Museum." *Nautical Research Journal*, June 1999.

———. "The Historic Dockyard Models of Annapolis." *Great Scale Modeling*, 2000.

Western Architect. "Death of Two Notable Architects." May 1915.

Whitehead, Russell F. "Harrie T. Lindeberg's Contribution to American Domestic Architecture." *Architectural Record*, April 1924.

Wright, Michael. "Bayberry Builders May Raze Home." *Southampton Press*, May 30, 2002.

———. "Zenk Doesn't See a Benefit in a Bayberry Golf Course." *Southampton Press*, May 30, 2002.

INDEX

PHOTOGRAPHY CREDITS

INTRODUCTION: 16, 17, 20, 22, 23, 26 Eric Woodward Collection; 18 top Library of Congress, Prints & Photographs Division; 18 bottom Mary Cummings Collection; 19 John Jermain Memorial Library, Long Island History Room; 21, 25, 27 Southampton Town Historian Collection

MONTAUK ASSOCIATION: 28, 29, 30, 31, 32, 33 Montauk Library, Carleton Kelsey Collection

ROSEMARY LODGE: 34, 35, 36, 37, 38, 39, 42 Jeff Heatley Photographer

THE DOLPHINS: 43, 44, 45, 46, 47, 48, Jeff Heatley Photographer

MAYCROFT: 49, 50 bottom, 51, 52 top, 52 bottom, 53 James Merrell Collection; 50 top Gary Lawrance Collection

PUDDING HILL: 56 East Hampton Library Long Island Collection; 57 Architecture & Building; 58, 59 Marco Ricca Photographer

VILLA MARIA: 60 Water Mill Museum; 61, 62, 63, 64, 65, 66, Jeff Heatley Photographer; 67 Andre T. Tchelistcheff, Architect

THE ART VILLAGE: 68, 69 Jeff Heatley Photographer; 70 Top, 70 Bottom Eric Woodward Collection; 71 Anne Surchin Collection; 73 Southampton Town Historian Collection

WILLIAM MERRITT CHASE HOMESTEAD: 74, 76 William Merritt Chase Archive, Parrish Art Museum; 75 Anne Surchin Collection

CLAVERACK: 78, 79 Jeff Heatley Photographer; 80, 81 "Courtesy of the Frances Loeb Library, Harvard Graduate School of Design"; 82, 83, 84 "© Amiaga Photographers, Inc."

THE ORCHARD: 86, 88, 89, Southampton Town Historian Collection; 87, 90, 96, 97, 98 Country Life in America; 91, 93 bottom, 94 American Estates & Gardens; 92, 93 top Architectural Review; 95 McKim, Mead & White Monograph; 99 top American Country Homes & Their Gardens

THE CREEKS: 100,101,102, 103,104, 105 top,105 bottom, 106 top, 106 bottom Nassau County Department of Parks, Recreation and Museums, Long Island Studies Institute Collection; 107 Country Life in America; 108 Library of Congress, Prints & Photographs Division

WOOLDON MANOR: 110, 117 top Country Life in America; 111, 112, 113 top, 113 bottom 114, 115 top, 115 bottom, 116 Architectural Record; 117 bottom, 122 Arts & Decoration; 118 top, 118 bottom, 119, 120 top, 120 bottom Hudson Nurseries

ONADUNE: 123 Gary Lawrance Collection; 124, 125, 126, 127 top, 127 bottom, 128 James Bleecker Photographer

MEADOWCROFT: 130, 132, 133 Jeff Heatley Photographer; 131 Courtesy of University of Pennsylvania Architectural Archive; 134 top, 134 bottom"© Amiaga Photographers, Inc."

RED MAPLES: 136 "Courtesy of the Frances Loeb Library, Harvard Graduate School of Design" 137, 142 top Orin Z. Finkle collection; 138, 141, 144 bottom Eric Woodward Collection; 139, 140, 144 top Gary Lawrance Collection; 142 bottom, 143 The Society for the Preservation of Long Island Antiquities

VILLA MILLE FIORI:146, 155 top "Courtesy of the Frances Loeb Library, Harvard Graduate School of Design"; 147, 148, 150, 155 bottom, 156 Architectural Record; 149 The Society for the Preservation of Long Island Antiquities; 151 Richard Marchand Collection; 152, 153 " The American Institute of Architects Library and Archives, Washington, D.C."; 154 Eric Woodward Collection

COXWOULD: 158, 160 Architecture; 159, 163 Judy Makrianes Collection; 161 Jeff Heatley Photographer

OLD TREES: 164,165 top, 165 bottom, 166, 167, 169, 170 Nassau County Department of Parks, Recreation and Museums, Long Island Studies Institute Collection; 168,171 James Bleecker photographer

MINDEN: 173 The Society for the Preservation of Long Island Antiquities; 174 top, 174 bottom, 175, 179, 180, 181 Bridgehampton Historical Society; 176 top, 176 bottom, 178 top, 178 bottom Nassau County Department of Parks, Recreation and Museums, Long Island Studies Institute Collection; 177 Country Life in America

BALLYSHEAR: 183, 186 top, 189 top Brickbuilder; 184, 187 top, 187 bottom, 188, 189 bottom, 190 top Nassau County Department of Parks, Recreation and Museums, Long Island Studies Institute Collection; 185, 190 bottom American Country Homes of Today; 186 bottom The Society for the Preservation of Long Island Antiquities; 191 Jeff Heatley Photographer

BLACK POINT: 193, 197, 198, 199, 200, 201, 202, 204 top, 204 bottom Southampton Historical Museum; 194 "Courtesy of the Frances Loeb Library, Harvard Graduate School of Design"; 195 Country Life in America; 196 Architectural Record; 203, 205 Gary Lawrance Collection

NID DE PAPILLON: 207 Gary Lawrance Collection; 208, 209, 210,211, 212 top Architectural Record; 212 bottom Orin Z. Finkle Collection

WOODHOUSE PLAYHOUSE: 214, 216, 217, 219 bottom Library of Congress, Prints & Photographs Division; 215, 220, 221 East Hampton Historical Society; 218 Gary Lawrance Collection; 219 top Nassau County Department of Parks, Recreation and Museums, Long Island Studies Institute Collection

BAYBERRY LAND: 222, 223 American Landscape Architecture; 224, 227, 232 bottom, 233 top, 234, 236; American Homes of Today; 225,228, 229, 230, 231, 232 top, 233 bottom, 235 Architectural Review; 226 Gary Lawrance Collection

CHESTERTOWN HOUSE: 238, 239, 240, 241, 242, 243 "Courtesy, The Winterthur Library: Winterthur Archives"

HEATHER DUNE: 246, 249, 250, 251, American Architect; 247 Architectural Record; 248, 252, 253 top, 253 bottom Arts & Decoration

PHOTOGRAPHY CREDITS

PORT OF MISSING MEN: 255, 256, 258 top, 259 bottom The Architect; 257 top The Architecture of John Russell Pope; 257 bottom, 258 bottom, 259 top, 260, 261 top, 262, 263, 264,265 Southampton Historical Museum

FOUR FOUNTAINS: 268, 269, 271,272,274,275, 277 The Architect; 270,273 Gary Lawrance Collection; 276 James Bleecker Photographer

OCEAN CASTLE: 279,280 top, 280 bottom, 282, 283, 284, 285, 286 Orin Z. Finkle Collection; 281 Gary Lawrance Collection

SUNSET COURT/ WESTERLY 287, 288, 289, 293, 294 Nassau County Department of Parks, Recreation and Museums, Long Island Studies Institute Collection; 290 top, 290 bottom 291, 292 top 292 bottom Arts & Decoration

THE BOUWERIE: 296, 298, 299, 300, 302 Avery Architectural and Fine Arts Library, Columbia University; 297, 301 Arts & Decoration

THE SHALLOWS: 304, 313 Arts & Decoration, 305, 306, 307 Avery Architectural and Fine Arts Library, Columbia University; 308, 309, 310, 311 Jeff Heatley Photographer; 312 top Library of Congress, Prints & Photographs Division

FLOOR PLANS BY RICHARD MARCHAND APPEAR ON PAGES: 40,41,54,55,85,99,109,121,129,135, 145,157,162,172,182,192,206,213,237, 244,245,254, 266, 278, 295, 303, 312

PORTFOLIO: 314 top left, bottom left, bottom right Gary Lawrance Collection; 314 top right John W. Rae, Jr. Collection; 315 top left, middle left, bottom left, bottom right Gary Lawrance Collection; 315top right Eric Woodward Collection; 315 middle right east Hampton Historical Society 316 top left, middle right, bottom left, bottom right Gary Lawrance Collection; 316 top right The Society for the Preservation of Long Island Antiquities; middle left Eric Woodward Collection; 317 Gary Lawrance Collection; 318 top left, top right, middle left, bottom left, bottom right Gary Lawrance Collection; middle right Anne Surchin Collection; 319 top left Anne Surchin Collection; top right, middle left, bottom left Gary Lawrance Collection; middle right Domestic Architecture of Harrie T. Lindeberg; bottom right Richard Marchand Collection; 320 top left American Country Homes of Today, top right, middle left, middle right, bottom left, bottom right Gary Lawrance Collection

COLOPHON

❦

ACANTHUS PRESS publishes fine books. We are interested in tracing—which often means rediscovering—the lineages of architecture and interior design. Just as we respect and are intrigued by building traditions, so we respect the traditions of good book design. Choices of type, paper, binding, and images, as well as printing production methods, are issues we consider and investigate with each Acanthus book. We see our mission as an enduring one—to create an Acanthus library of books, thematically and visually interrelated, reflecting variations on design themes that are elegant, subtle, and timeless.

The typeface used throughout this book is Goudy, designed by Frederic Goudy in 1908. It is named for his estate in Marlboro, New York.

Edited by William A. Morrison

Copyedited by Angela Buckley

Printed on Japanese Fine Art Matte paper

Bound with T-Saifu Japanese cloth

Printed and bound by Regent Publishing Services Limited, Hong Kong

ACANTHUS PRESS

FINE BOOKS

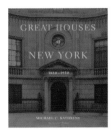    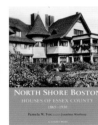 

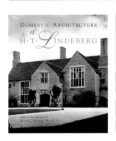 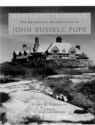  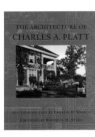  

SERIES

20th Century Decorators : Urban and Suburban Domestic Architecture

The American Architect : Architecture of Leisure